CREATED BY DAVID SCHULNER

DAVID SCHULNER
AARON GINSBURG
WADE MCINTYRE
WRITERS

JUAN JOSE RYP
ARTIST

ANDY TROY
COLORIST

RUS WOOTON
LETTERER

SEAN MACKIEWICZ
EDITOR

JUAN JOSE RYP
AND ANDY TROY
COVER

CREATED BY DAVID SCHULNER

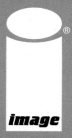

IMAGE COMICS, INC.
Robert Kirkman – Chief Operating Officer
Erik Larsen – Chief Financial Officer
Todd McFarlane – President
Marc Silvestri – Chief Executive Officer
Jim Valentino – Vice-President

Eric Stephenson – Publisher
Ron Richards – Director of Business Development
Jennifer de Guzman – Director of Trade Book Sales
Kat Salazar – Director of PR & Marketing
Corey Murphy – Director of Retail Sales
Jeremy Sullivan – Director of Digital Sales
Emilio Bautista – Sales Assistant
Branwyn Bigglestone – Senior Accounts Manager
Emily Miller – Accounts Manager
Jessica Ambriz – Administrative Assistant
Tyler Shainline – Events Coordinator
David Brothers – Content Manager
Jonathan Chan – Production Manager
Drew Gill – Art Director
Meredith Wallace – Print Manager
Monica Garcia – Senior Production Artist
Addison Duke – Production Artist
Tricia Ramos – Production Assistant
IMAGECOMICS.COM

For SKYBOUND ENTERTAINMENT
Robert Kirkman - CEO
Sean Mackiewicz - Editorial Director
Shawn Kirkham - Director of Business Development
Brian Huntington - Online Editorial Director
June Alian - Publicity Director
Rachel Skidmore - Director of Media Development
Helen Leigh - Assistant Editor
Dan Petersen - Operations Manager
Sarah Effinger - Office Manager
Nick Palmer - Operations Coordinator
Lizzy Iverson - Administrative Assistant
Stephan Murillo - Administrative Assistant

International inquiries: foreign@skybound.com
Licensing inquiries: contact@skybound.com

WWW.SKYBOUND.COM

CLONE VOL. 4 TP. ISBN: 978-1-63215-036-3. First Printing. Published by Image Comics, Inc. Office of publication: 2001 Center Street, 6th Floor, Berkeley, CA 94704.

CHAPTER 16

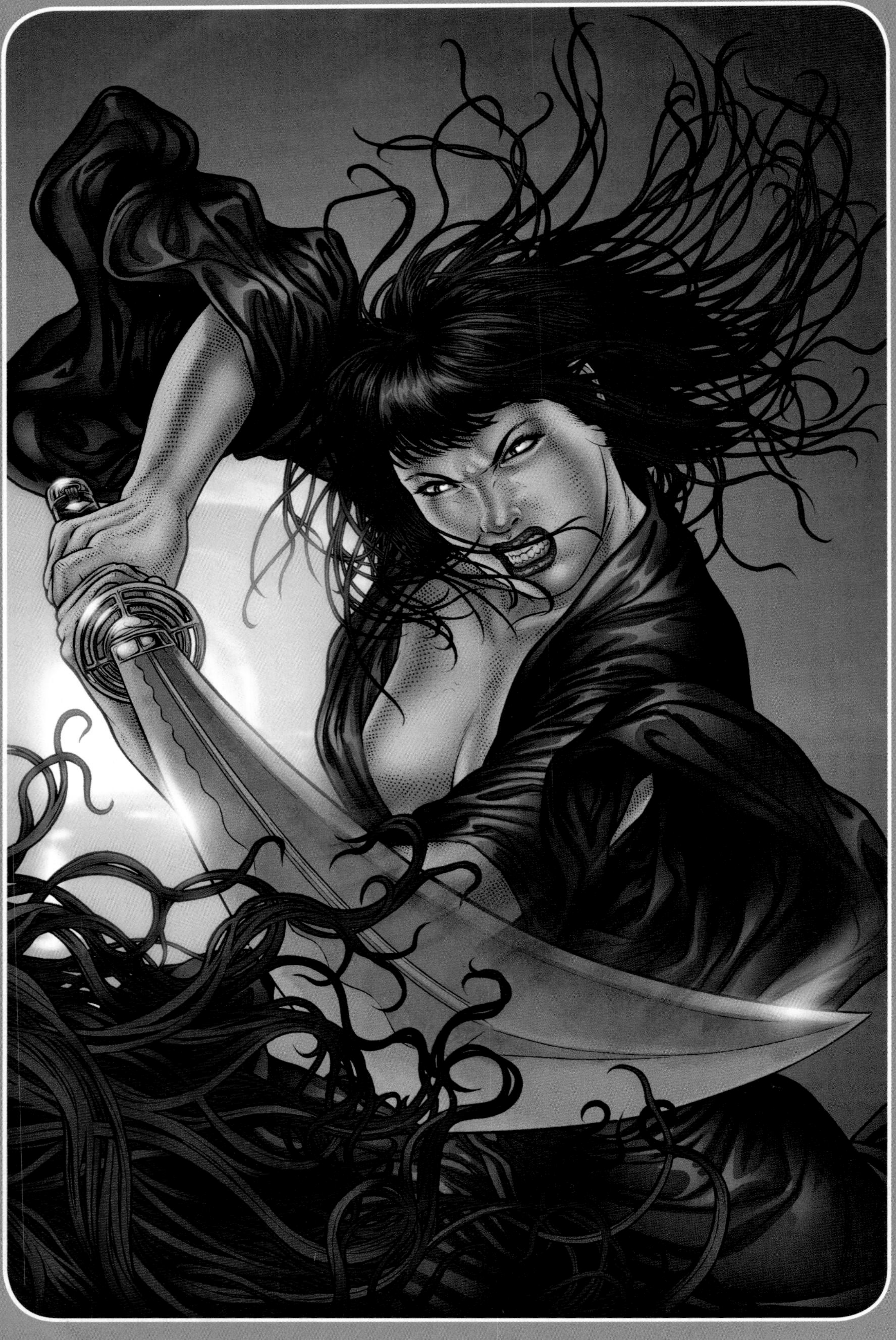

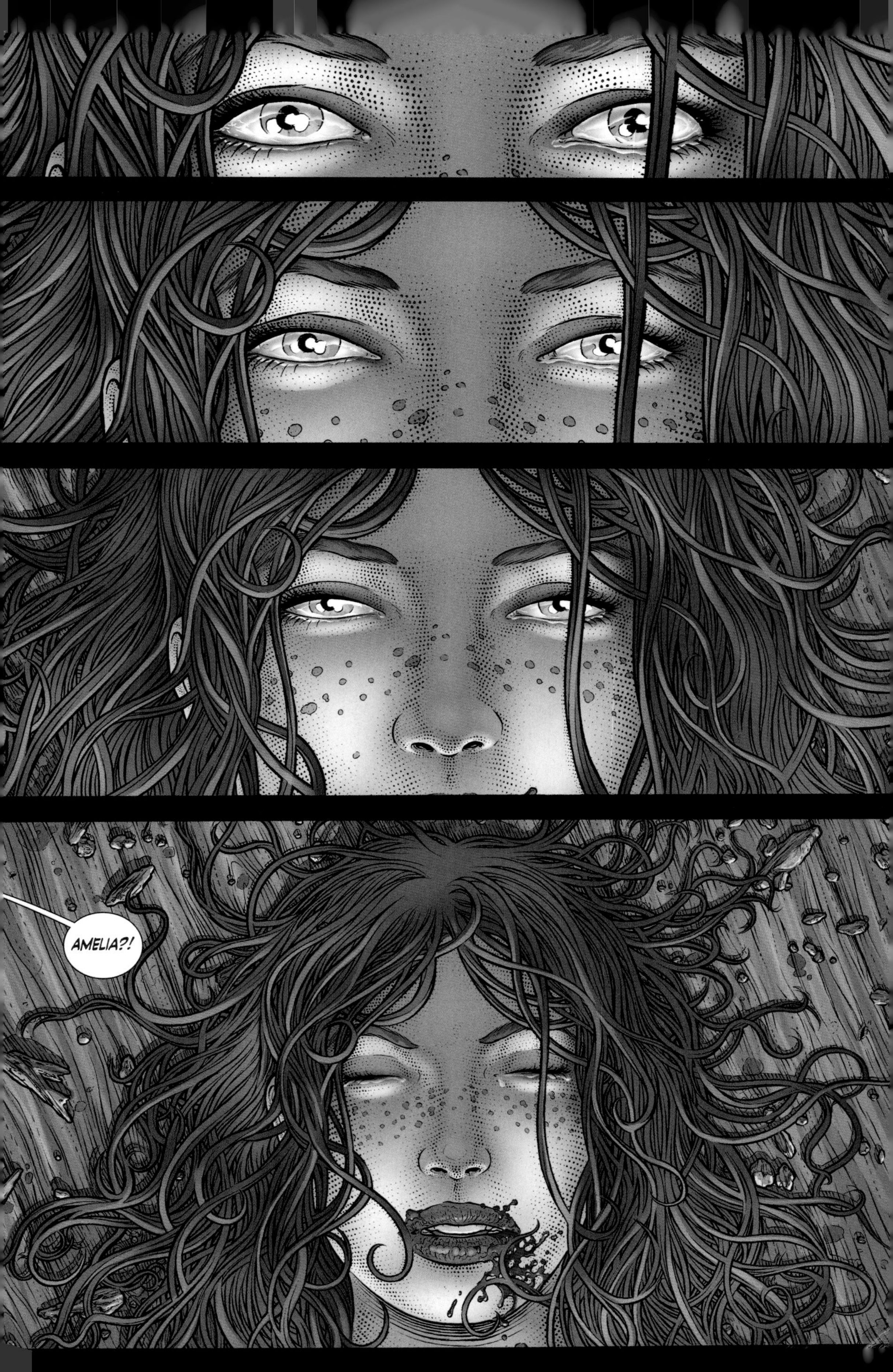

AMELIA?!

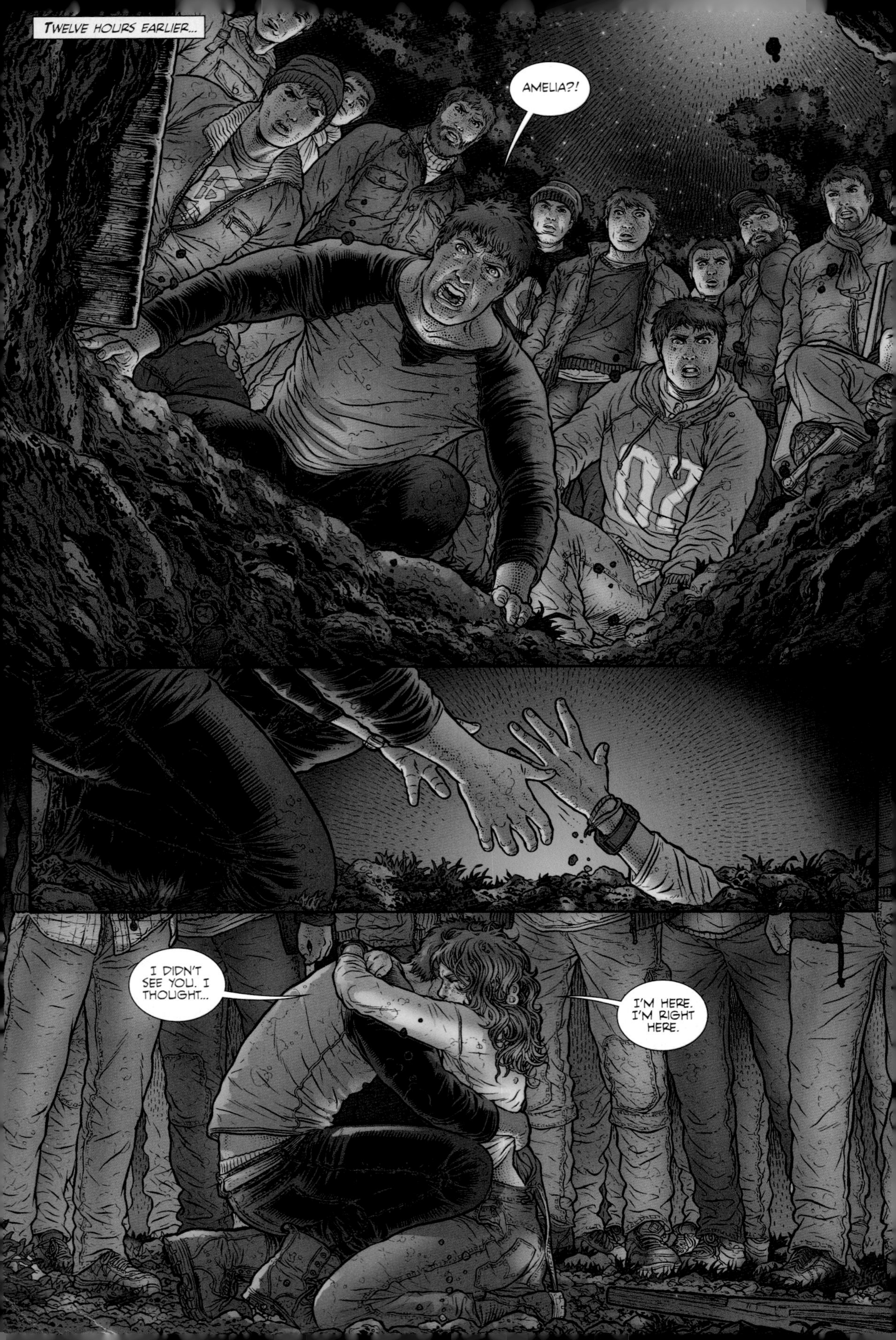
TWELVE HOURS EARLIER...
AMELIA?!
I DIDN'T SEE YOU. I THOUGHT...
I'M HERE. I'M RIGHT HERE.

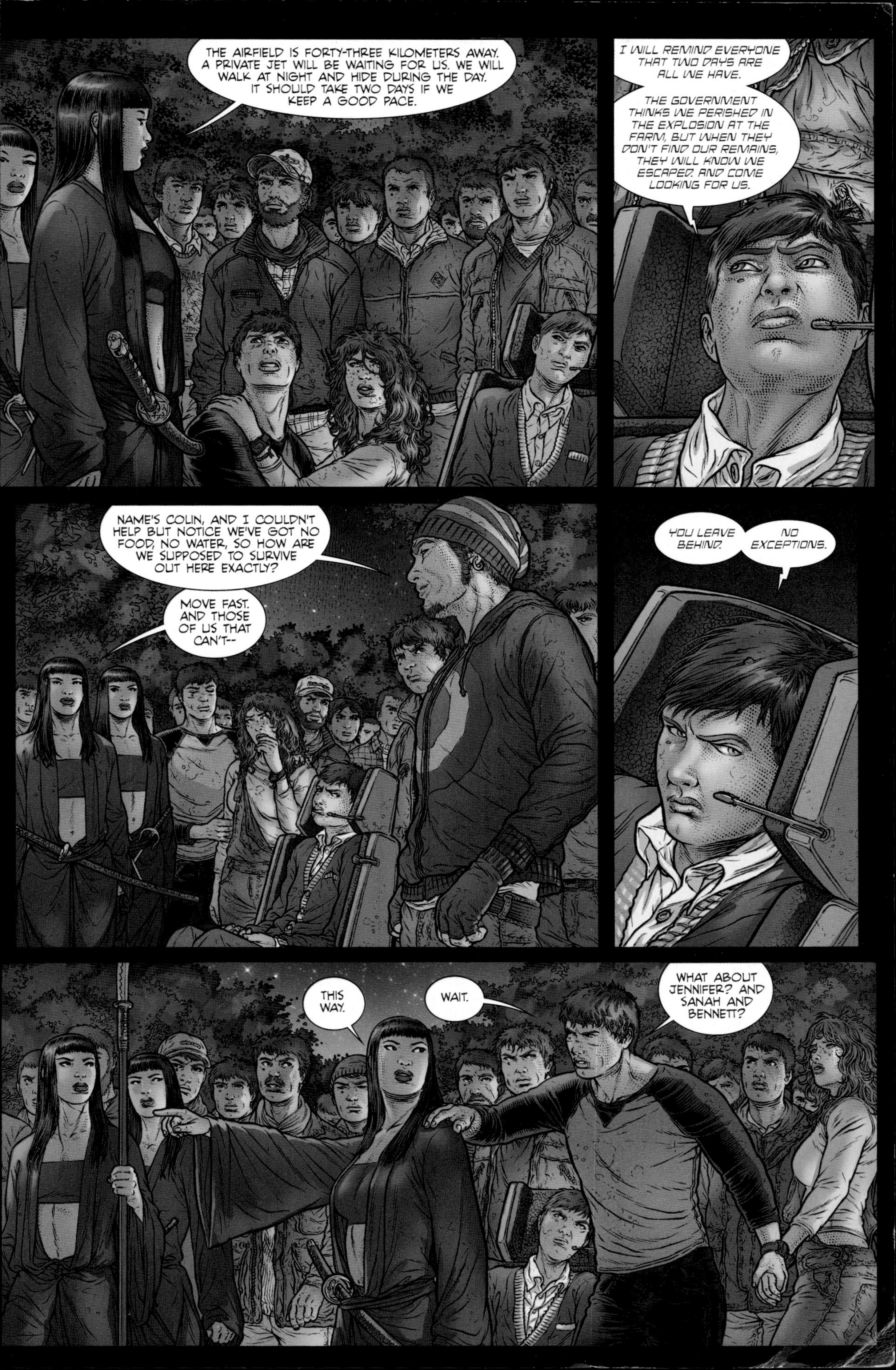
THE AIRFIELD IS FORTY-THREE KILOMETERS AWAY. A PRIVATE JET WILL BE WAITING FOR US. WE WILL WALK AT NIGHT AND HIDE DURING THE DAY. IT SHOULD TAKE TWO DAYS IF WE KEEP A GOOD PACE.
I WILL REMIND EVERYONE THAT TWO DAYS ARE ALL WE HAVE.
THE GOVERNMENT THINKS WE PERISHED IN THE EXPLOSION AT THE FARM, BUT WHEN THEY DON'T FIND OUR REMAINS, THEY WILL KNOW WE ESCAPED. AND COME LOOKING FOR US.
NAME'S COLIN, AND I COULDN'T HELP BUT NOTICE WE'VE GOT NO FOOD, NO WATER, SO HOW ARE WE SUPPOSED TO SURVIVE OUT HERE EXACTLY?
MOVE FAST. AND THOSE OF US THAT CAN'T--
YOU LEAVE BEHIND.
NO EXCEPTIONS.
THIS WAY.
WAIT.
WHAT ABOUT JENNIFER? AND SANAH AND BENNETT?

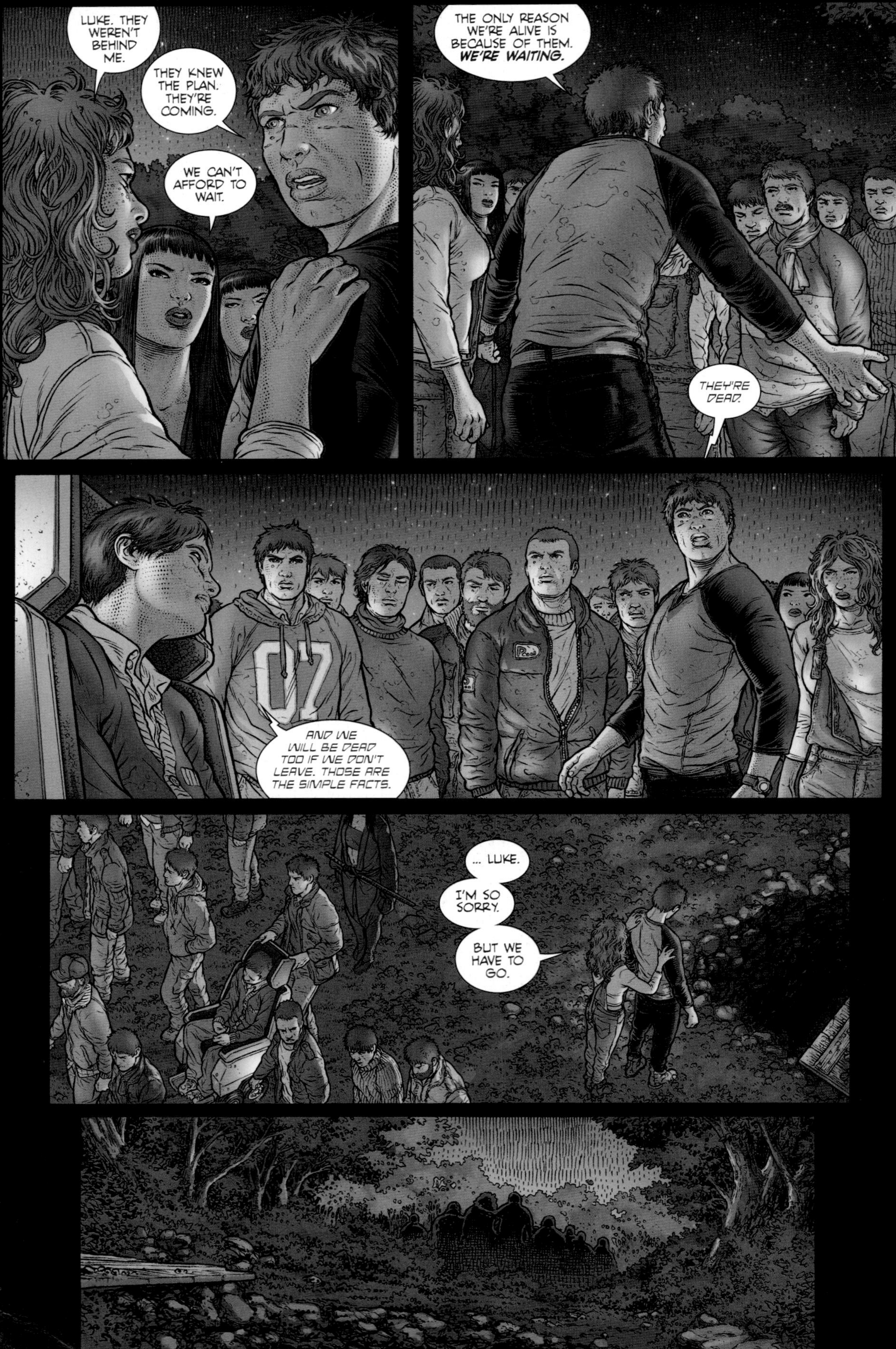
LUKE. THEY WEREN'T BEHIND ME.
THEY KNEW THE PLAN. THEY'RE COMING.
WE CAN'T AFFORD TO WAIT.
THE ONLY REASON WE'RE ALIVE IS BECAUSE OF THEM. WE'RE WAITING.
THEY'RE DEAD.
AND WE WILL BE DEAD TOO IF WE DON'T LEAVE. THOSE ARE THE SIMPLE FACTS.
... LUKE.
I'M SO SORRY.
BUT WE HAVE TO GO.

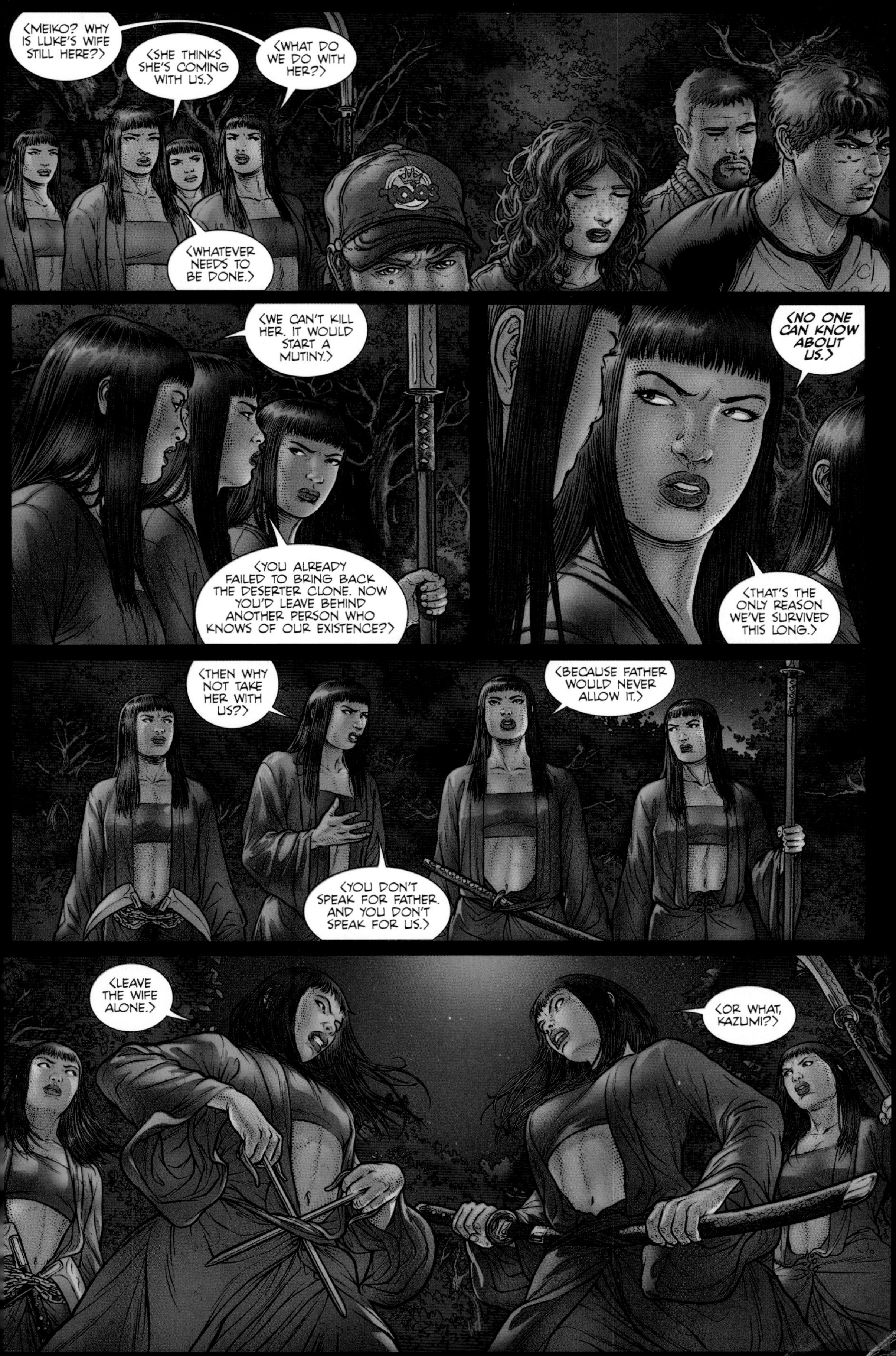

<MEIKO? WHY IS LUKE'S WIFE STILL HERE?>
<SHE THINKS SHE'S COMING WITH US.>
<WHAT DO WE DO WITH HER?>
<WHATEVER NEEDS TO BE DONE.>
<WE CAN'T KILL HER. IT WOULD START A MUTINY.>
<YOU ALREADY FAILED TO BRING BACK THE DESERTER CLONE. NOW YOU'D LEAVE BEHIND ANOTHER PERSON WHO KNOWS OF OUR EXISTENCE?>
<NO ONE CAN KNOW ABOUT US.>
<THAT'S THE ONLY REASON WE'VE SURVIVED THIS LONG.>
<THEN WHY NOT TAKE HER WITH US?>
<BECAUSE FATHER WOULD NEVER ALLOW IT.>
<YOU DON'T SPEAK FOR FATHER. AND YOU DON'T SPEAK FOR US.>
<LEAVE THE WIFE ALONE.>
<OR WHAT, KAZUMI?>

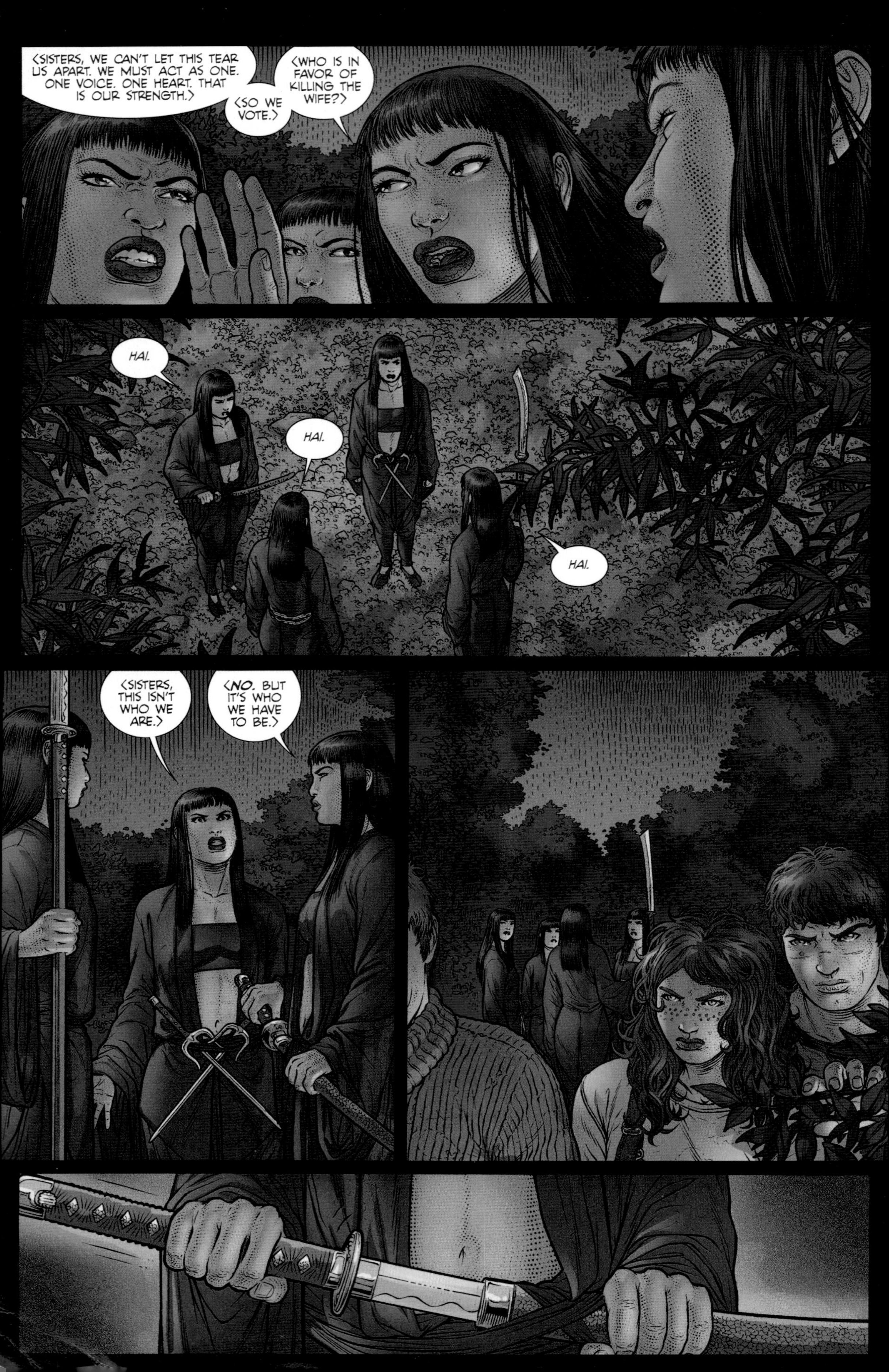
<SISTERS, WE CAN'T LET THIS TEAR US APART. WE MUST ACT AS ONE. ONE VOICE. ONE HEART. THAT IS OUR STRENGTH.>
<SO WE VOTE.>
<WHO IS IN FAVOR OF KILLING THE WIFE?>
HAI.
HAI.
HAI.
<SISTERS, THIS ISN'T WHO WE ARE.>
<NO. BUT IT'S WHO WE HAVE TO BE.>

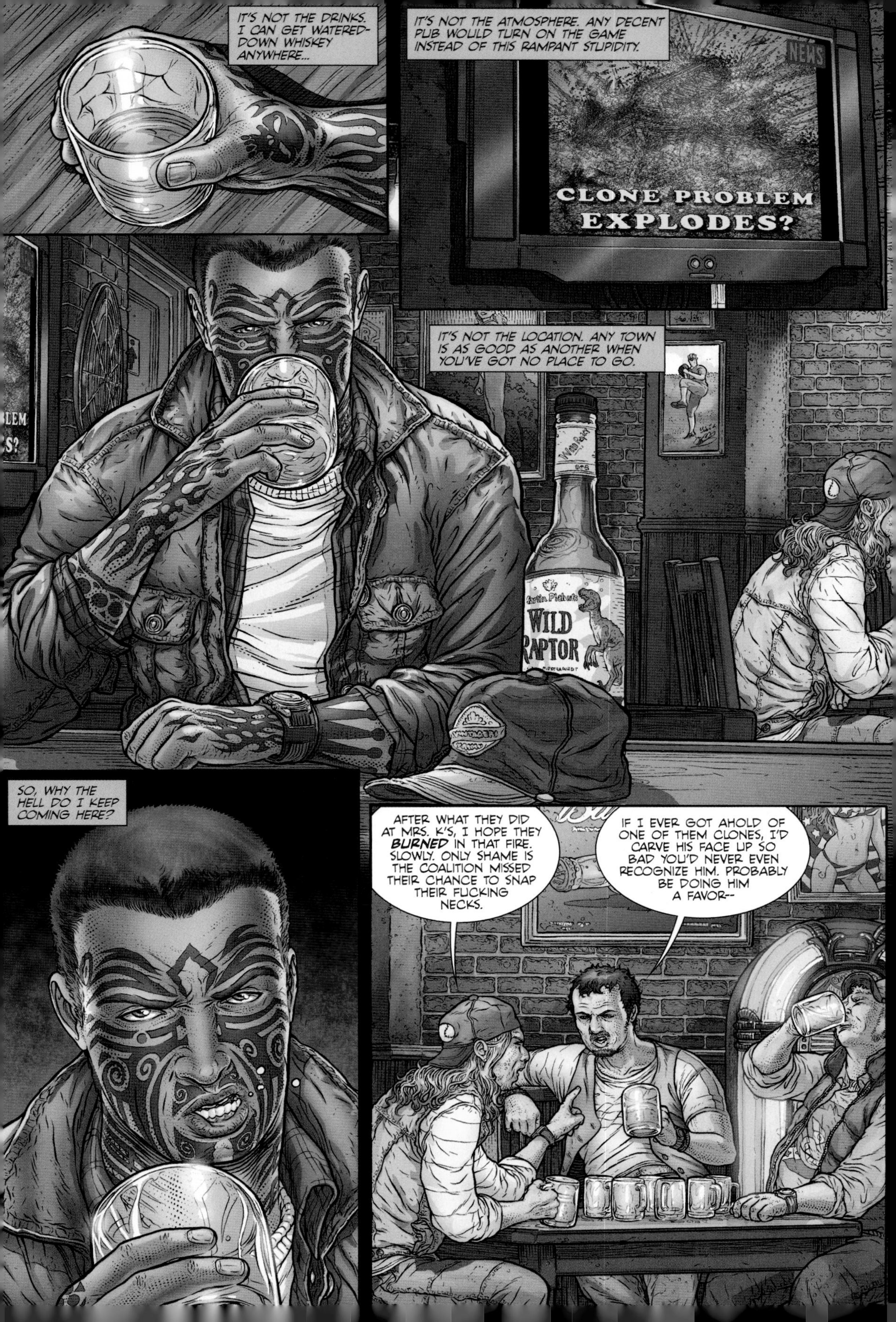
IT'S NOT THE DRINKS. I CAN GET WATERED-DOWN WHISKEY ANYWHERE...
IT'S NOT THE ATMOSPHERE. ANY DECENT PUB WOULD TURN ON THE GAME INSTEAD OF THIS RAMPANT STUPIDITY.
NEWS
CLONE PROBLEM EXPLODES?
IT'S NOT THE LOCATION. ANY TOWN IS AS GOOD AS ANOTHER WHEN YOU'VE GOT NO PLACE TO GO.
WILD RAPTOR
SO, WHY THE HELL DO I KEEP COMING HERE?
AFTER WHAT THEY DID AT MRS. K'S, I HOPE THEY BURNED IN THAT FIRE. SLOWLY. ONLY SHAME IS THE COALITION MISSED THEIR CHANCE TO SNAP THEIR FUCKING NECKS.
IF I EVER GOT AHOLD OF ONE OF THEM CLONES, I'D CARVE HIS FACE UP SO BAD YOU'D NEVER EVEN RECOGNIZE HIM. PROBABLY BE DOING HIM A FAVOR--

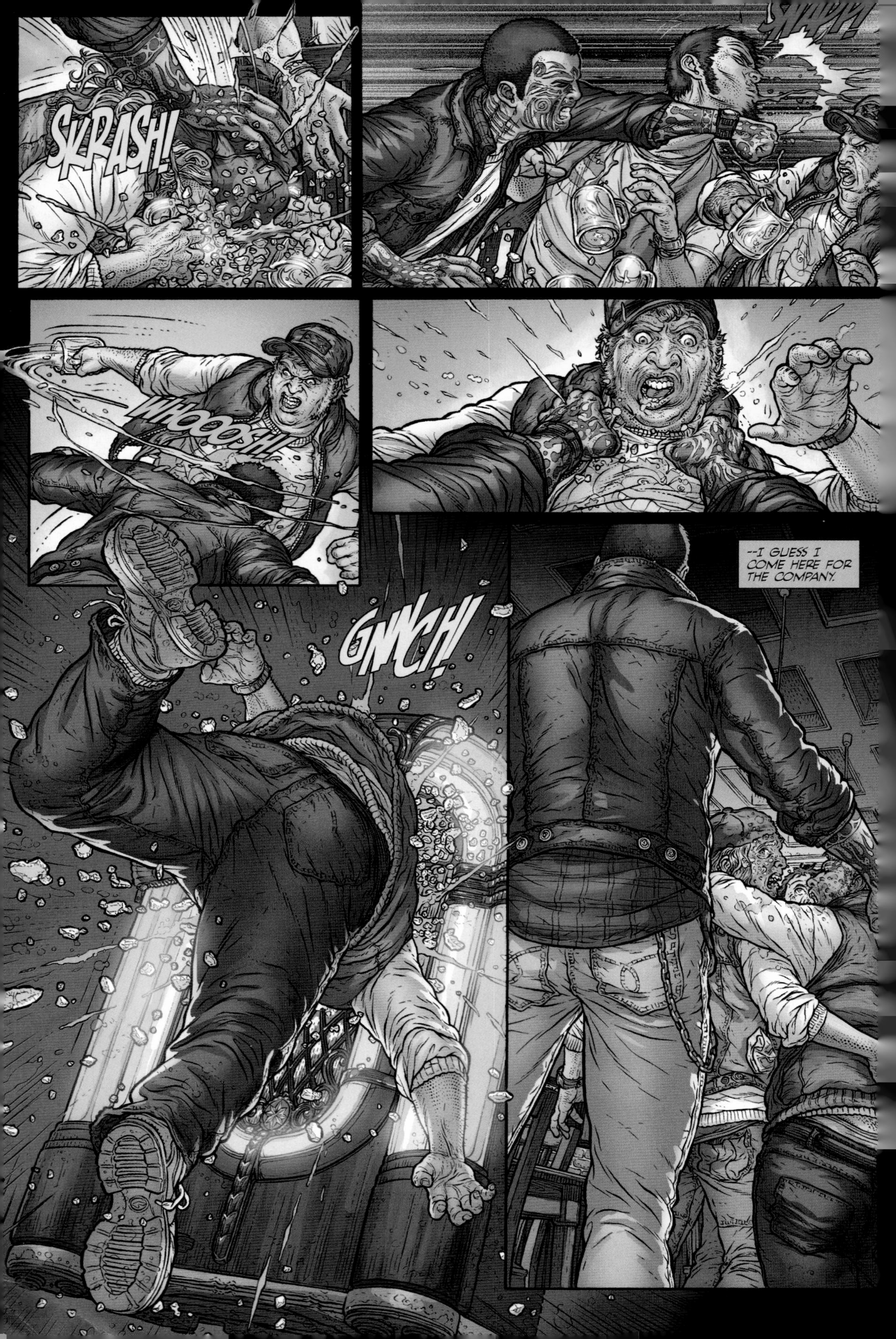
SKRASH!
SNAPP!
WHOOOSH!
GNNCH!
--I GUESS I COME HERE FOR THE COMPANY.

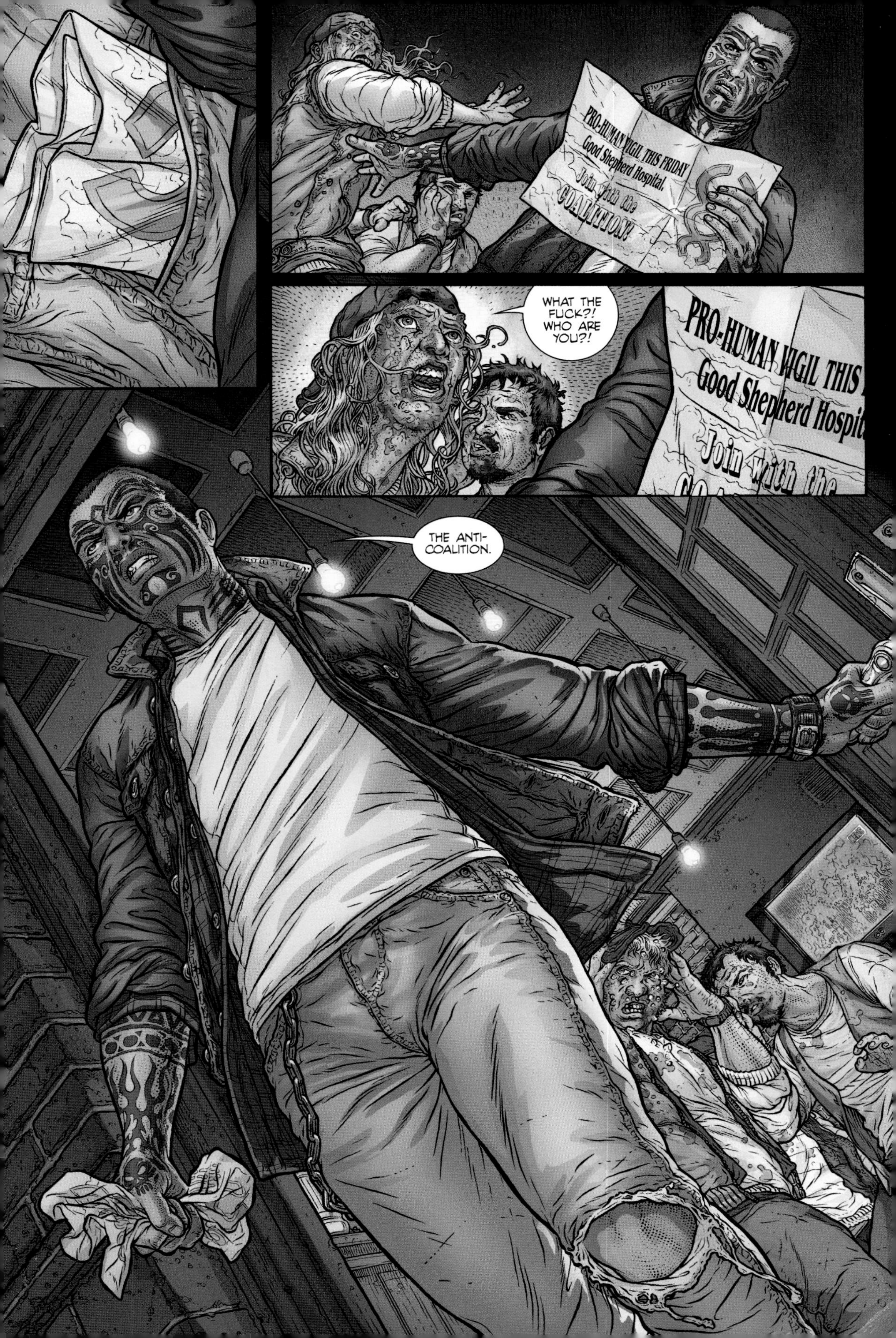
PRO-HUMAN VIGIL THIS FRIDAY
Good Shepherd Hospital.
Join with the COALITION!
WHAT THE FUCK?! WHO ARE YOU?!
PRO-HUMAN VIGIL THIS
Good Shepherd
Join with the
THE ANTI-COALITION.

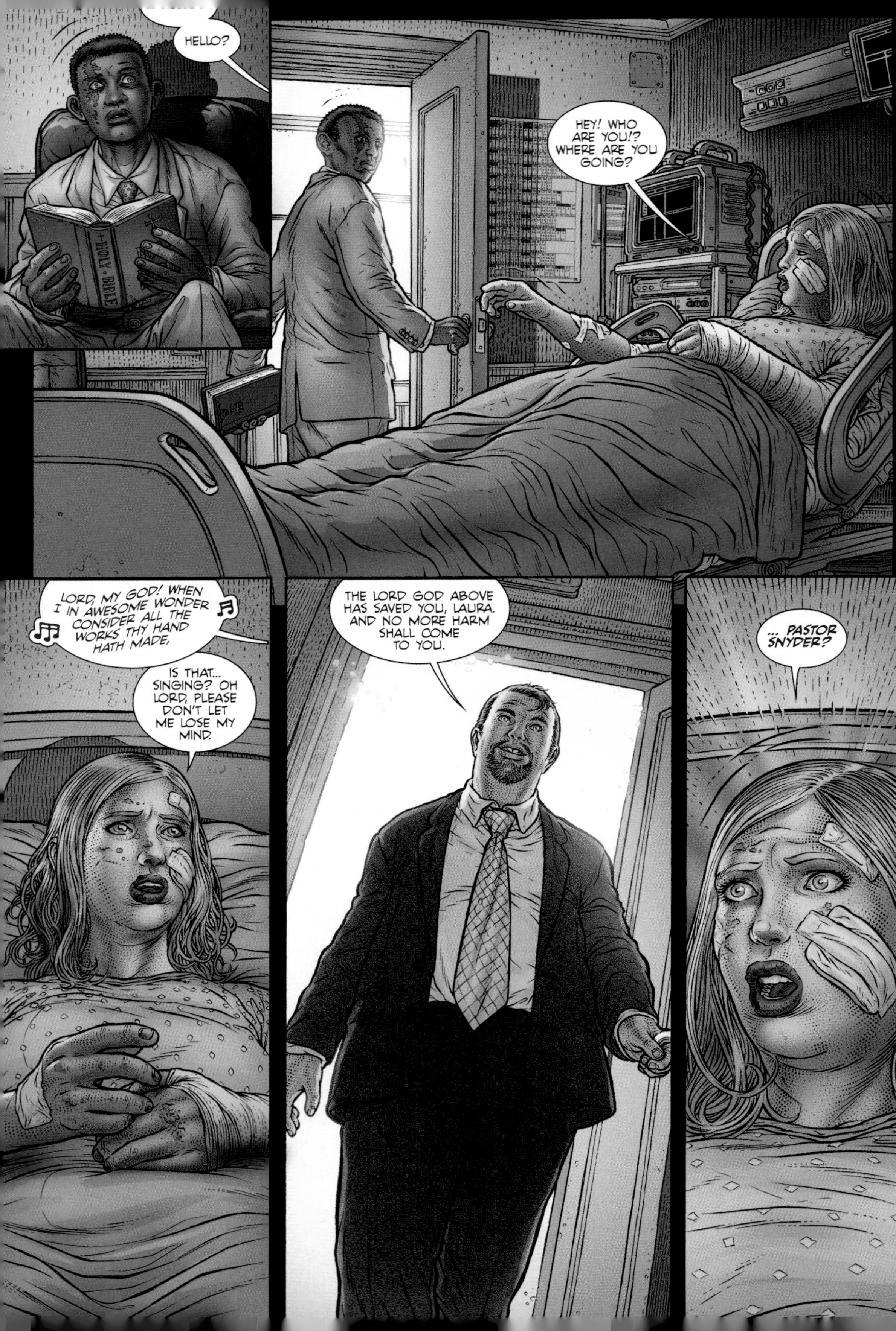
HELLO?
HEY! WHO ARE YOU!? WHERE ARE YOU GOING?
LORD, MY GOD! WHEN I IN AWESOME WONDER CONSIDER ALL THE WORKS THY HAND HATH MADE,
IS THAT... SINGING? OH LORD, PLEASE DON'T LET ME LOSE MY MIND.
THE LORD GOD ABOVE HAS SAVED YOU, LAURA. AND NO MORE HARM SHALL COME TO YOU.
... PASTOR SNYDER?

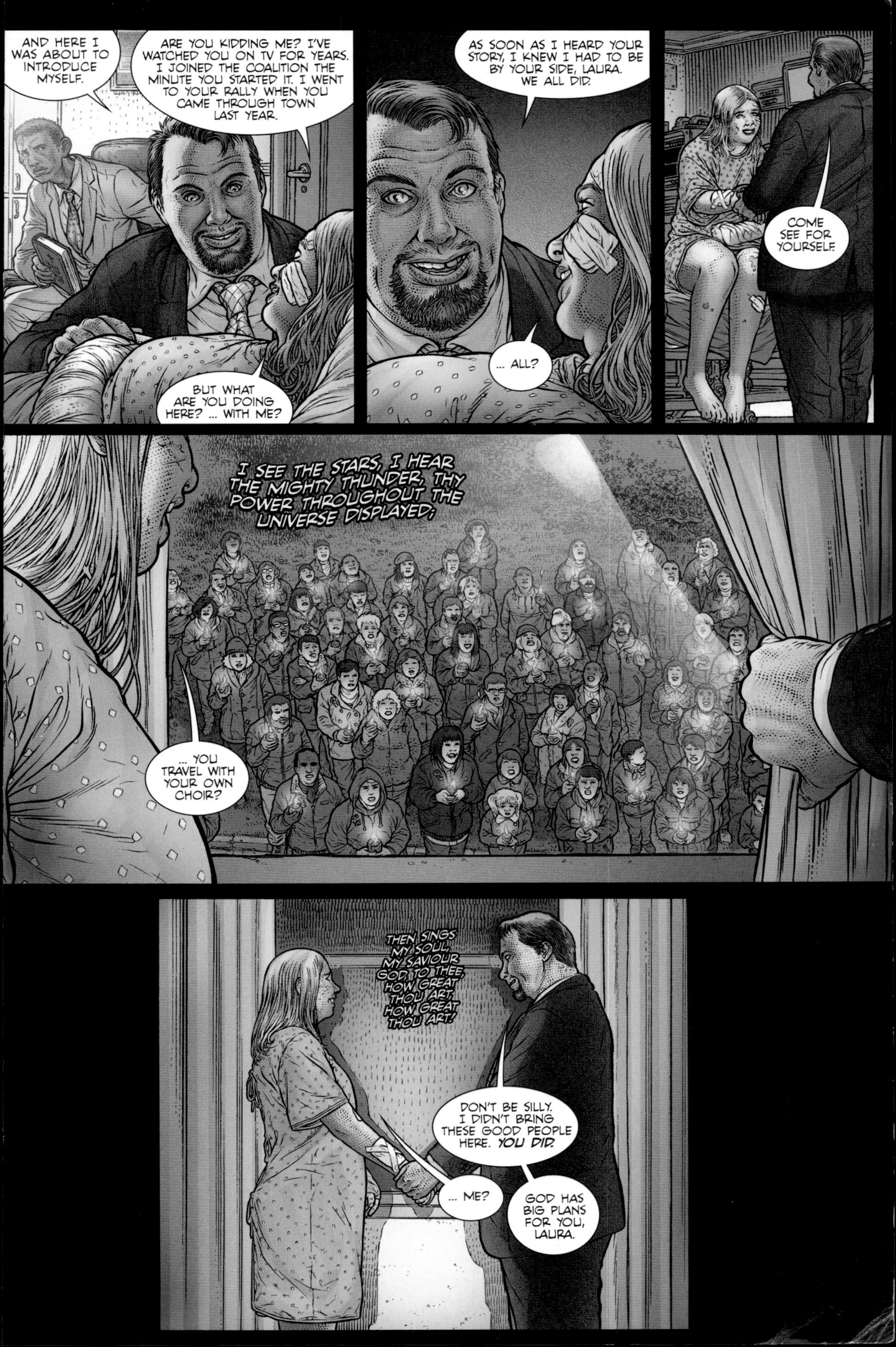
AND HERE I WAS ABOUT TO INTRODUCE MYSELF.
ARE YOU KIDDING ME? I'VE WATCHED YOU ON TV FOR YEARS. I JOINED THE COALITION THE MINUTE YOU STARTED IT. I WENT TO YOUR RALLY WHEN YOU CAME THROUGH TOWN LAST YEAR.
BUT WHAT ARE YOU DOING HERE? ... WITH ME?
AS SOON AS I HEARD YOUR STORY, I KNEW I HAD TO BE BY YOUR SIDE, LAURA. WE ALL DID.
... ALL?
COME SEE FOR YOURSELF.
I SEE THE STARS, I HEAR THE MIGHTY THUNDER, THY POWER THROUGHOUT THE UNIVERSE DISPLAYED;
... YOU TRAVEL WITH YOUR OWN CHOIR?
THEN SINGS MY SOUL, MY SAVIOUR GOD, TO THEE, HOW GREAT THOU ART, HOW GREAT THOU ART!
DON'T BE SILLY. I DIDN'T BRING THESE GOOD PEOPLE HERE. YOU DID.
... ME?
GOD HAS BIG PLANS FOR YOU, LAURA.

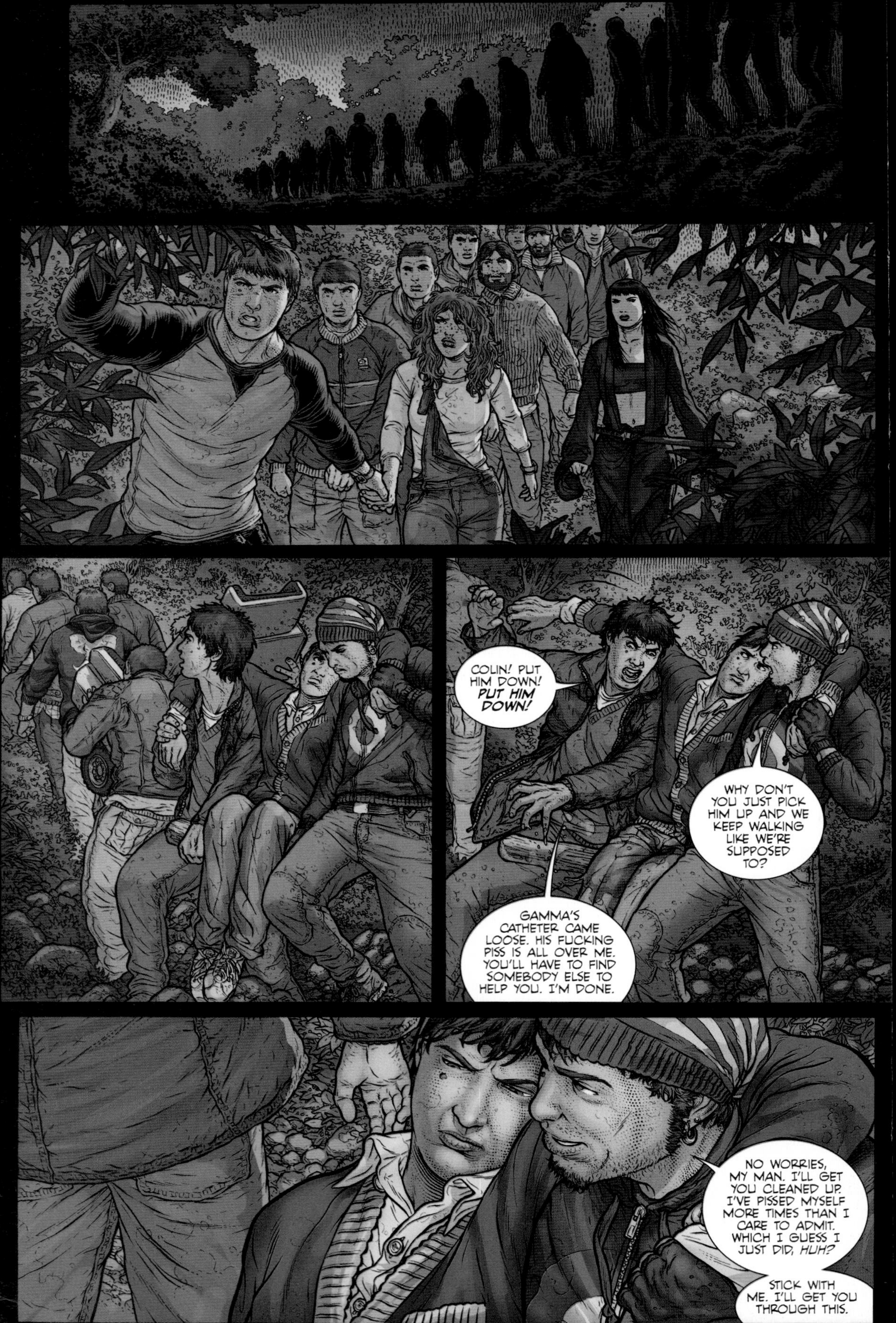

COLIN! PUT HIM DOWN! *PUT HIM DOWN!*
GAMMA'S CATHETER CAME LOOSE. HIS FUCKING PISS IS ALL OVER ME. YOU'LL HAVE TO FIND SOMEBODY ELSE TO HELP YOU. I'M DONE.
WHY DON'T YOU JUST PICK HIM UP AND WE KEEP WALKING LIKE WE'RE SUPPOSED TO?
NO WORRIES, MY MAN. I'LL GET YOU CLEANED UP. I'VE PISSED MYSELF MORE TIMES THAN I CARE TO ADMIT. WHICH I GUESS I JUST DID, *HUH?*
STICK WITH ME. I'LL GET YOU THROUGH THIS.

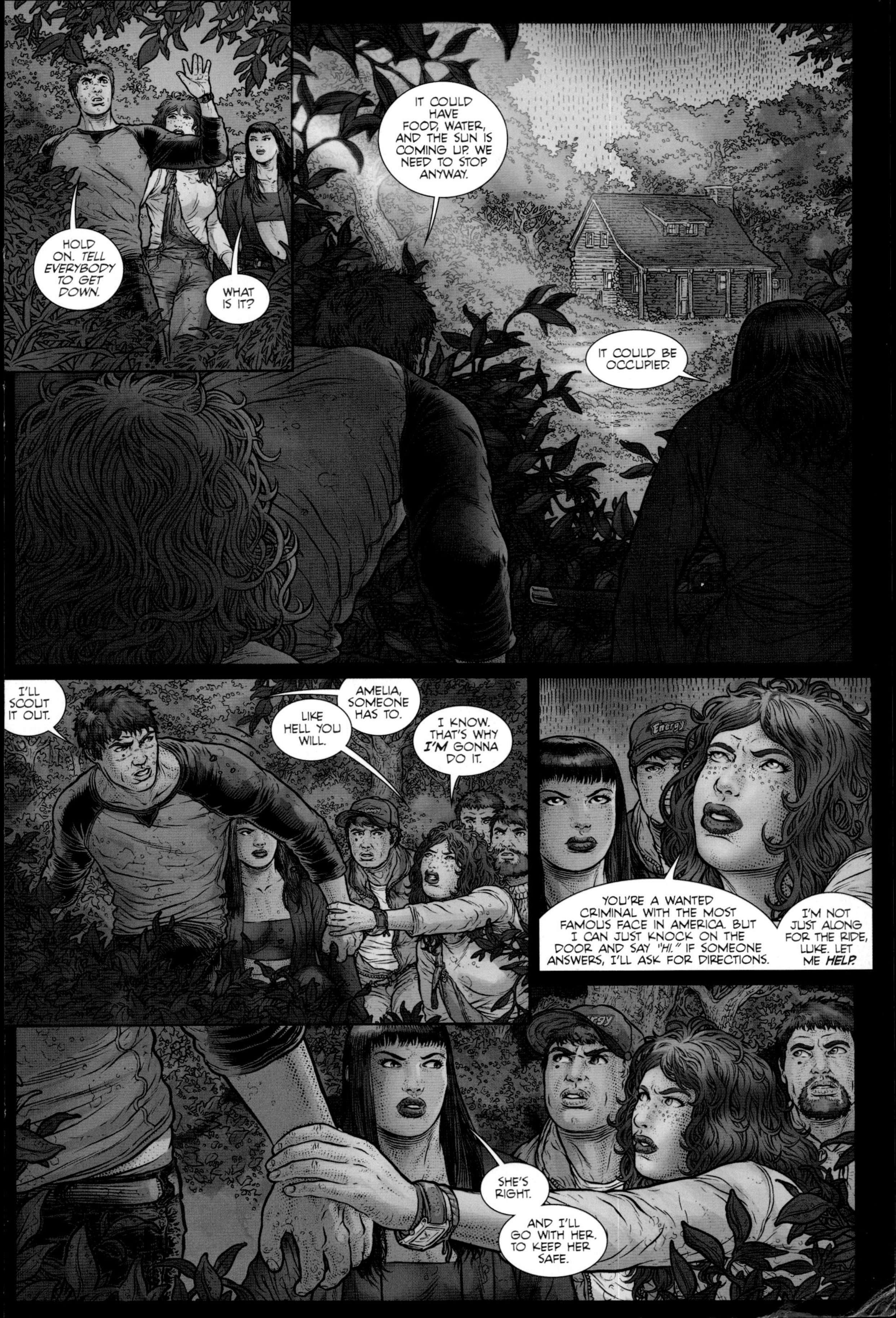
HOLD ON. *TELL EVERYBODY* TO GET DOWN.
WHAT IS IT?
IT COULD HAVE FOOD, WATER, AND THE SUN IS COMING UP. WE NEED TO STOP ANYWAY.
IT COULD BE OCCUPIED.
I'LL SCOUT IT OUT.
LIKE HELL YOU WILL.
AMELIA, SOMEONE HAS TO.
I KNOW. THAT'S WHY ***I'M*** GONNA DO IT.
YOU'RE A WANTED CRIMINAL WITH THE MOST FAMOUS FACE IN AMERICA. BUT I CAN JUST KNOCK ON THE DOOR AND SAY *"HI."* IF SOMEONE ANSWERS, I'LL ASK FOR DIRECTIONS.
I'M NOT JUST ALONG FOR THE RIDE, LUKE. LET ME ***HELP.***
SHE'S RIGHT.
AND I'LL GO WITH HER. TO KEEP HER SAFE.

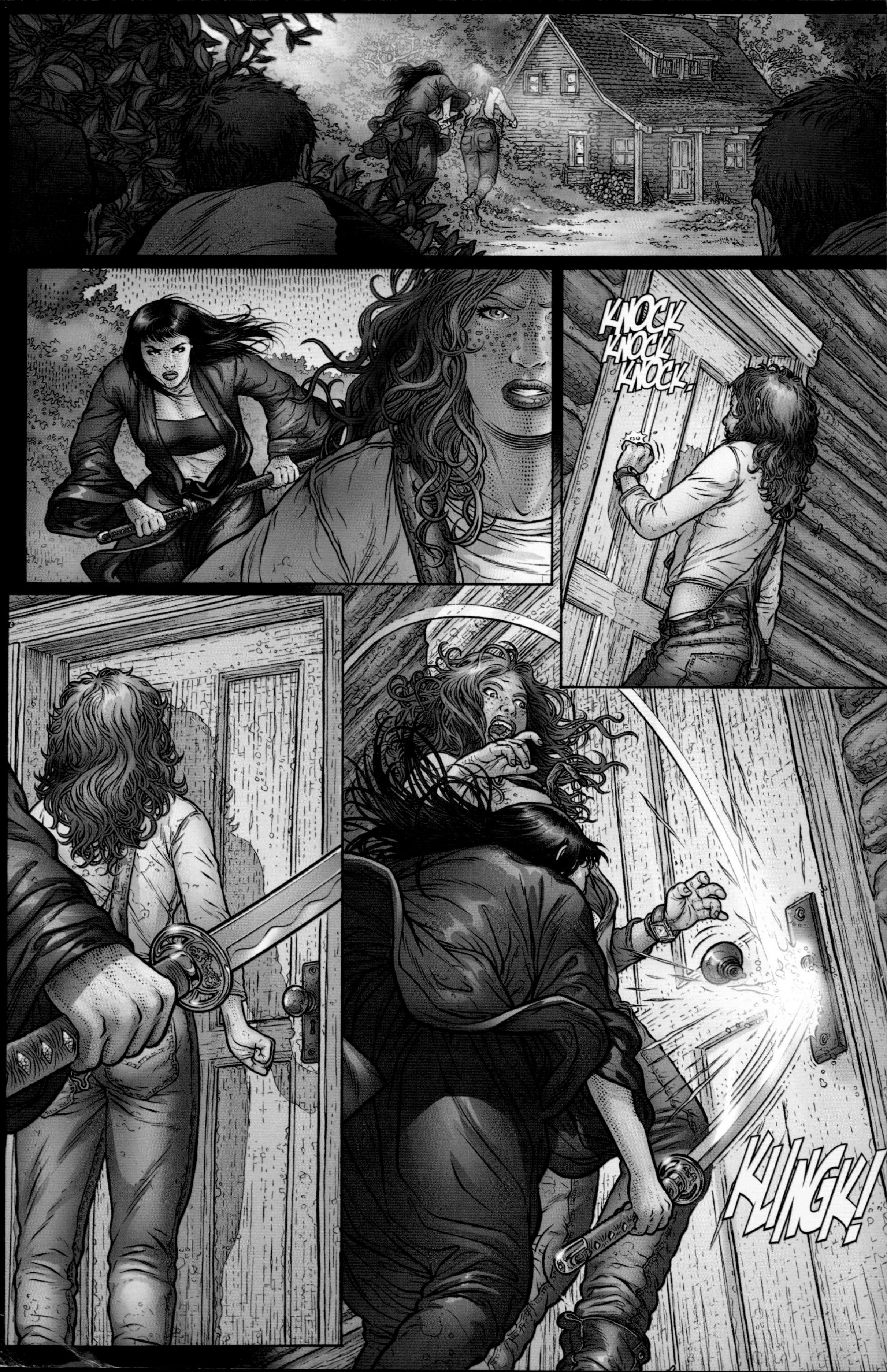

KNOCK KNOCK KNOCK.
KLINGK!

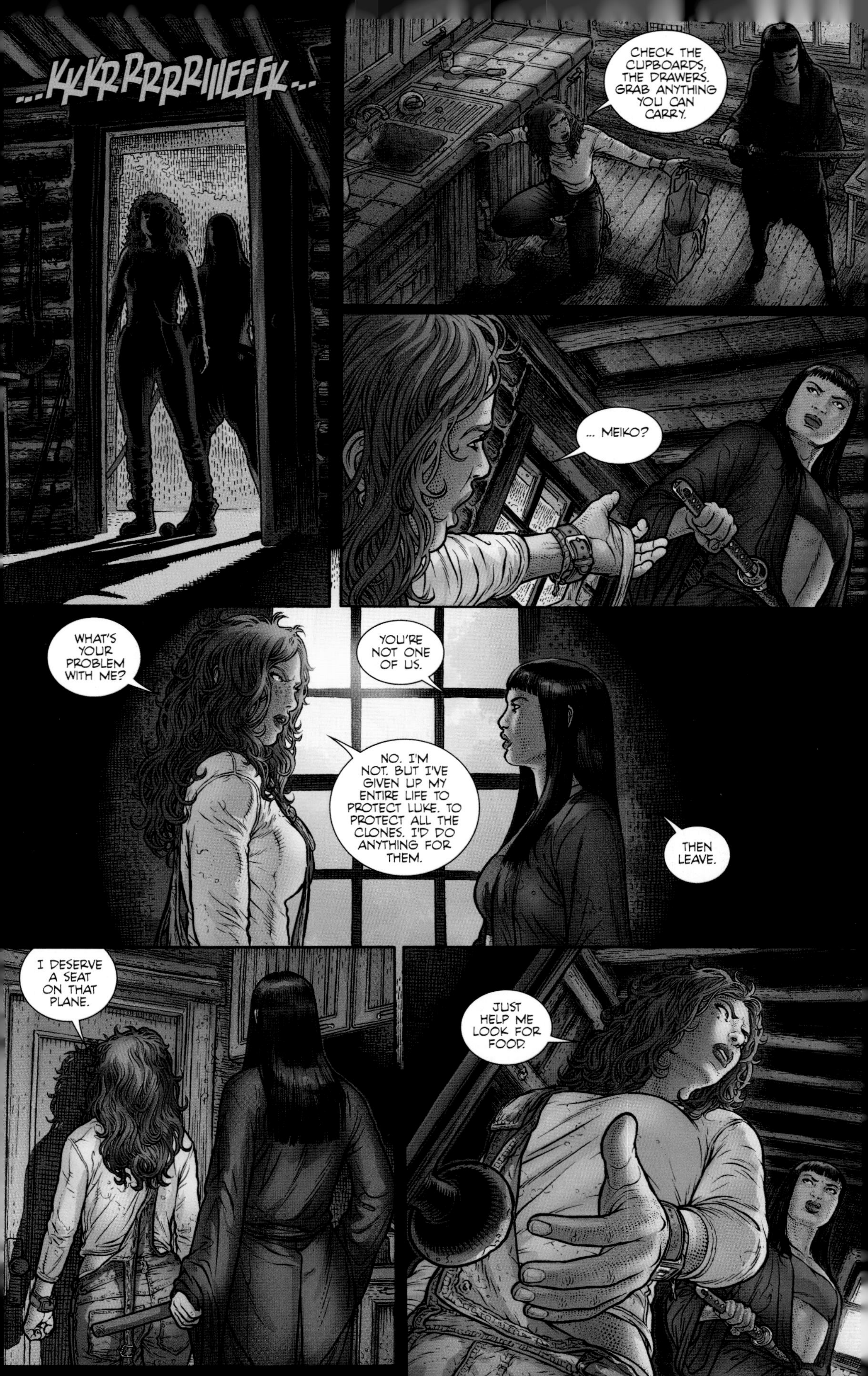
...KKKRRRRRIIIEEEK...
CHECK THE CUPBOARDS, THE DRAWERS. GRAB ANYTHING YOU CAN CARRY.
... MEIKO?
WHAT'S YOUR PROBLEM WITH ME?
YOU'RE NOT ONE OF US.
NO. I'M NOT. BUT I'VE GIVEN UP MY ENTIRE LIFE TO PROTECT LUKE. TO PROTECT ALL THE CLONES. I'D DO ANYTHING FOR THEM.
THEN LEAVE.
I DESERVE A SEAT ON THAT PLANE.
JUST HELP ME LOOK FOR FOOD.

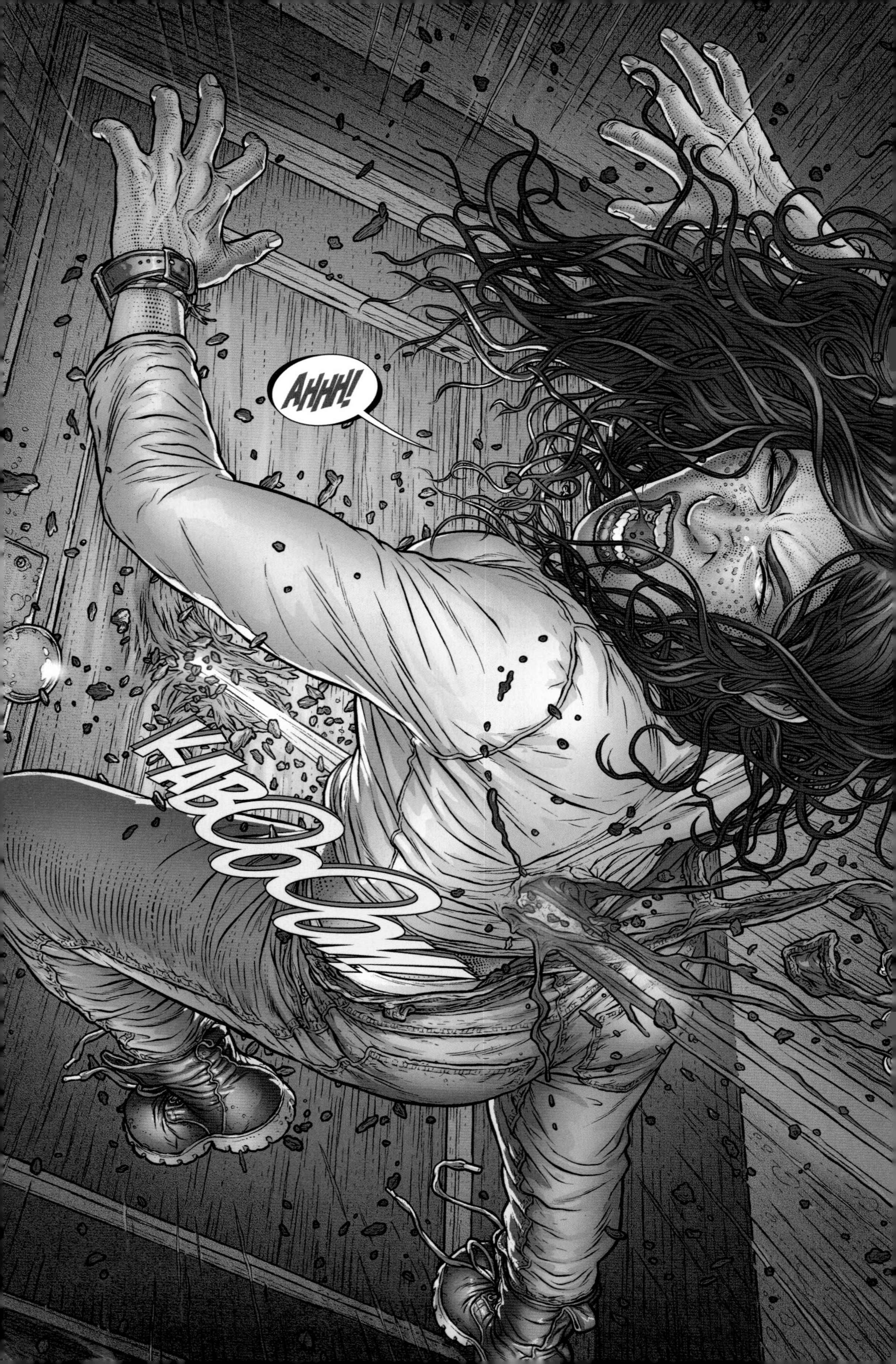
AHHH!
KABOOOOM!

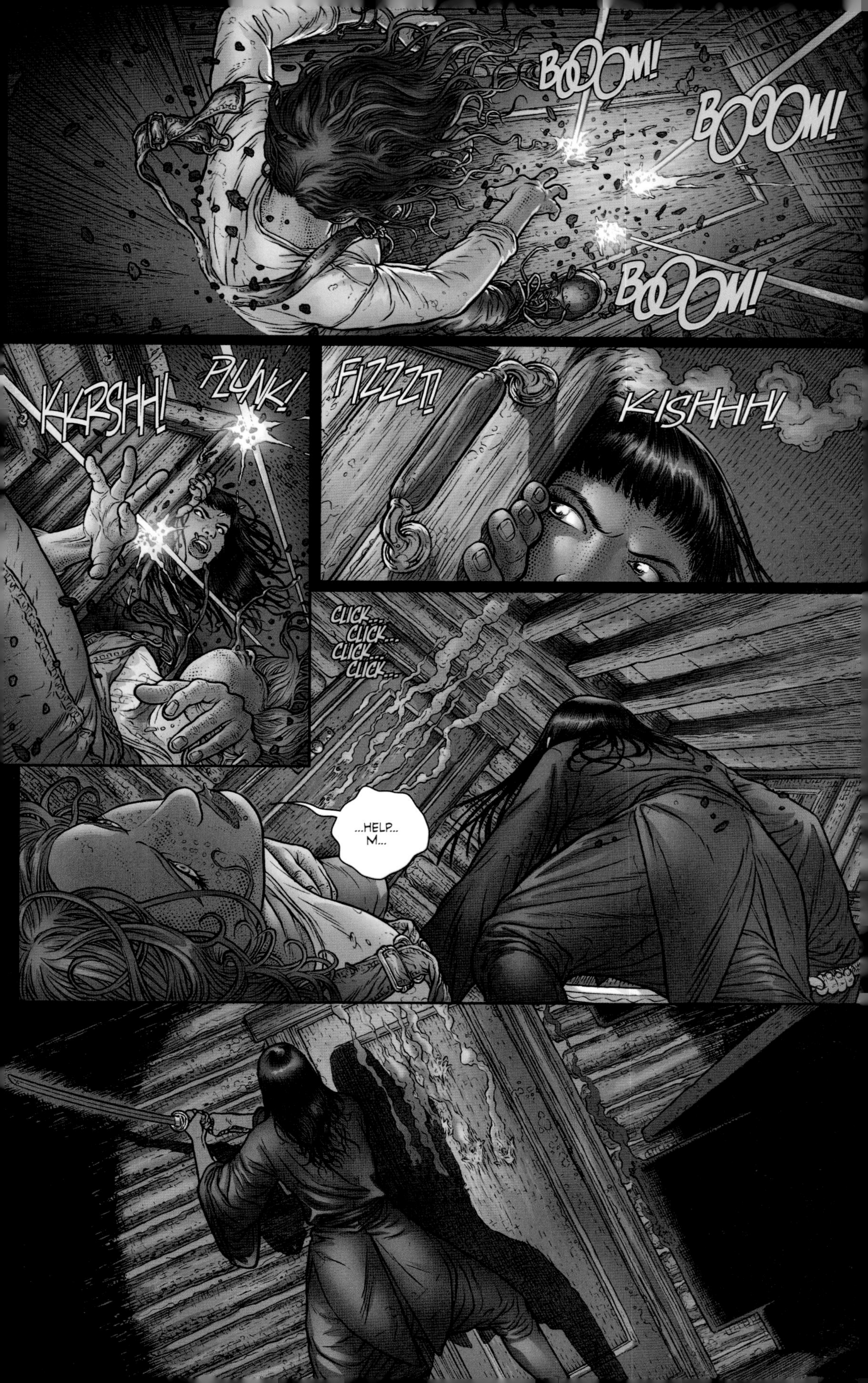
BOOOM!
BOOOM!
BOOOM!
KKRSHH!
PLUNK!
FIZZZT!
KISHHH!
CLICK... CLICK... CLICK... CLICK...
...HELP... M...

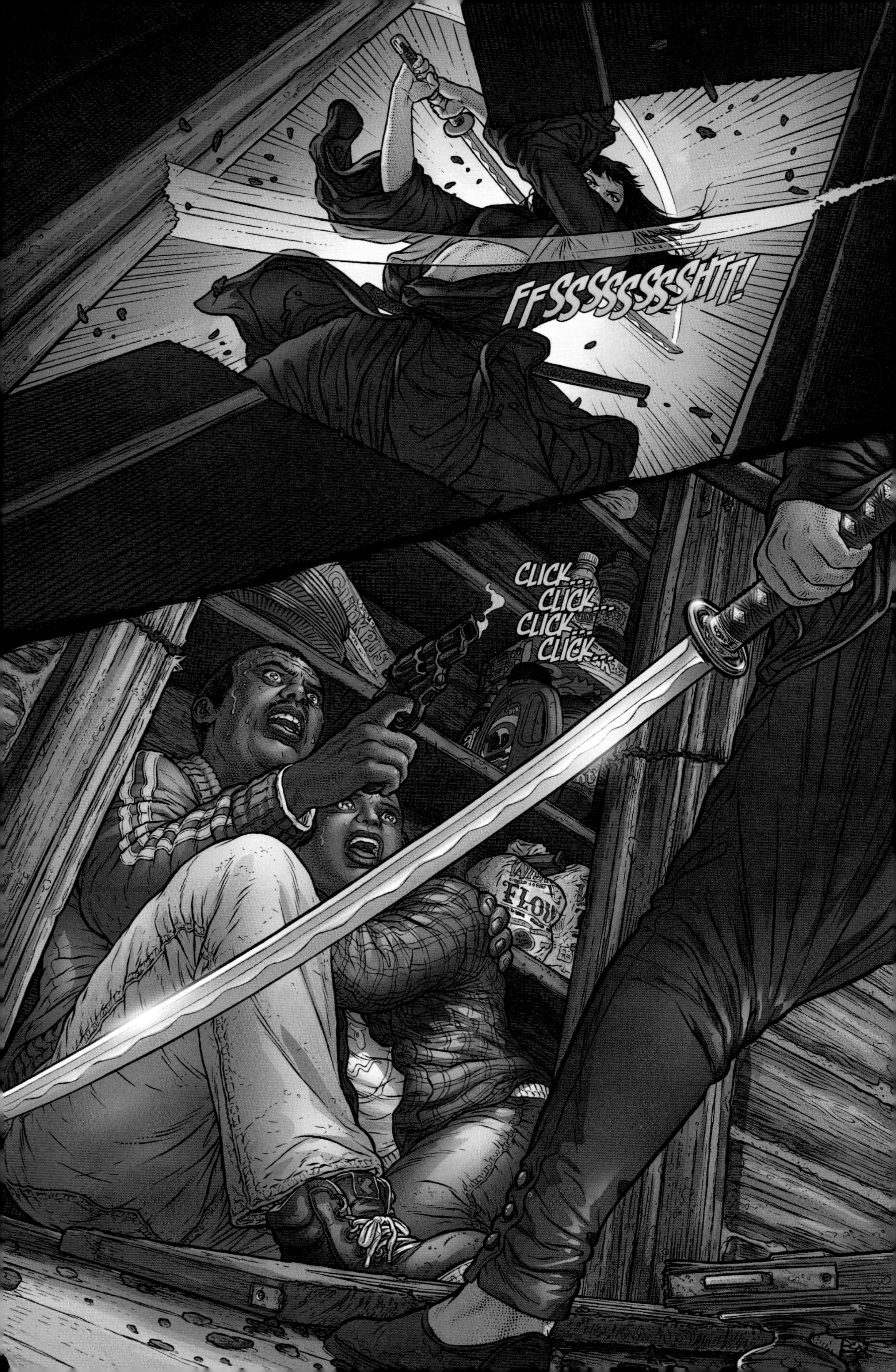

FFSSSSSSSSHTT!
CLICK...
CLICK...
CLICK...
CLICK...

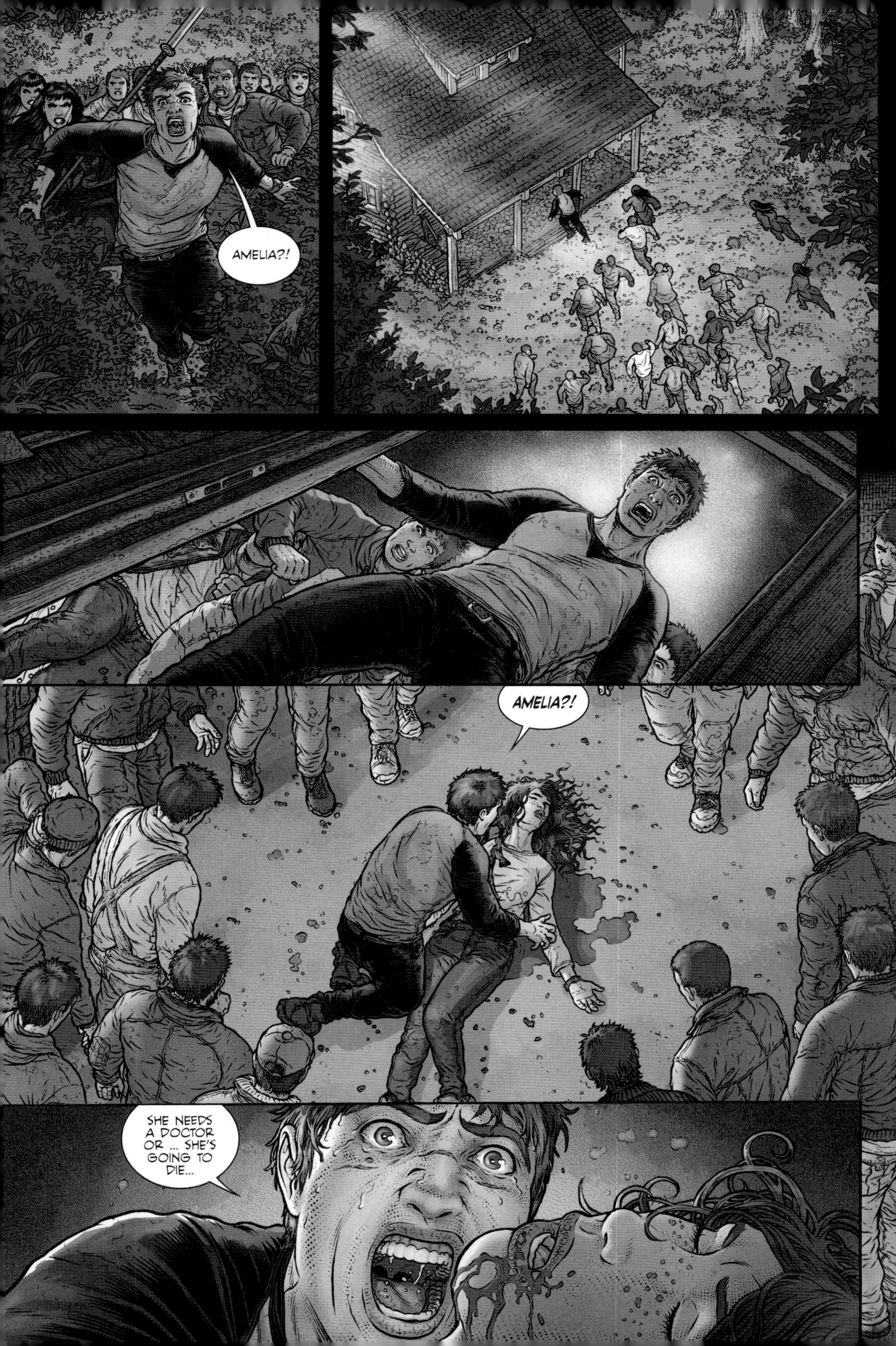
AMELIA?!
AMELIA?!
SHE NEEDS A DOCTOR OR ... SHE'S GOING TO DIE...

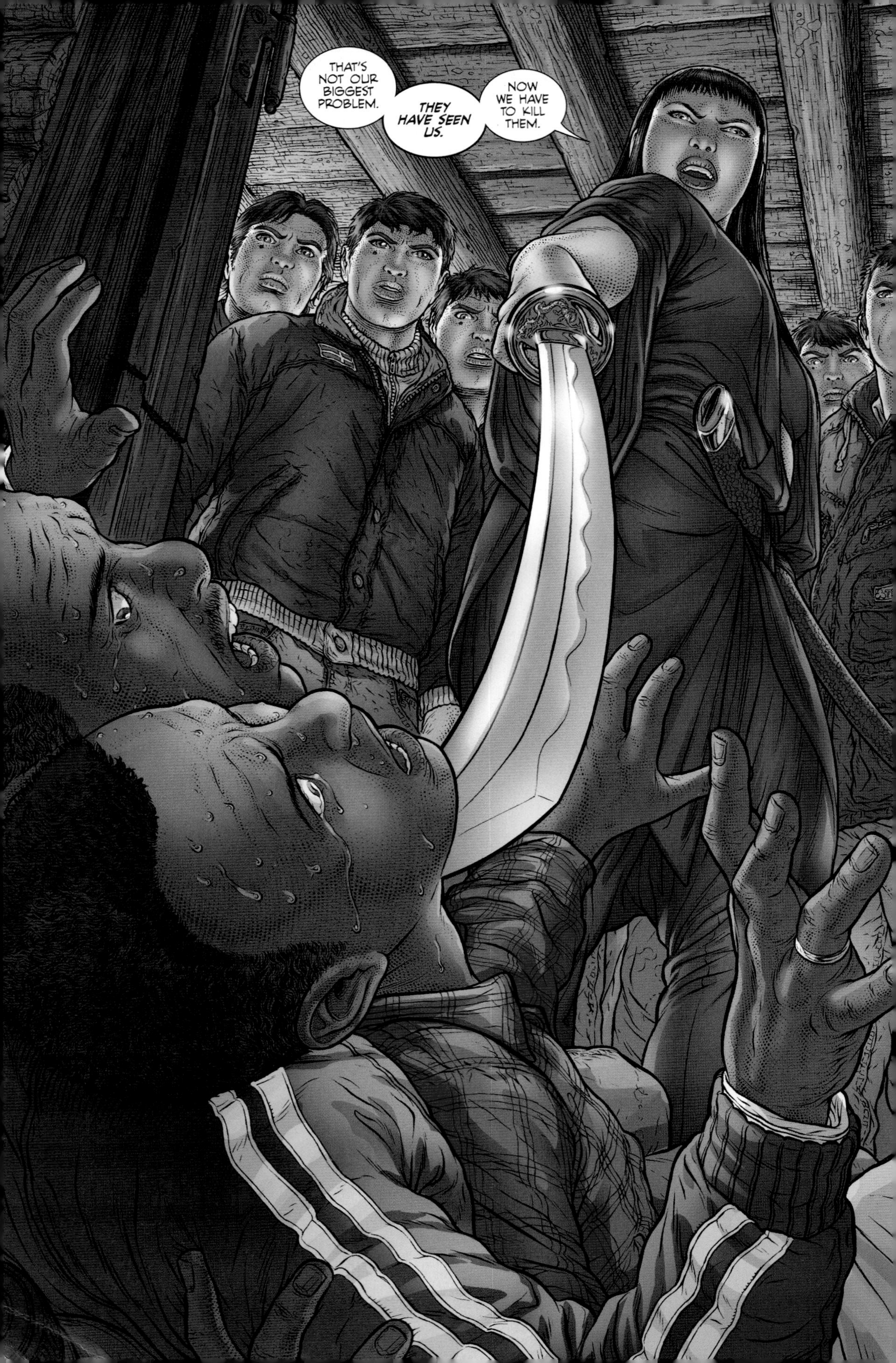
THAT'S NOT OUR BIGGEST PROBLEM.
THEY HAVE SEEN US.
NOW WE HAVE TO KILL THEM.

CHAPTER 17

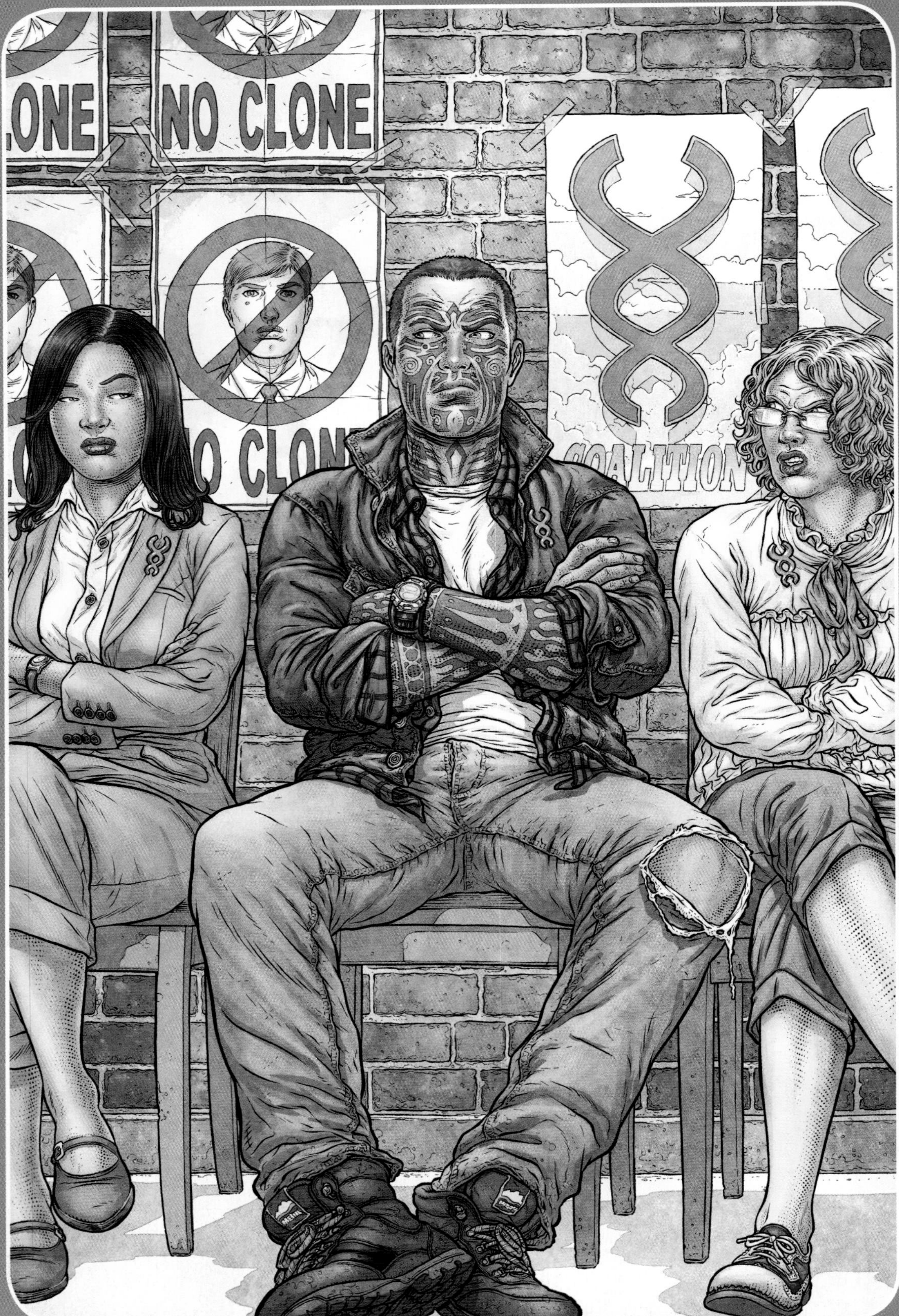
NO CLONE
LONE
NO CLON
COALITION

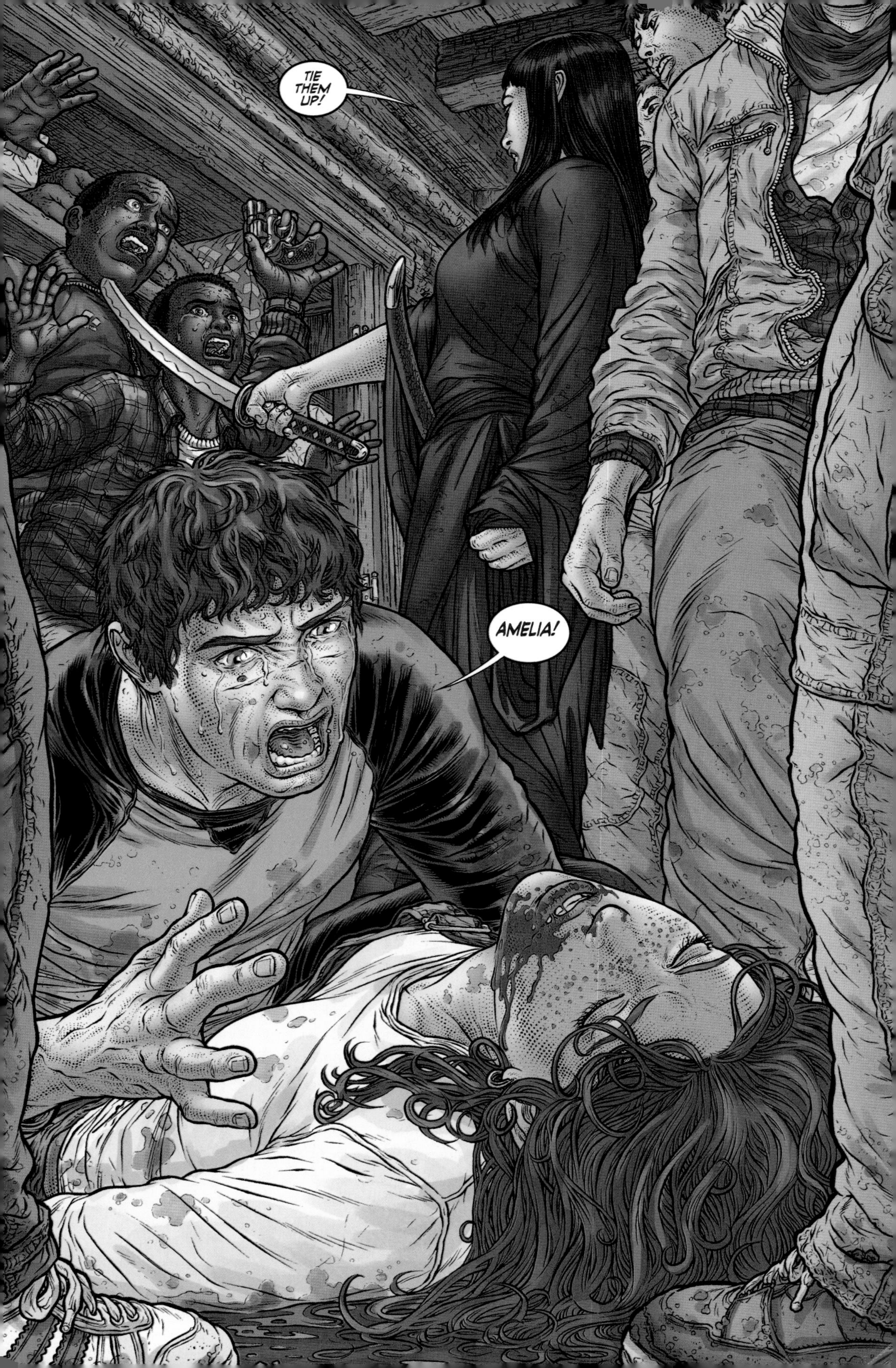
TIE THEM UP!
AMELIA!

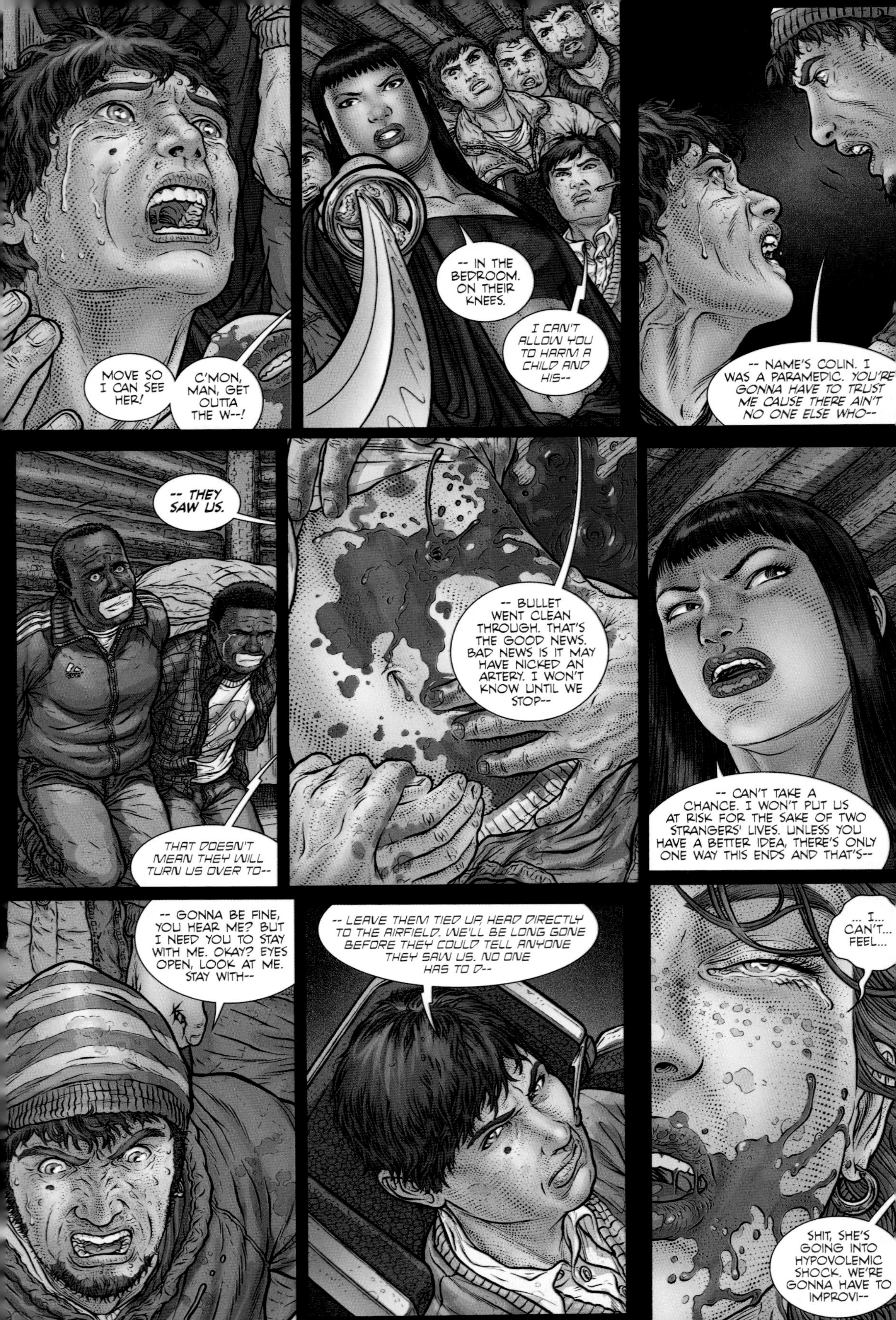
MOVE SO I CAN SEE HER!
C'MON, MAN, GET OUTTA THE W--!
-- IN THE BEDROOM. ON THEIR KNEES.
I CAN'T ALLOW YOU TO HARM A CHILD AND HIS--
-- NAME'S COLIN. I WAS A PARAMEDIC. YOU'RE GONNA HAVE TO TRUST ME CAUSE THERE AIN'T NO ONE ELSE WHO--
-- THEY SAW US.
THAT DOESN'T MEAN THEY WILL TURN US OVER TO--
-- BULLET WENT CLEAN THROUGH. THAT'S THE GOOD NEWS. BAD NEWS IS IT MAY HAVE NICKED AN ARTERY. I WON'T KNOW UNTIL WE STOP--
-- CAN'T TAKE A CHANCE. I WON'T PUT US AT RISK FOR THE SAKE OF TWO STRANGERS' LIVES. UNLESS YOU HAVE A BETTER IDEA, THERE'S ONLY ONE WAY THIS ENDS AND THAT'S--
-- GONNA BE FINE, YOU HEAR ME? BUT I NEED YOU TO STAY WITH ME. OKAY? EYES OPEN, LOOK AT ME. STAY WITH--
-- LEAVE THEM TIED UP, HEAD DIRECTLY TO THE AIRFIELD. WE'LL BE LONG GONE BEFORE THEY COULD TELL ANYONE THEY SAW US. NO ONE HAS TO D--
... I... CAN'T... FEEL...
SHIT, SHE'S GOING INTO HYPOVOLEMIC SHOCK. WE'RE GONNA HAVE TO IMPROVI--

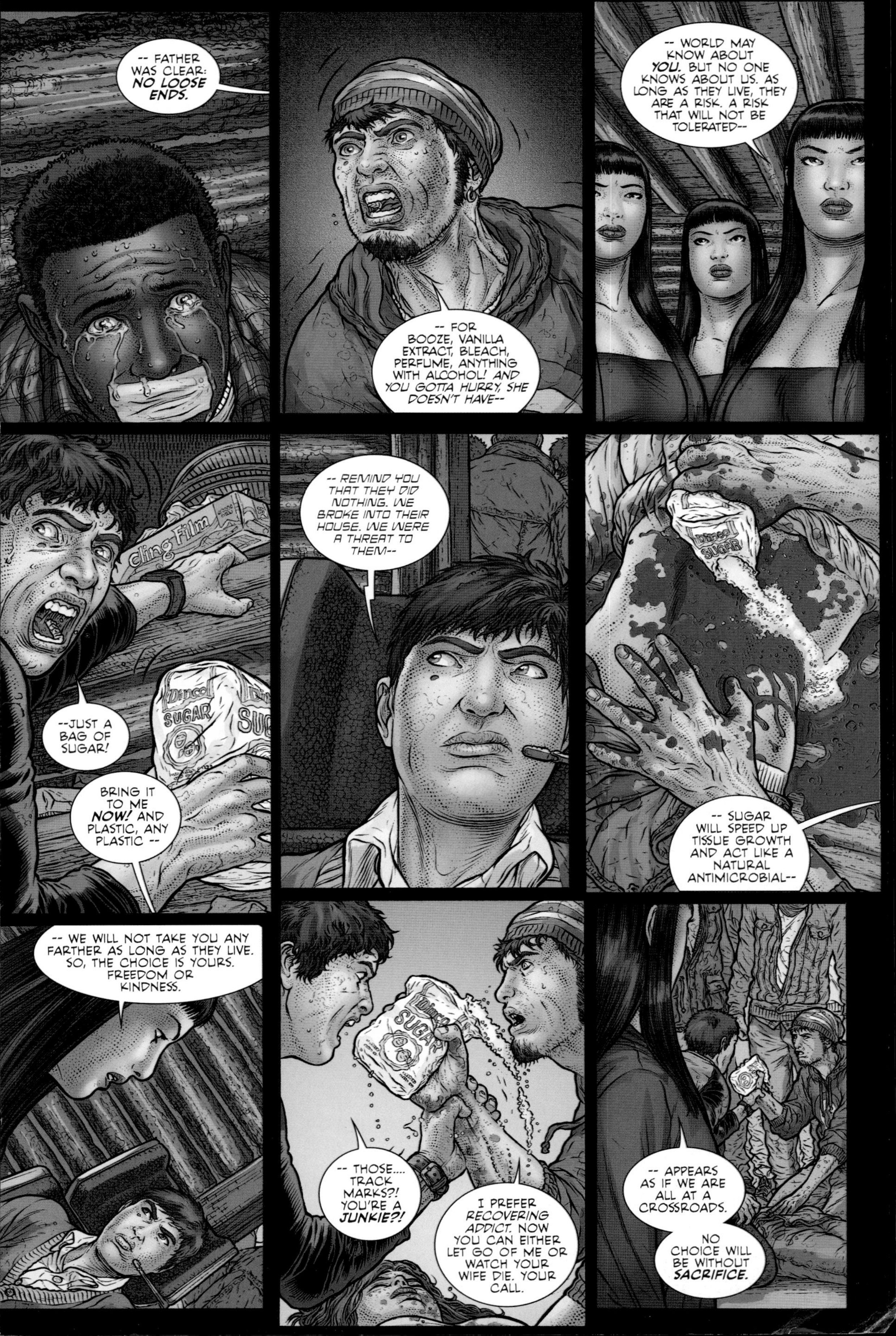
-- FATHER WAS CLEAR: *NO LOOSE ENDS.*
-- FOR BOOZE, VANILLA EXTRACT, BLEACH, PERFUME, ANYTHING WITH ALCOHOL! *AND YOU GOTTA HURRY, SHE DOESN'T HAVE--*
-- WORLD MAY KNOW ABOUT *YOU.* BUT NO ONE KNOWS ABOUT US. AS LONG AS THEY LIVE, THEY ARE A RISK. A RISK THAT WILL NOT BE TOLERATED--
Cling Film
--JUST A BAG OF SUGAR!
BRING IT TO ME *NOW!* AND PLASTIC, ANY PLASTIC --
-- REMIND YOU THAT THEY DID NOTHING. WE BROKE INTO THEIR HOUSE. WE WERE A THREAT TO THEM--
SUGAR
-- SUGAR WILL SPEED UP TISSUE GROWTH AND ACT LIKE A NATURAL ANTIMICROBIAL--
-- WE WILL NOT TAKE YOU ANY FARTHER AS LONG AS THEY LIVE. SO, THE CHOICE IS YOURS. FREEDOM OR KINDNESS.
SUGAR
-- THOSE.... TRACK MARKS?! YOU'RE A *JUNKIE?!*
I PREFER *RECOVERING ADDICT.* NOW YOU CAN EITHER LET GO OF ME OR WATCH YOUR WIFE DIE. YOUR CALL.
-- APPEARS AS IF WE ARE ALL AT A CROSSROADS.
NO CHOICE WILL BE WITHOUT *SACRIFICE.*

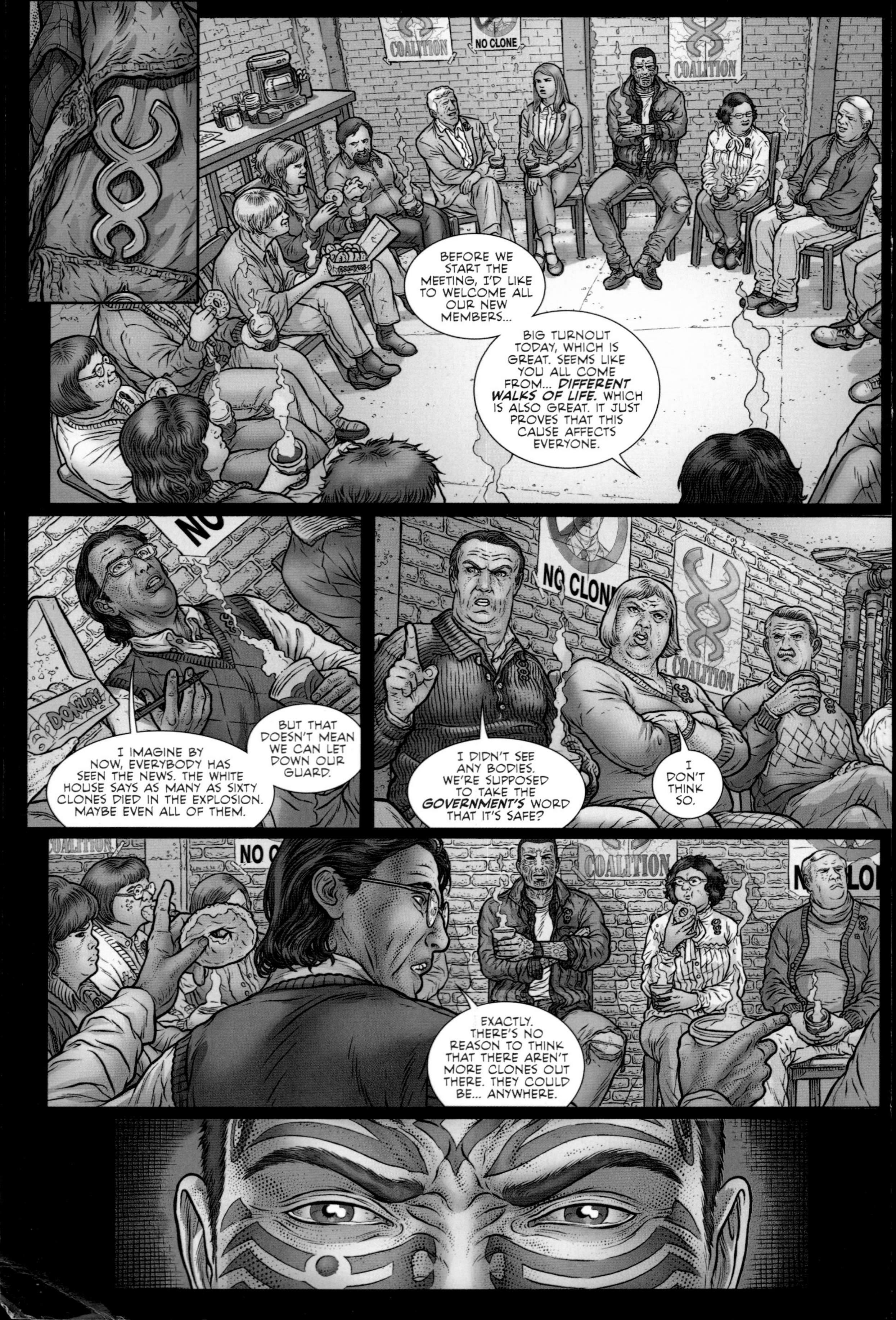
COALITION
NO CLONE
COALITION
BEFORE WE START THE MEETING, I'D LIKE TO WELCOME ALL OUR NEW MEMBERS...
BIG TURNOUT TODAY, WHICH IS GREAT. SEEMS LIKE YOU ALL COME FROM... *DIFFERENT WALKS OF LIFE.* WHICH IS ALSO GREAT. IT JUST PROVES THAT THIS CAUSE AFFECTS EVERYONE.
DONUTS
I IMAGINE BY NOW, EVERYBODY HAS SEEN THE NEWS. THE WHITE HOUSE SAYS AS MANY AS SIXTY CLONES DIED IN THE EXPLOSION. MAYBE EVEN ALL OF THEM.
BUT THAT DOESN'T MEAN WE CAN LET DOWN OUR GUARD.
NO CLONE
COALITION
I DIDN'T SEE ANY BODIES. WE'RE SUPPOSED TO TAKE THE *GOVERNMENT'S* WORD THAT IT'S SAFE?
I DON'T THINK SO.
COALITION
COALITION
EXACTLY. THERE'S NO REASON TO THINK THAT THERE AREN'T MORE CLONES OUT THERE. THEY COULD BE... ANYWHERE.

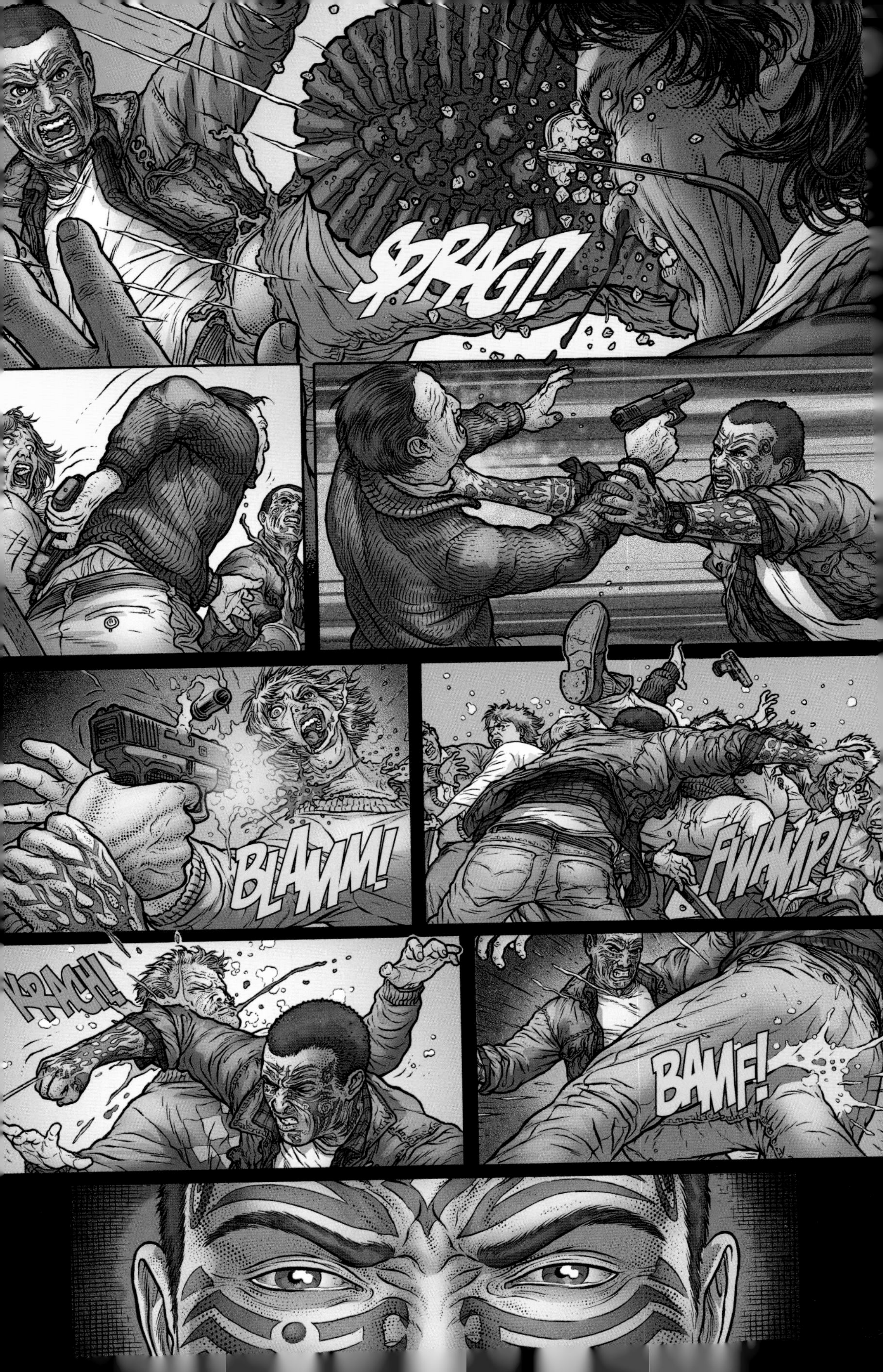
SPRAG!!
BLAMM!
FWAMP!
KRACH!
BAMF!

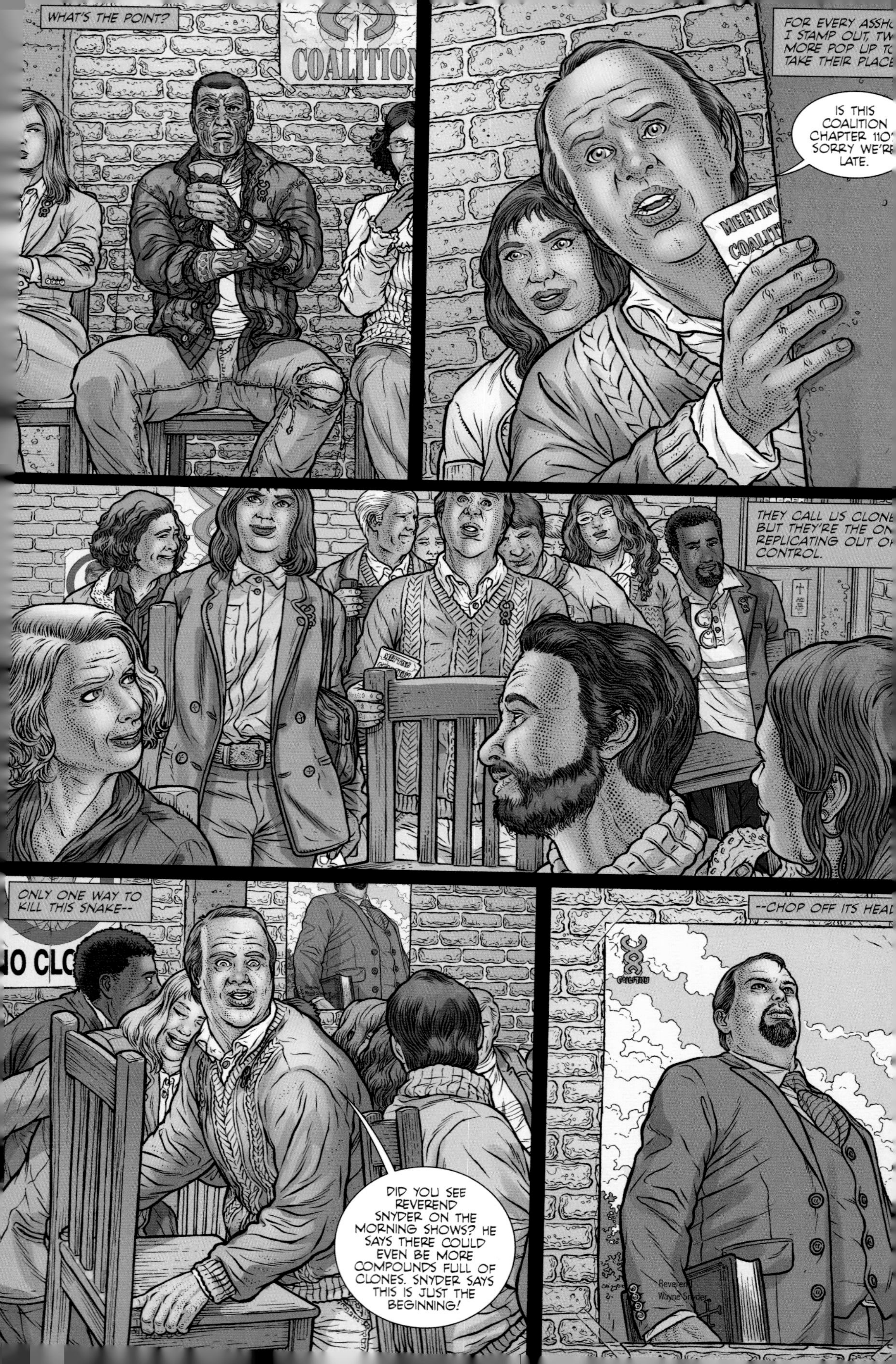
WHAT'S THE POINT?
COALITION
FOR EVERY ASSHO
I STAMP OUT, TW
MORE POP UP TO
TAKE THEIR PLACE
IS THIS COALITION CHAPTER 110 SORRY WE'R LATE.
MEETING COALIT
THEY CALL US CLONE
BUT THEY'RE THE ON
REPLICATING OUT O
CONTROL.
ONLY ONE WAY TO KILL THIS SNAKE--
NO CLO
DID YOU SEE REVEREND SNYDER ON THE MORNING SHOWS? HE SAYS THERE COULD EVEN BE MORE COMPOUNDS FULL OF CLONES. SNYDER SAYS THIS IS JUST THE BEGINNING!
--CHOP OFF ITS HEA
Wayne Snyder

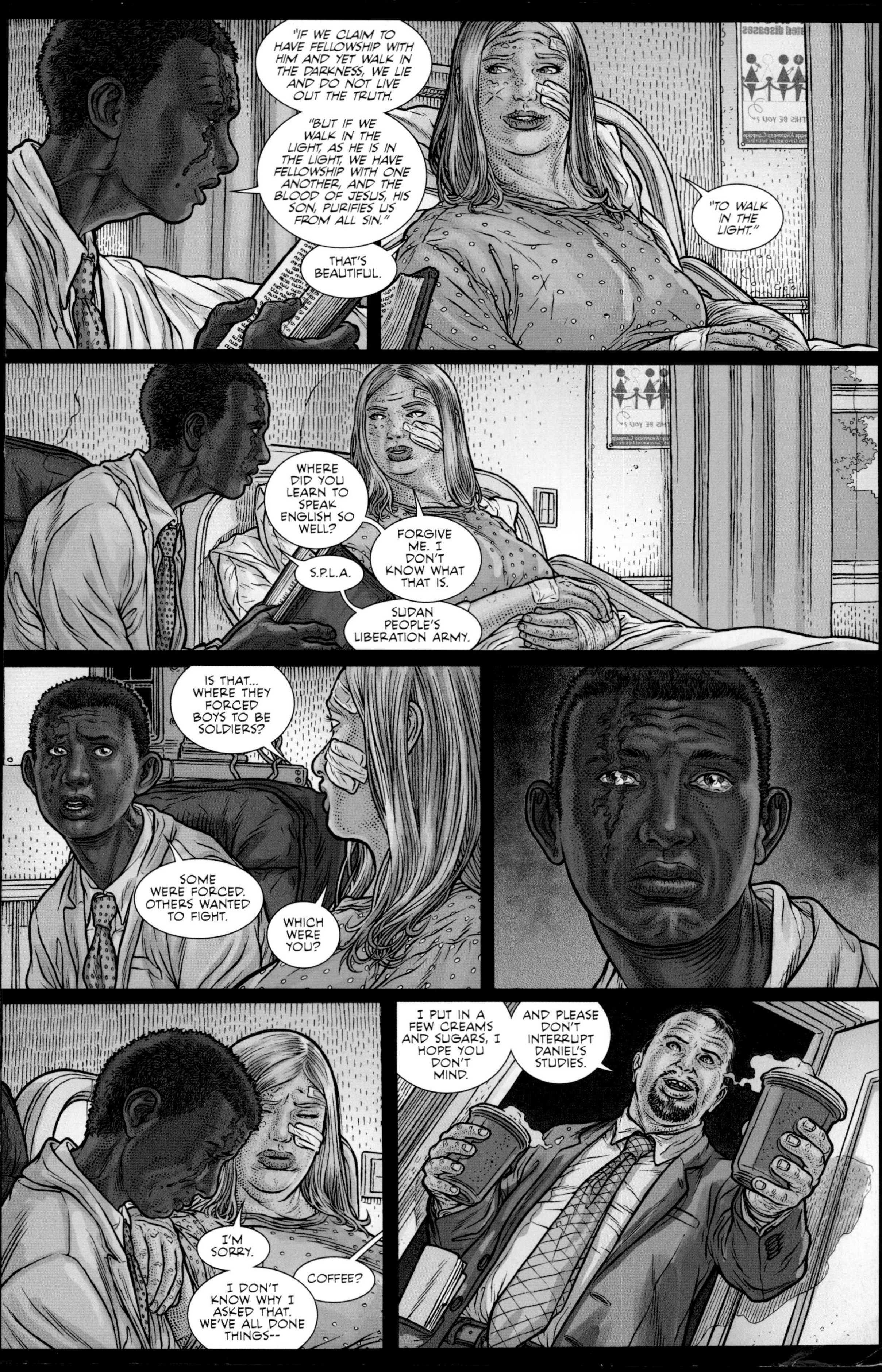
"IF WE CLAIM TO HAVE FELLOWSHIP WITH HIM AND YET WALK IN THE DARKNESS, WE LIE AND DO NOT LIVE OUT THE TRUTH.
"BUT IF WE WALK IN THE LIGHT, AS HE IS IN THE LIGHT, WE HAVE FELLOWSHIP WITH ONE ANOTHER, AND THE BLOOD OF JESUS, HIS SON, PURIFIES US FROM ALL SIN."
THAT'S BEAUTIFUL.
"TO WALK IN THE LIGHT."
WHERE DID YOU LEARN TO SPEAK ENGLISH SO WELL?
S.P.L.A.
FORGIVE ME. I DON'T KNOW WHAT THAT IS.
SUDAN PEOPLE'S LIBERATION ARMY.
IS THAT... WHERE THEY FORCED BOYS TO BE SOLDIERS?
SOME WERE FORCED. OTHERS WANTED TO FIGHT.
WHICH WERE YOU?
I'M SORRY.
I DON'T KNOW WHY I ASKED THAT. WE'VE ALL DONE THINGS--
COFFEE?
I PUT IN A FEW CREAMS AND SUGARS, I HOPE YOU DON'T MIND.
AND PLEASE DON'T INTERRUPT DANIEL'S STUDIES.

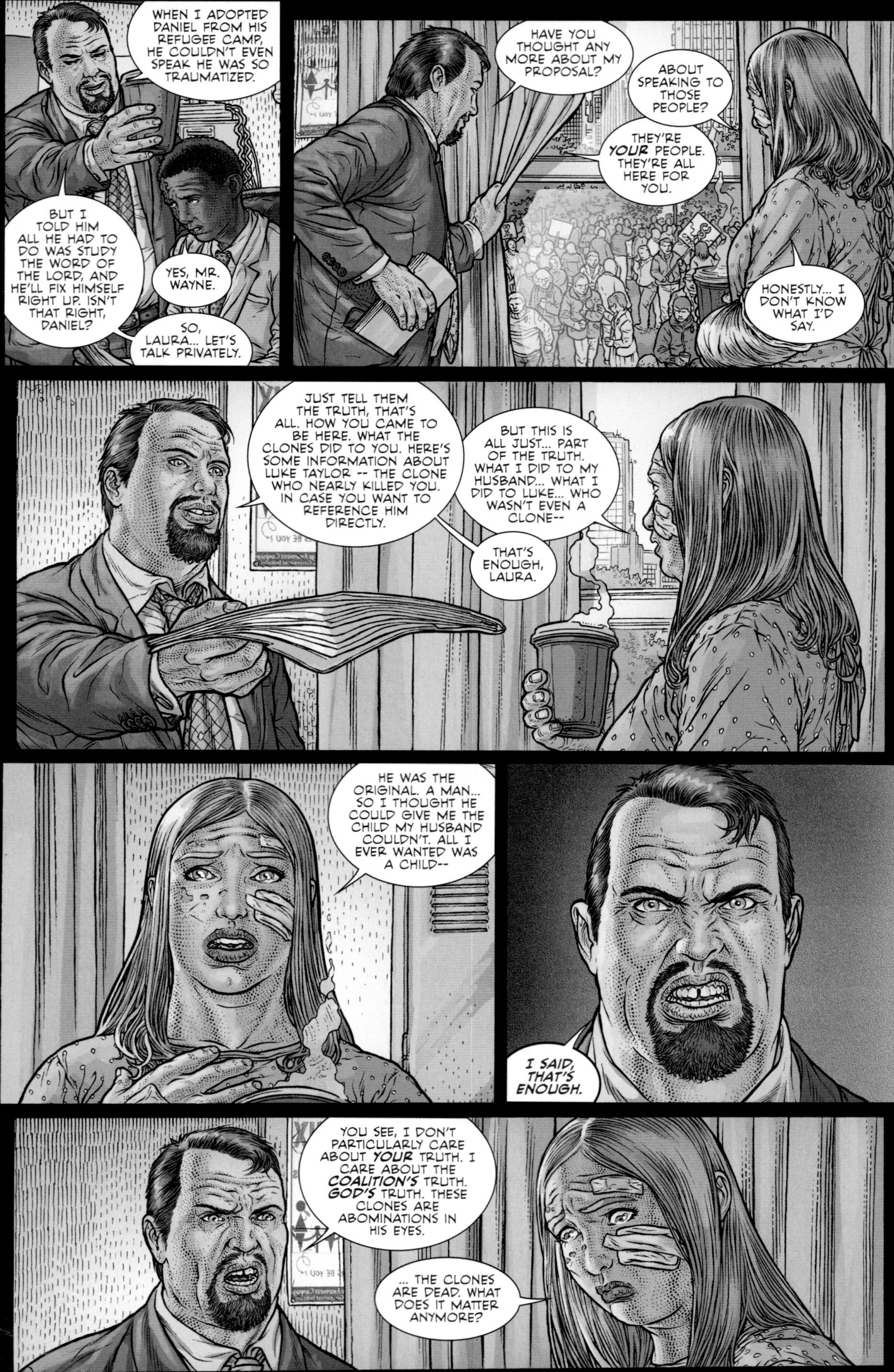
WHEN I ADOPTED DANIEL FROM HIS REFUGEE CAMP, HE COULDN'T EVEN SPEAK HE WAS SO TRAUMATIZED.
BUT I TOLD HIM ALL HE HAD TO DO WAS STUDY THE WORD OF THE LORD, AND HE'LL FIX HIMSELF RIGHT UP. ISN'T THAT RIGHT, DANIEL?
YES, MR. WAYNE.
SO, LAURA... LET'S TALK PRIVATELY.
HAVE YOU THOUGHT ANY MORE ABOUT MY PROPOSAL?
ABOUT SPEAKING TO THOSE PEOPLE?
THEY'RE YOUR PEOPLE. THEY'RE ALL HERE FOR YOU.
HONESTLY... I DON'T KNOW WHAT I'D SAY.
JUST TELL THEM THE TRUTH, THAT'S ALL. HOW YOU CAME TO BE HERE. WHAT THE CLONES DID TO YOU. HERE'S SOME INFORMATION ABOUT LUKE TAYLOR -- THE CLONE WHO NEARLY KILLED YOU. IN CASE YOU WANT TO REFERENCE HIM DIRECTLY.
BUT THIS IS ALL JUST... PART OF THE TRUTH. WHAT I DID TO MY HUSBAND... WHAT I DID TO LUKE... WHO WASN'T EVEN A CLONE--
THAT'S ENOUGH, LAURA.
HE WAS THE ORIGINAL. A MAN... SO I THOUGHT HE COULD GIVE ME THE CHILD MY HUSBAND COULDN'T. ALL I EVER WANTED WAS A CHILD--
I SAID, THAT'S ENOUGH.
YOU SEE, I DON'T PARTICULARLY CARE ABOUT YOUR TRUTH. I CARE ABOUT THE COALITION'S TRUTH. GOD'S TRUTH. THESE CLONES ARE ABOMINATIONS IN HIS EYES.
... THE CLONES ARE DEAD. WHAT DOES IT MATTER ANYMORE?

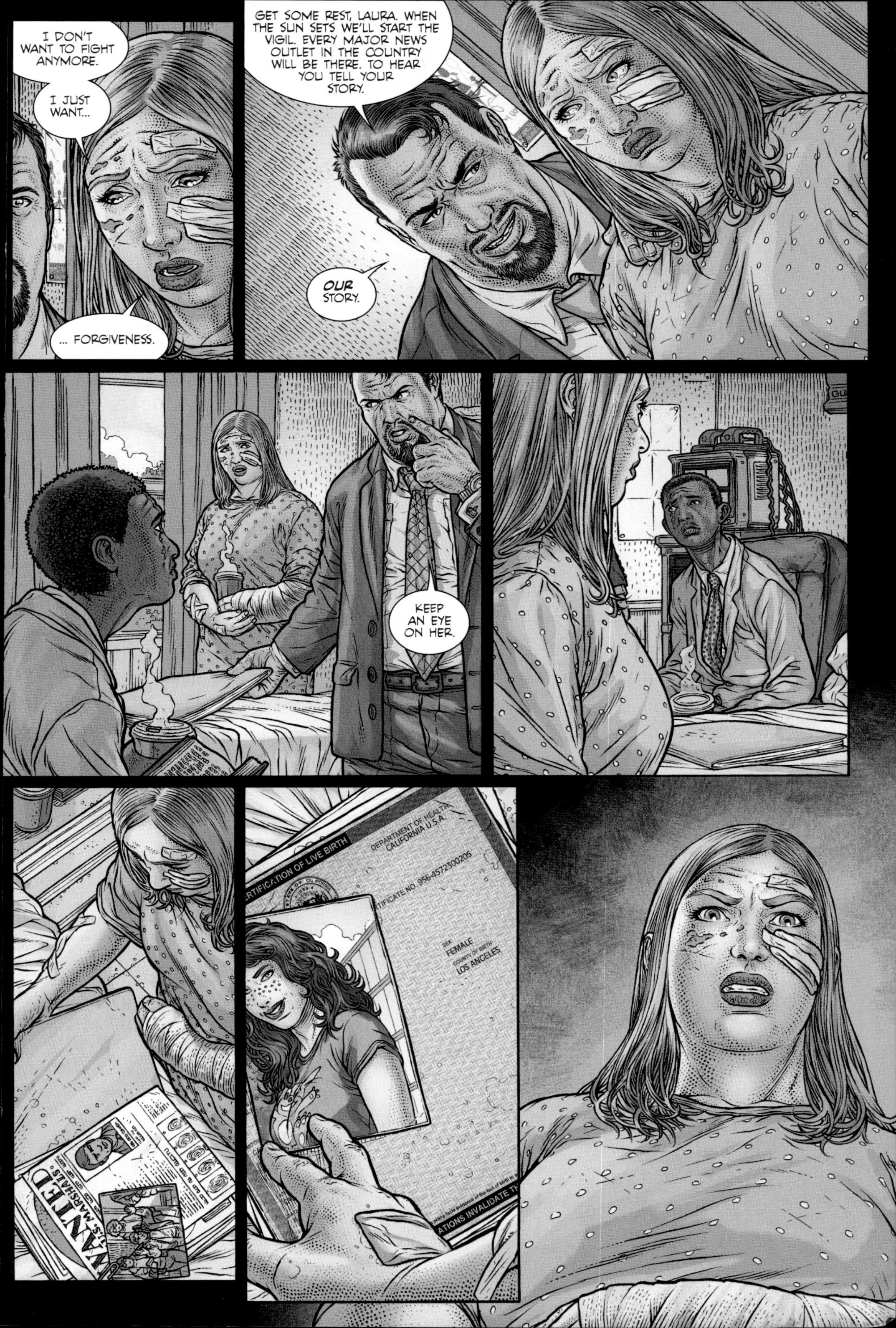

I DON'T WANT TO FIGHT ANYMORE.
I JUST WANT...
... FORGIVENESS.
GET SOME REST, LAURA. WHEN THE SUN SETS WE'LL START THE VIGIL. EVERY MAJOR NEWS OUTLET IN THE COUNTRY WILL BE THERE. TO HEAR YOU TELL YOUR STORY.
OUR STORY.
KEEP AN EYE ON HER.
WANTED
U.S. MARSHALS
DEPARTMENT OF HEALTH
CALIFORNIA U.S.A.
CERTIFICATION OF LIVE BIRTH
CERTIFICATE NO. 956-4572300205
SEX
FEMALE
COUNTY OF BIRTH
LOS ANGELES
ATIONS INVALIDATE TH

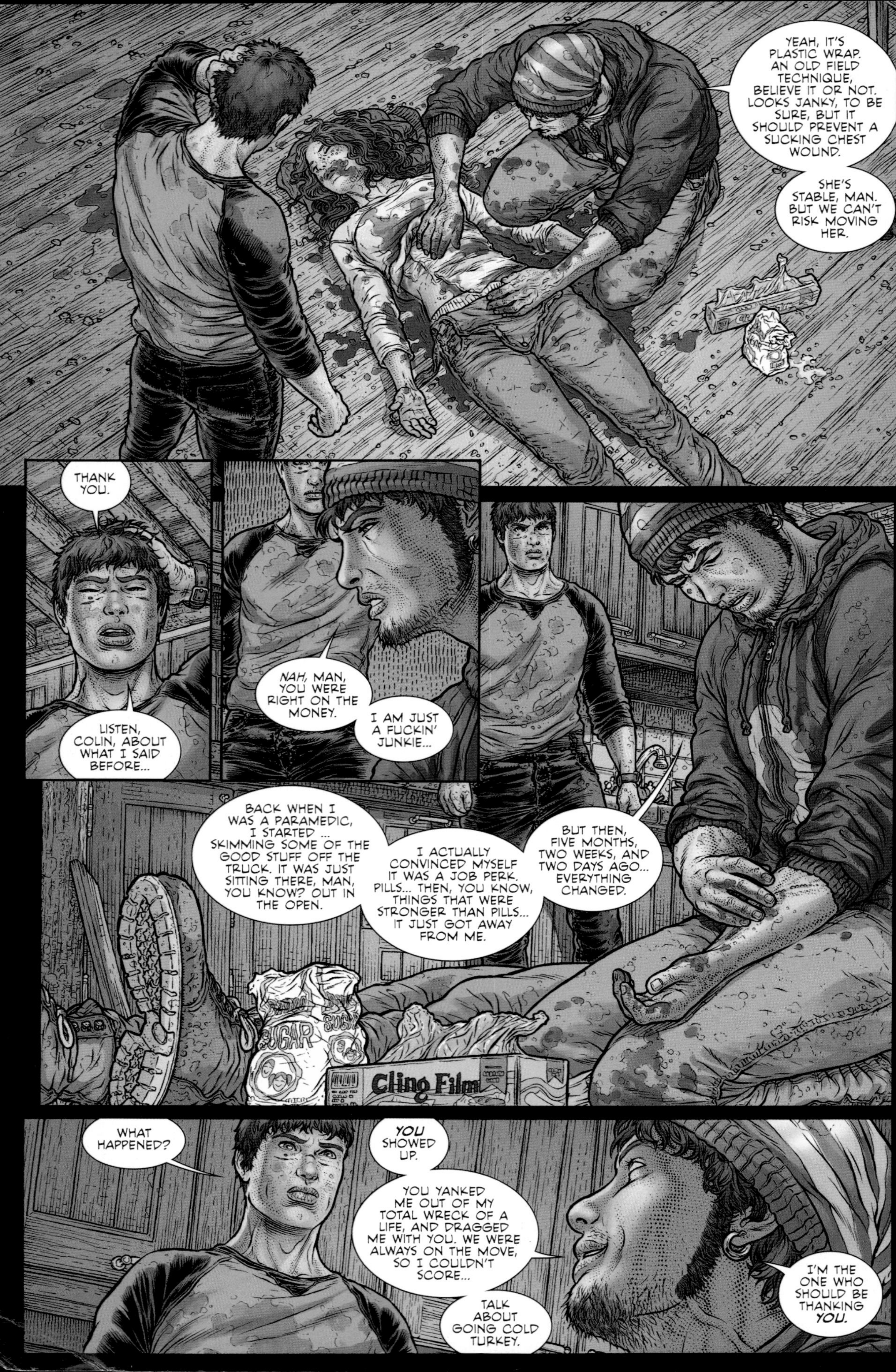
YEAH, IT'S PLASTIC WRAP. AN OLD FIELD TECHNIQUE, BELIEVE IT OR NOT. LOOKS JANKY, TO BE SURE, BUT IT SHOULD PREVENT A SUCKING CHEST WOUND.
SHE'S STABLE, MAN. BUT WE CAN'T RISK MOVING HER.
THANK YOU.
LISTEN, COLIN, ABOUT WHAT I SAID BEFORE...
NAH, MAN, YOU WERE RIGHT ON THE MONEY.
I AM JUST A FUCKIN' JUNKIE...
BACK WHEN I WAS A PARAMEDIC, I STARTED ... SKIMMING SOME OF THE GOOD STUFF OFF THE TRUCK. IT WAS JUST SITTING THERE, MAN, YOU KNOW? OUT IN THE OPEN.
I ACTUALLY CONVINCED MYSELF IT WAS A JOB PERK. PILLS... THEN, YOU KNOW, THINGS THAT WERE STRONGER THAN PILLS... IT JUST GOT AWAY FROM ME.
BUT THEN, FIVE MONTHS, TWO WEEKS, AND TWO DAYS AGO... EVERYTHING CHANGED.
SUGAR
SUGAR
Cling Film
WHAT HAPPENED?
YOU SHOWED UP.
YOU YANKED ME OUT OF MY TOTAL WRECK OF A LIFE, AND DRAGGED ME WITH YOU. WE WERE ALWAYS ON THE MOVE, SO I COULDN'T SCORE...
TALK ABOUT GOING COLD TURKEY.
I'M THE ONE WHO SHOULD BE THANKING *YOU*.

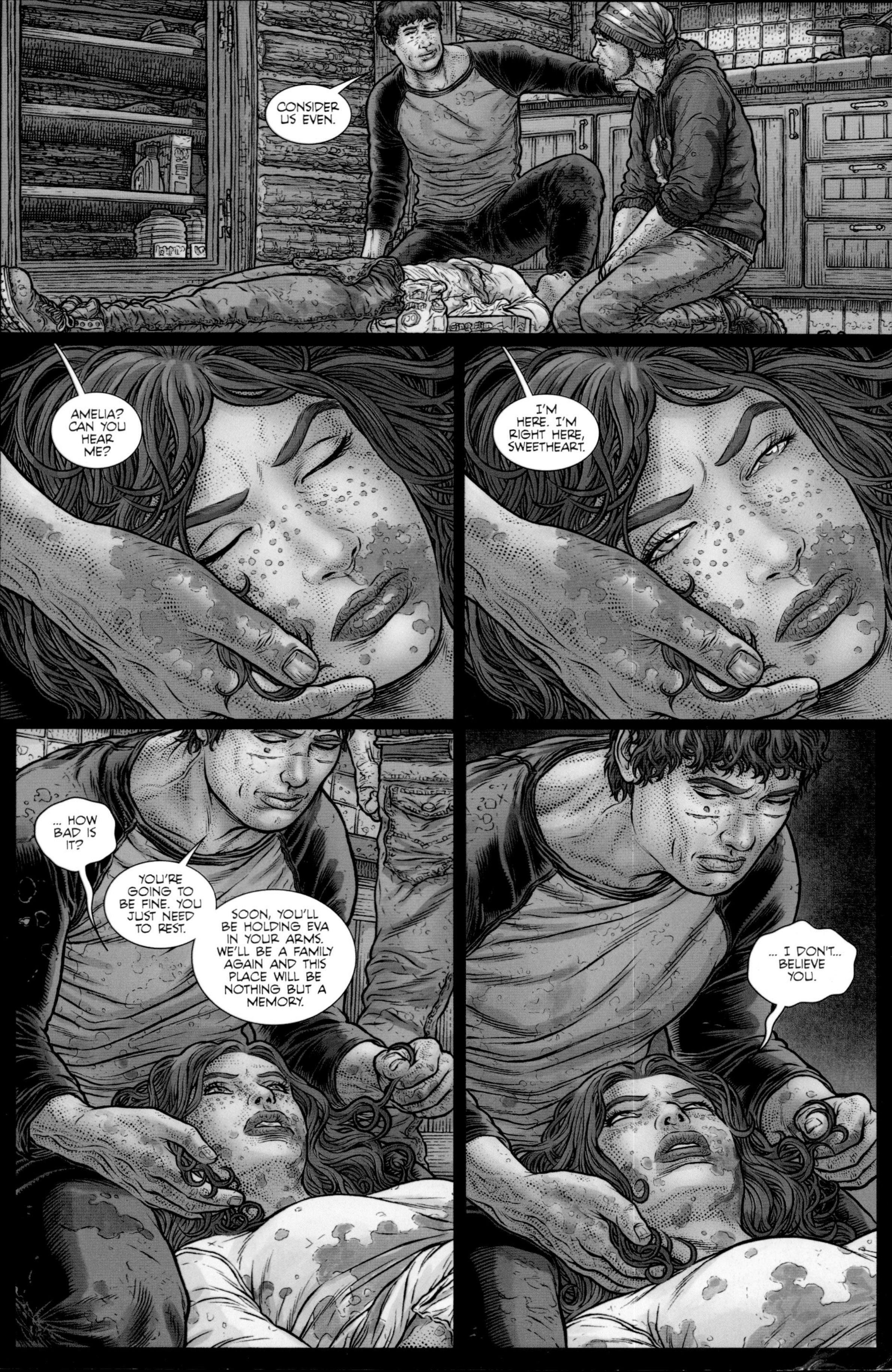
CONSIDER US EVEN.
AMELIA? CAN YOU HEAR ME?
I'M HERE. I'M RIGHT HERE, SWEETHEART.
... HOW BAD IS IT?
YOU'RE GOING TO BE FINE. YOU JUST NEED TO REST.
SOON, YOU'LL BE HOLDING EVA IN YOUR ARMS. WE'LL BE A FAMILY AGAIN AND THIS PLACE WILL BE NOTHING BUT A MEMORY.
... I DON'T... BELIEVE YOU.

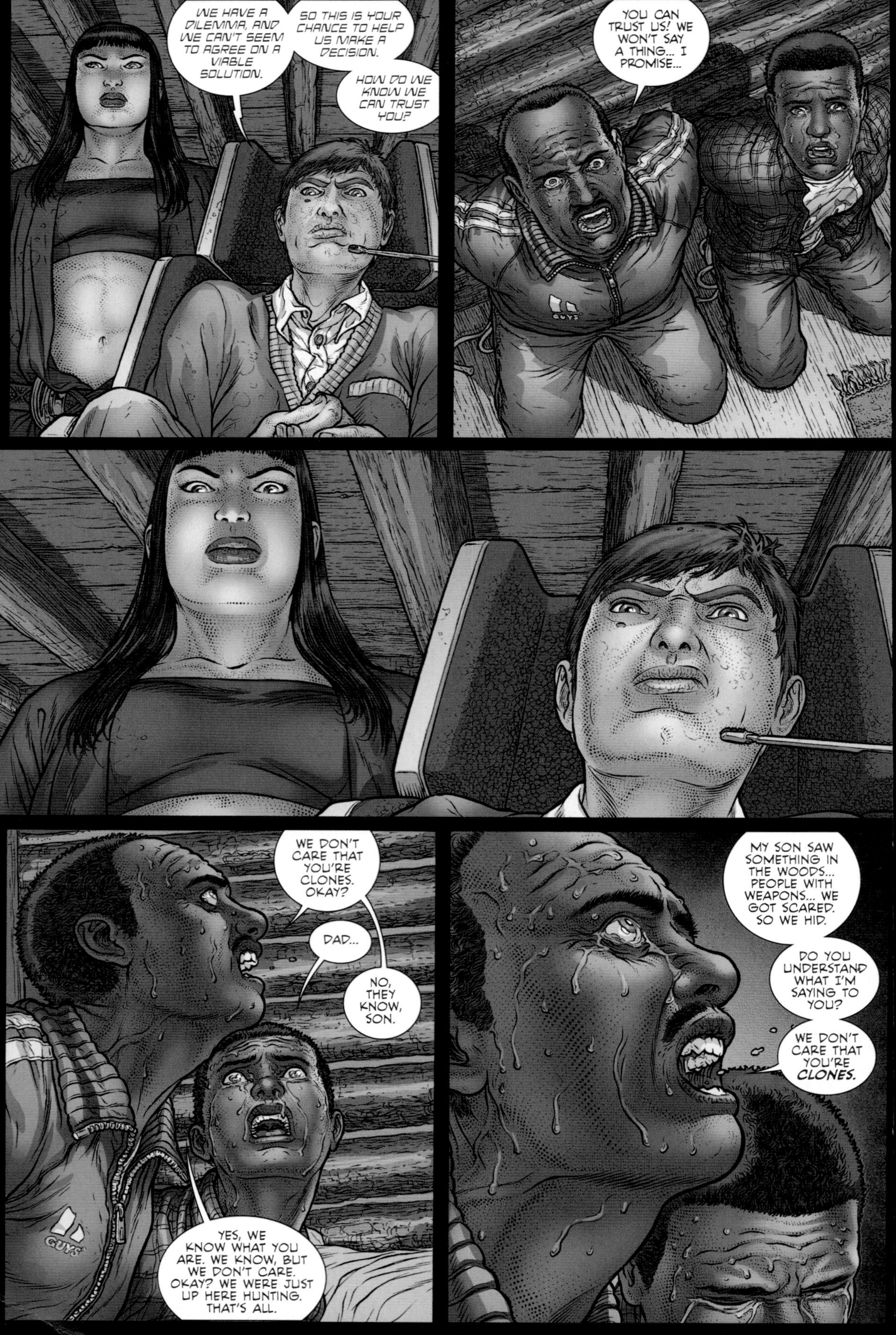
WE HAVE A DILEMMA, AND WE CAN'T SEEM TO AGREE ON A VIABLE SOLUTION.
SO THIS IS YOUR CHANCE TO HELP US MAKE A DECISION.
HOW DO WE KNOW WE CAN TRUST YOU?
YOU CAN TRUST US! WE WON'T SAY A THING... I PROMISE...
WE DON'T CARE THAT YOU'RE CLONES. OKAY?
DAD...
NO, THEY KNOW, SON.
YES, WE KNOW WHAT YOU ARE. WE KNOW, BUT WE DON'T CARE. OKAY? WE WERE JUST UP HERE HUNTING. THAT'S ALL.
MY SON SAW SOMETHING IN THE WOODS... PEOPLE WITH WEAPONS... WE GOT SCARED. SO WE HID.
DO YOU UNDERSTAND WHAT I'M SAYING TO YOU?
WE DON'T CARE THAT YOU'RE ***CLONES.***

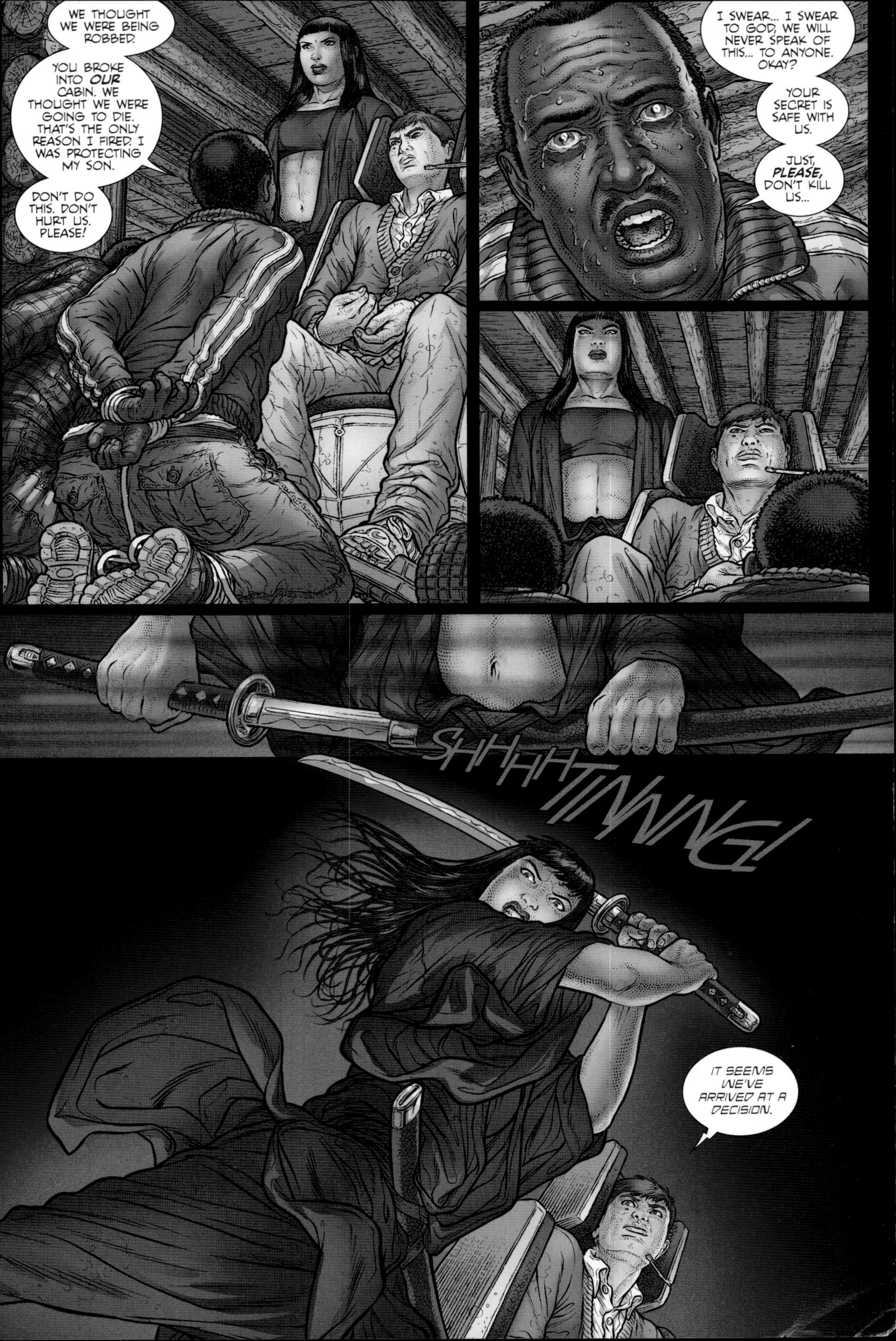
WE THOUGHT WE WERE BEING ROBBED.
YOU BROKE INTO OUR CABIN. WE THOUGHT WE WERE GOING TO DIE. THAT'S THE ONLY REASON I FIRED. I WAS PROTECTING MY SON.
DON'T DO THIS. DON'T HURT US. PLEASE!
I SWEAR... I SWEAR TO GOD, WE WILL NEVER SPEAK OF THIS... TO ANYONE. OKAY?
YOUR SECRET IS SAFE WITH US.
JUST, PLEASE, DON'T KILL US...
SHHHHTINNNG!
IT SEEMS WE'VE ARRIVED AT A DECISION.

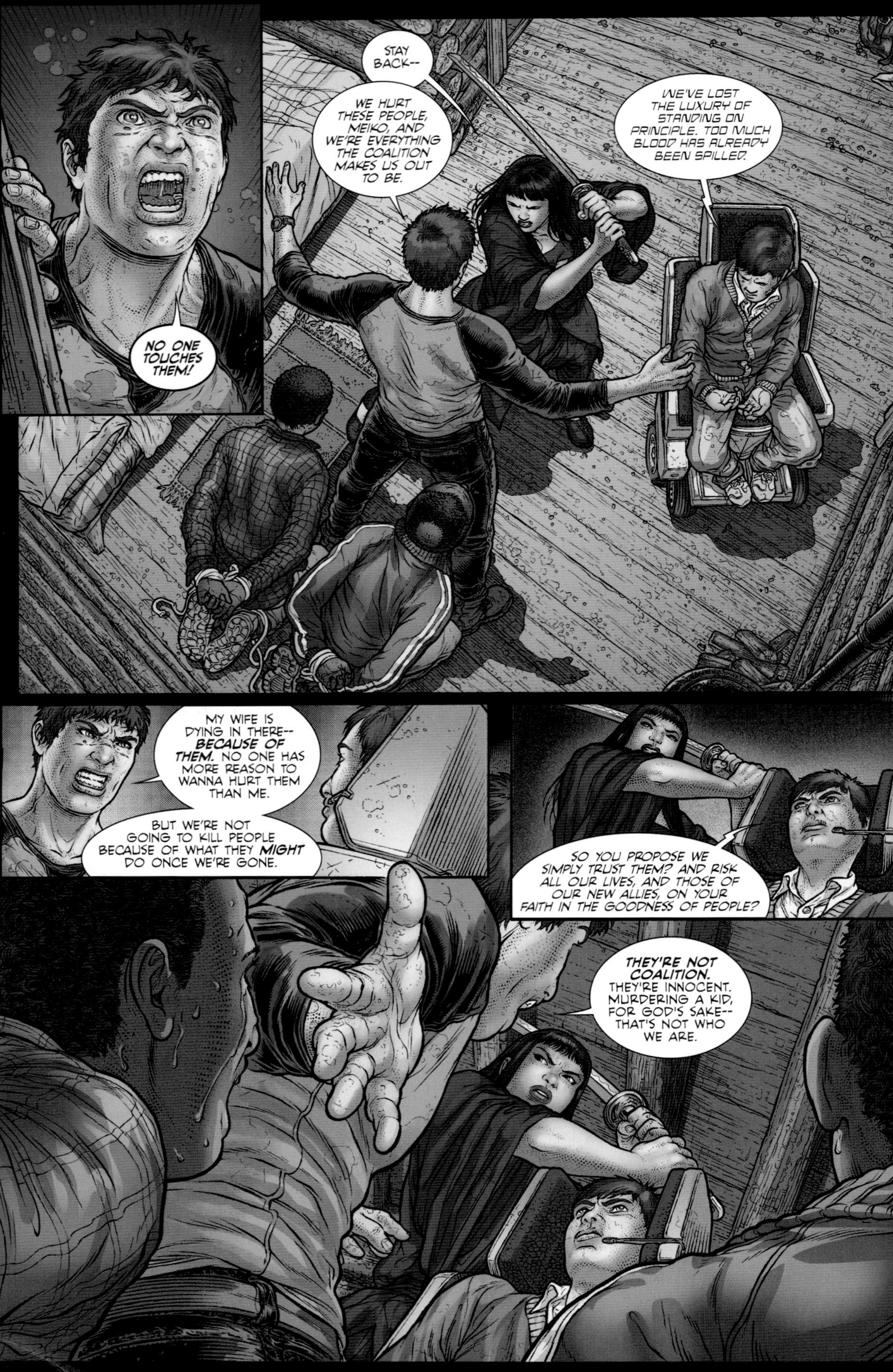
NO ONE TOUCHES THEM!
STAY BACK--
WE HURT THESE PEOPLE, MEIKO, AND WE'RE EVERYTHING THE COALITION MAKES US OUT TO BE.
WE'VE LOST THE LUXURY OF STANDING ON PRINCIPLE. TOO MUCH BLOOD HAS ALREADY BEEN SPILLED.
MY WIFE IS DYING IN THERE-- BECAUSE OF THEM. NO ONE HAS MORE REASON TO WANNA HURT THEM THAN ME.
BUT WE'RE NOT GOING TO KILL PEOPLE BECAUSE OF WHAT THEY MIGHT DO ONCE WE'RE GONE.
SO YOU PROPOSE WE SIMPLY TRUST THEM? AND RISK ALL OUR LIVES, AND THOSE OF OUR NEW ALLIES, ON YOUR FAITH IN THE GOODNESS OF PEOPLE?
THEY'RE NOT COALITION. THEY'RE INNOCENT. MURDERING A KID, FOR GOD'S SAKE-- THAT'S NOT WHO WE ARE.

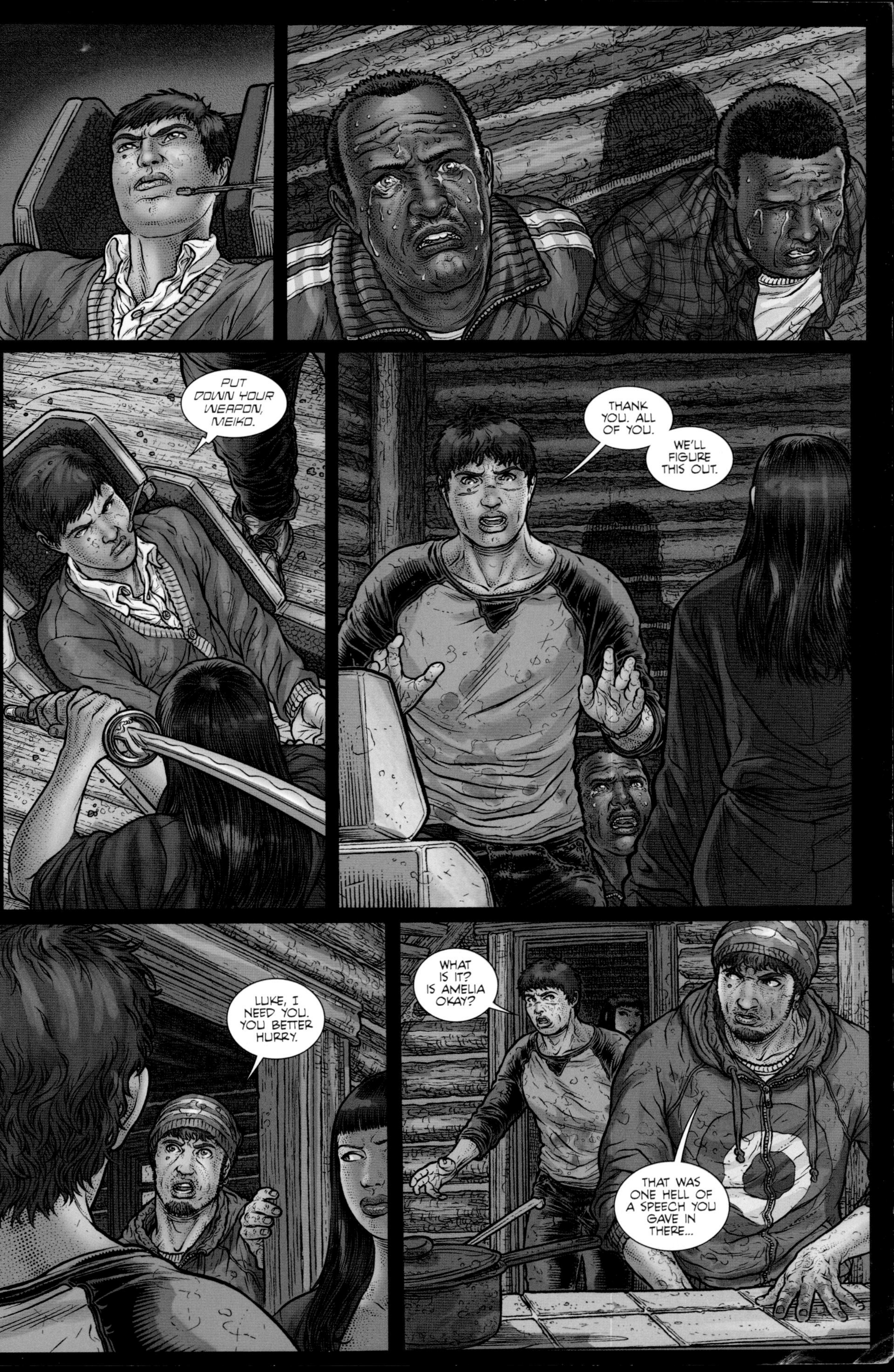
PUT DOWN YOUR WEAPON, MEIKO.
THANK YOU. ALL OF YOU.
WE'LL FIGURE THIS OUT.
LUKE, I NEED YOU. YOU BETTER HURRY.
WHAT IS IT? IS AMELIA OKAY?
THAT WAS ONE HELL OF A SPEECH YOU GAVE IN THERE...

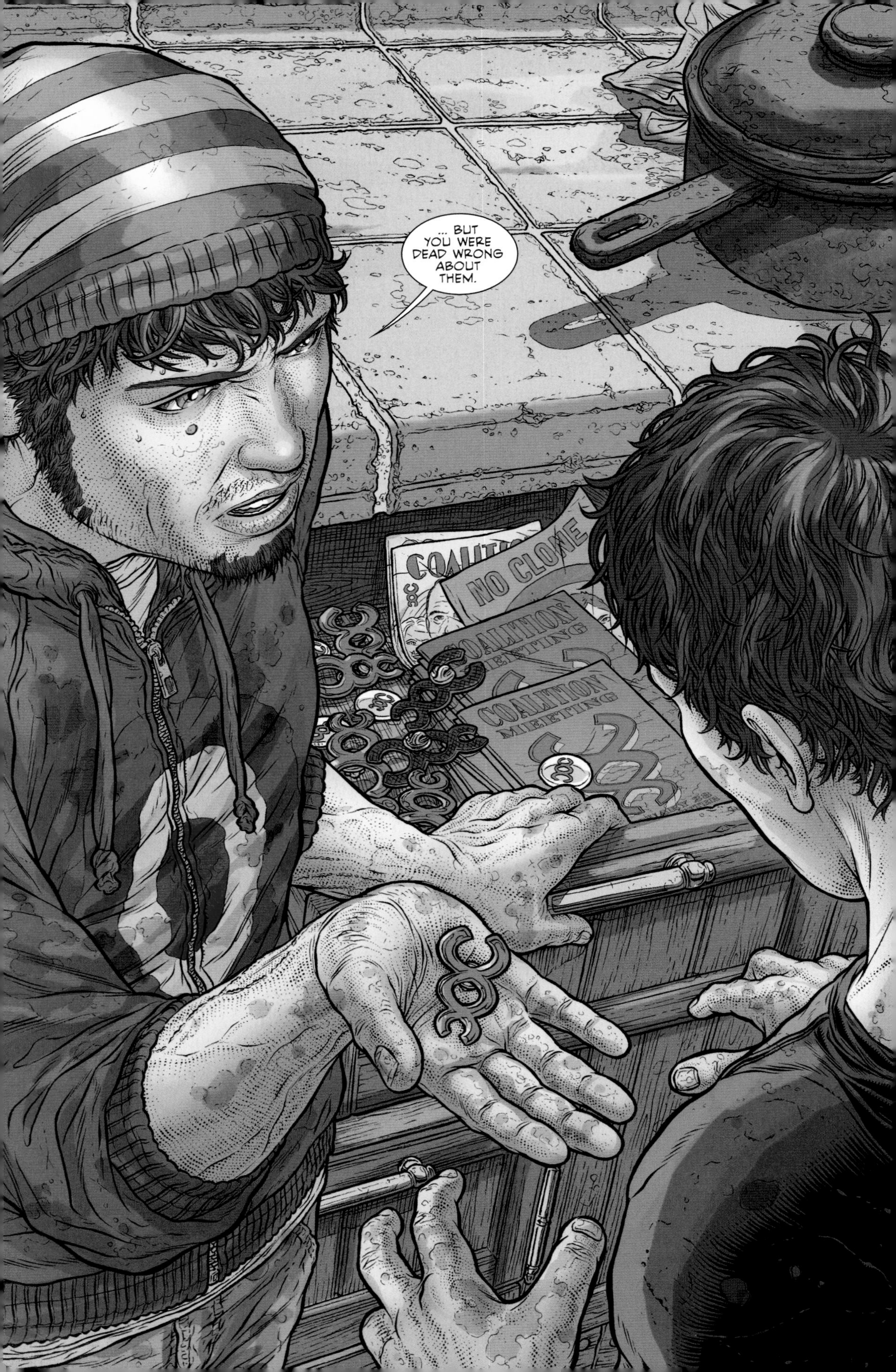
... BUT YOU WERE DEAD WRONG ABOUT THEM.
NO CLONE
COALITION MEETING
COALITION MEETING

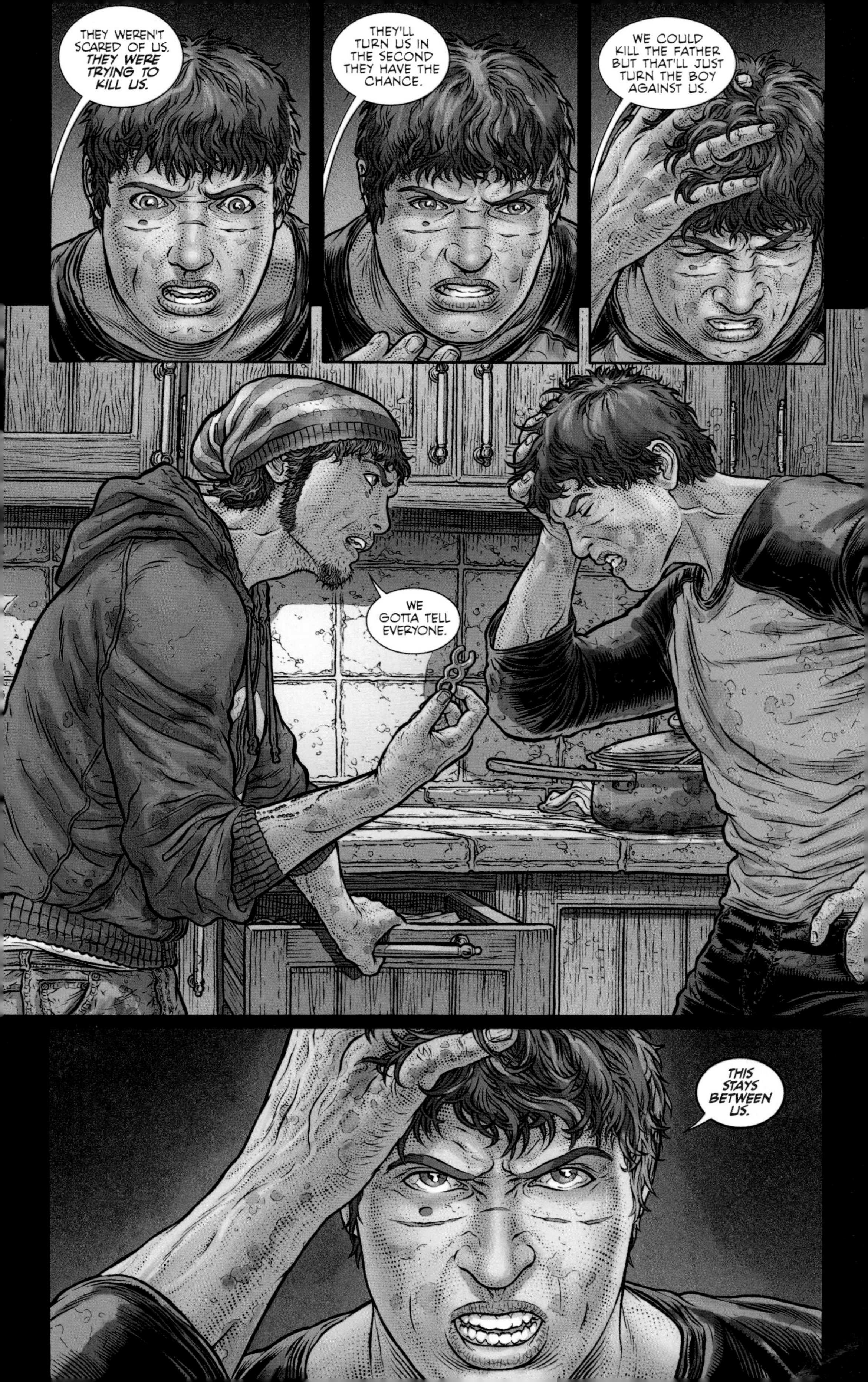
THEY WEREN'T SCARED OF US. ***THEY WERE TRYING TO KILL US.***
THEY'LL TURN US IN THE SECOND THEY HAVE THE CHANCE.
WE COULD KILL THE FATHER BUT THAT'LL JUST TURN THE BOY AGAINST US.
WE GOTTA TELL EVERYONE.
THIS STAYS BETWEEN US.

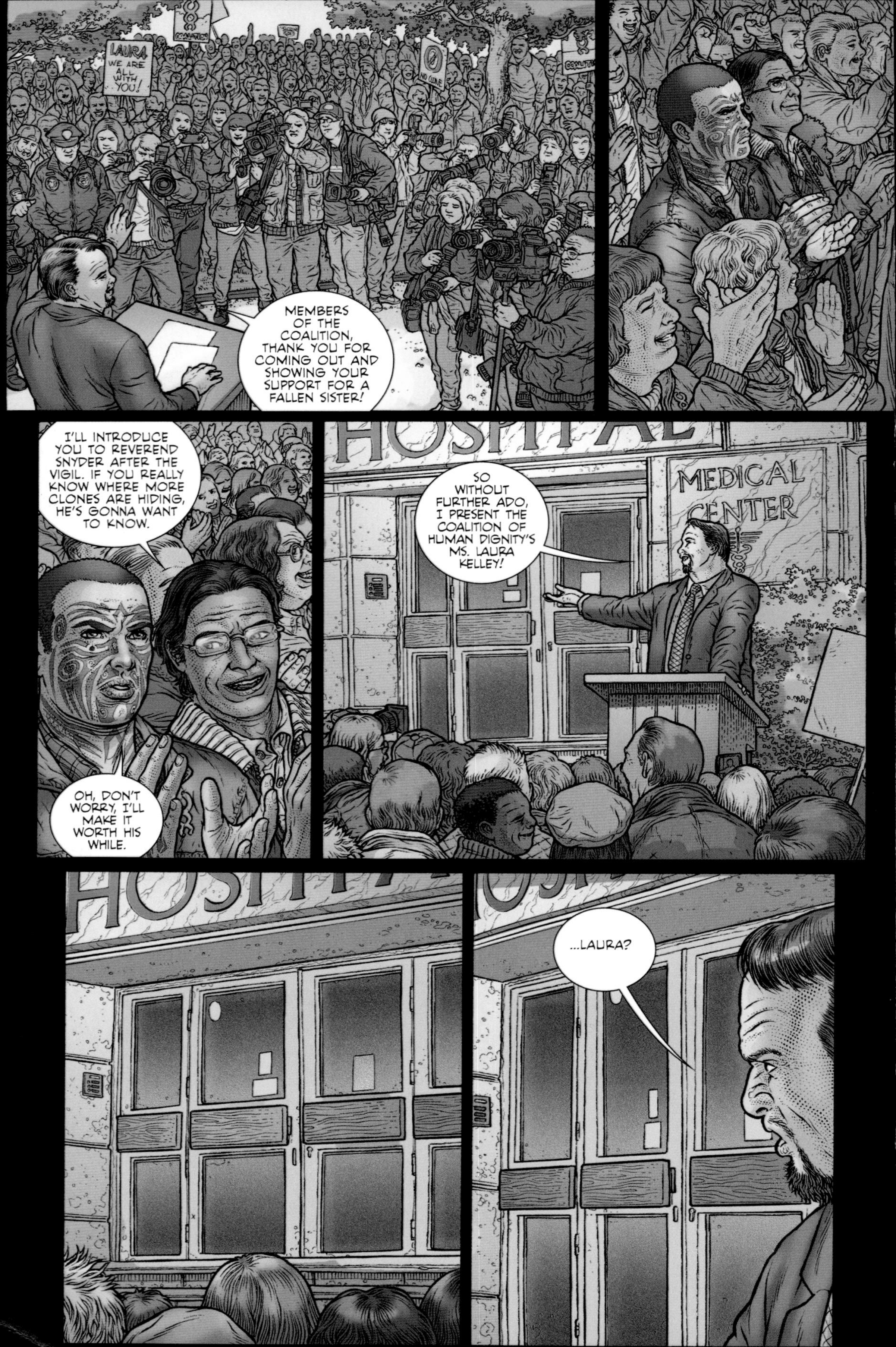
LAURA WE ARE ALL WITH YOU!
COALITION
NO CLONE
MEMBERS OF THE COALITION, THANK YOU FOR COMING OUT AND SHOWING YOUR SUPPORT FOR A FALLEN SISTER!
I'LL INTRODUCE YOU TO REVEREND SNYDER AFTER THE VIGIL. IF YOU REALLY KNOW WHERE MORE CLONES ARE HIDING, HE'S GONNA WANT TO KNOW.
OH, DON'T WORRY, I'LL MAKE IT WORTH HIS WHILE.
HOSPITAL
MEDICAL CENTER
SO WITHOUT FURTHER ADO, I PRESENT THE COALITION OF HUMAN DIGNITY'S MS. LAURA KELLEY!
...LAURA?

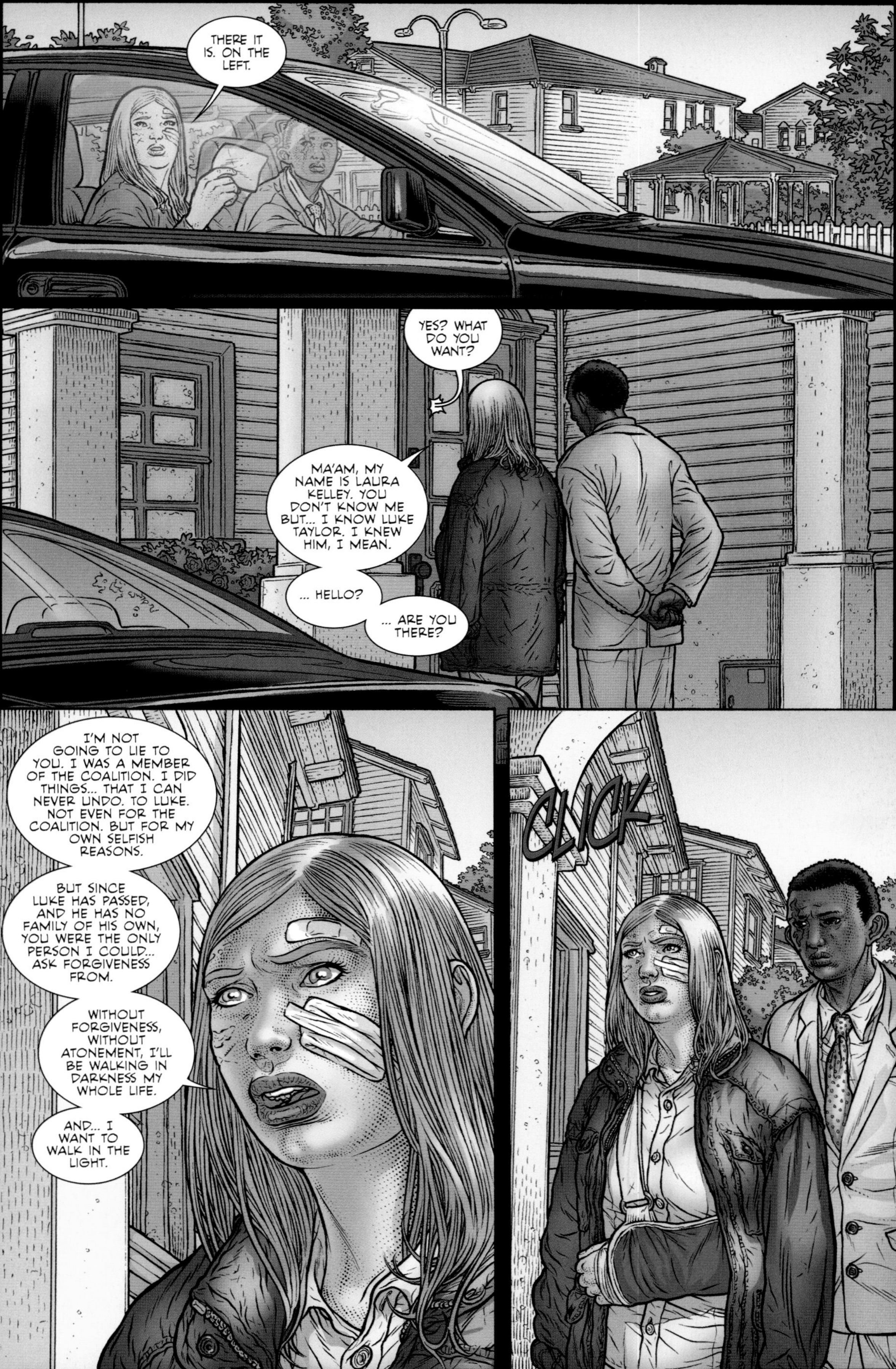
THERE IT IS. ON THE LEFT.
YES? WHAT DO YOU WANT?
MA'AM, MY NAME IS LAURA KELLEY. YOU DON'T KNOW ME BUT... I KNOW LUKE TAYLOR. I KNEW HIM, I MEAN.
... HELLO?
... ARE YOU THERE?
I'M NOT GOING TO LIE TO YOU. I WAS A MEMBER OF THE COALITION. I DID THINGS... THAT I CAN NEVER UNDO. TO LUKE. NOT EVEN FOR THE COALITION. BUT FOR MY OWN SELFISH REASONS.
BUT SINCE LUKE HAS PASSED, AND HE HAS NO FAMILY OF HIS OWN, YOU WERE THE ONLY PERSON I COULD... ASK FORGIVENESS FROM.
WITHOUT FORGIVENESS, WITHOUT ATONEMENT, I'LL BE WALKING IN DARKNESS MY WHOLE LIFE.
AND... I WANT TO WALK IN THE LIGHT.
CLICK

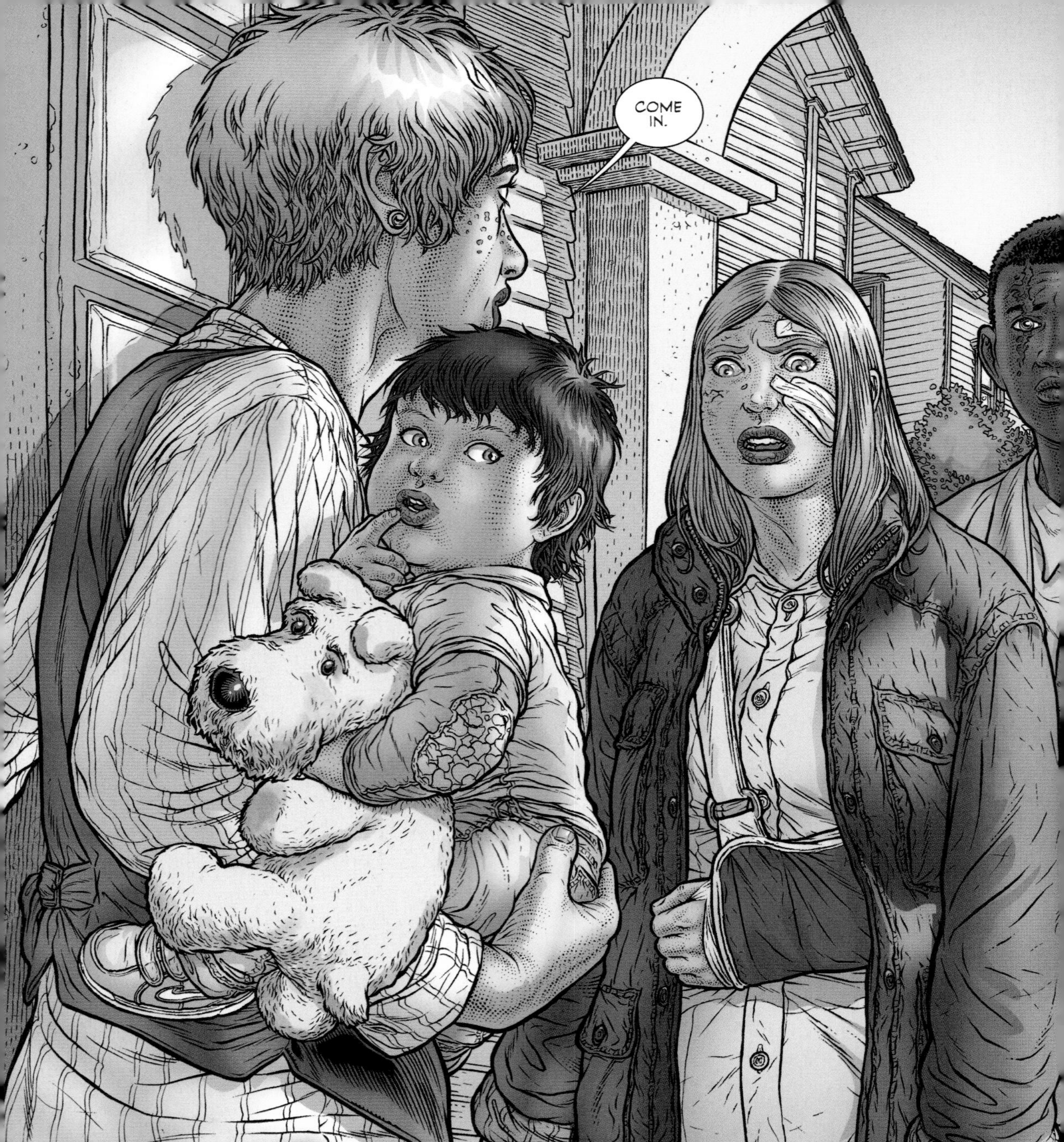
COME IN.

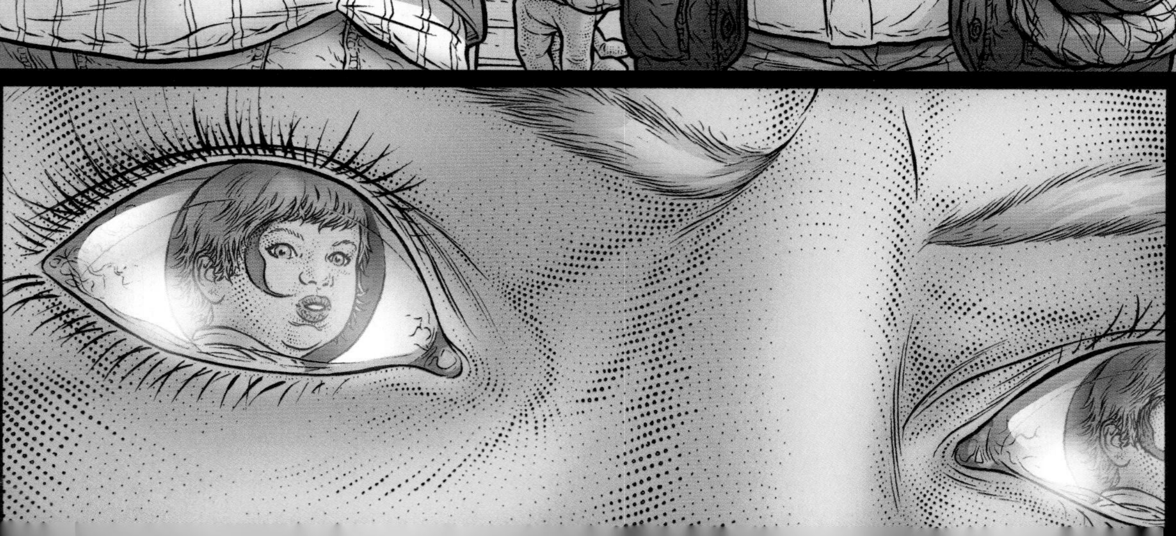

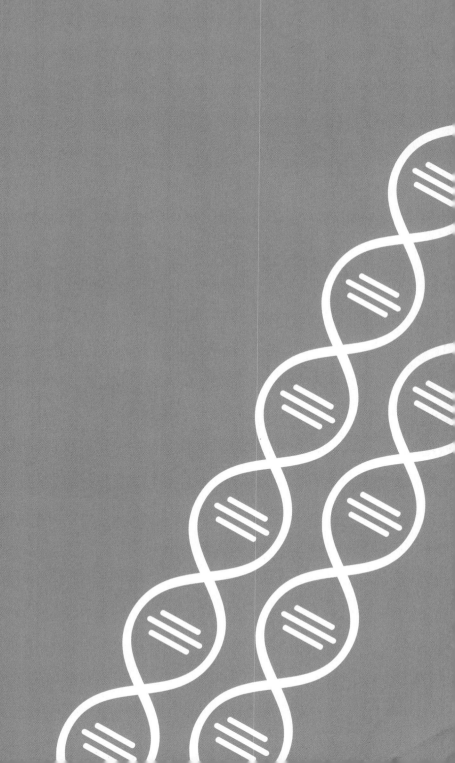

CHAPTER 18

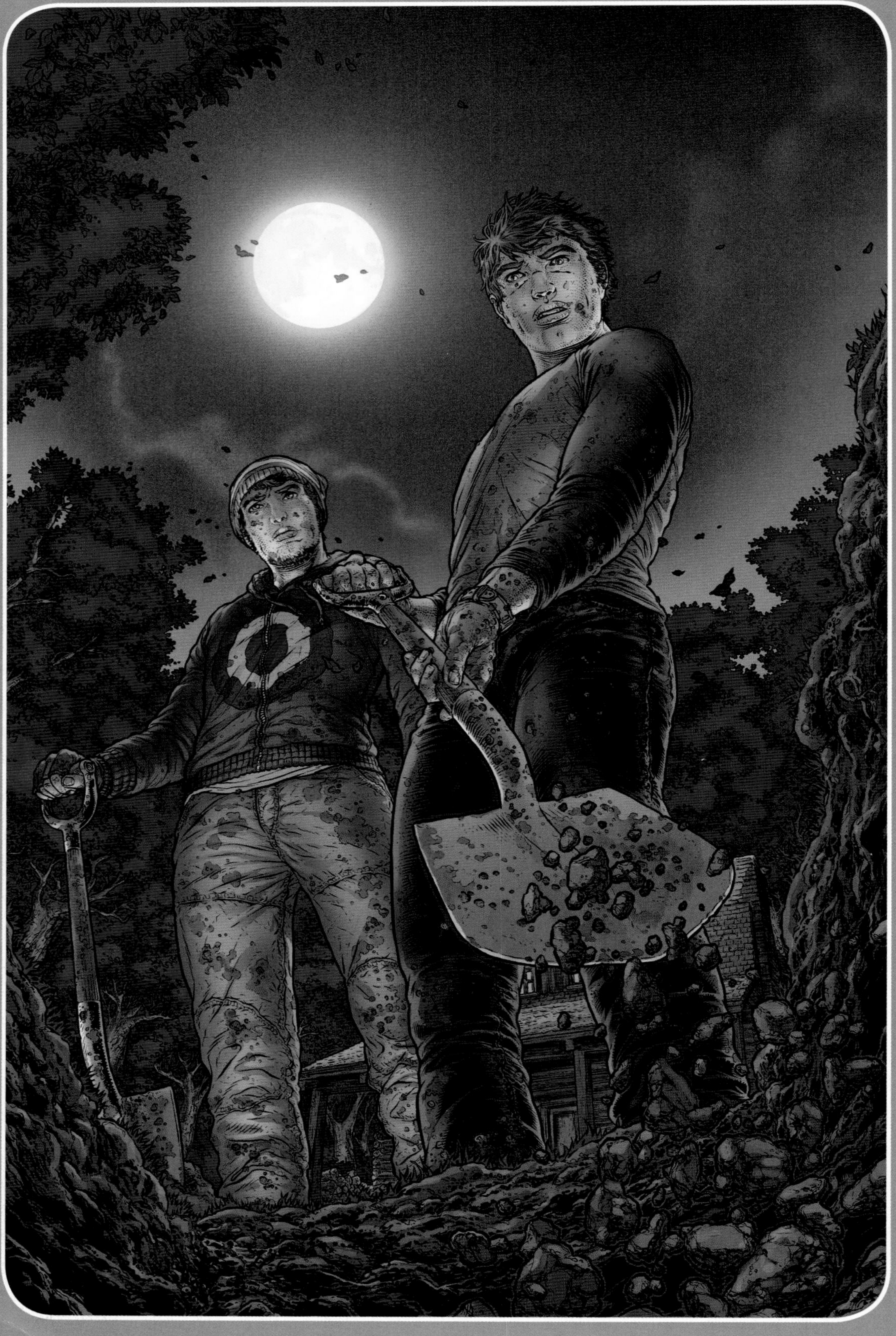

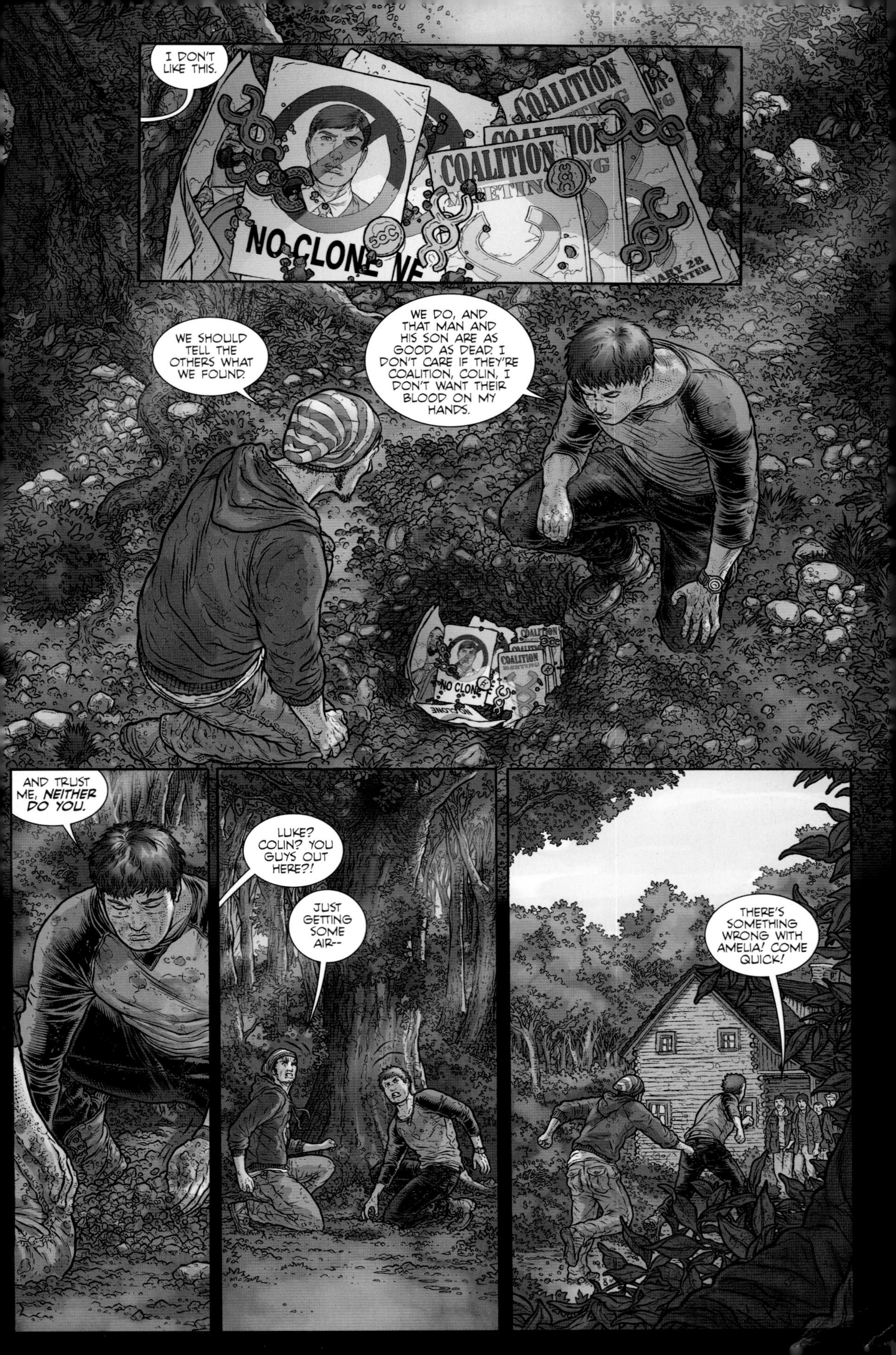

I DON'T LIKE THIS.
NO CLONE NE
COALITION
COALITION
COALITION MEETING
WE SHOULD TELL THE OTHERS WHAT WE FOUND.
WE DO, AND THAT MAN AND HIS SON ARE AS GOOD AS DEAD. I DON'T CARE IF THEY'RE COALITION, COLIN, I DON'T WANT THEIR BLOOD ON MY HANDS.
AND TRUST ME, *NEITHER DO YOU.*
LUKE? COLIN? YOU GUYS OUT HERE?!
JUST GETTING SOME AIR--
THERE'S SOMETHING WRONG WITH AMELIA! COME QUICK!

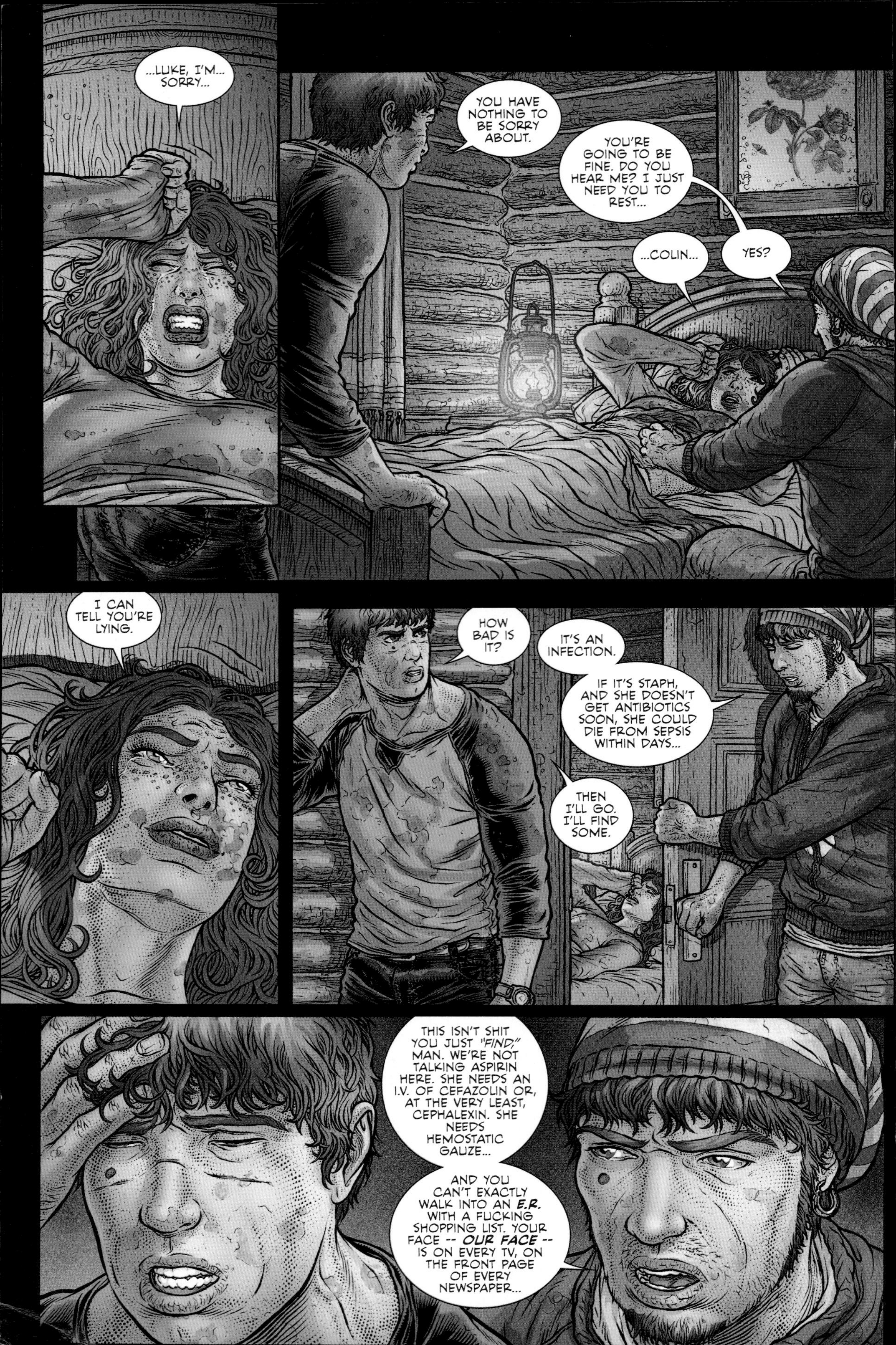
...LUKE, I'M... SORRY...
YOU HAVE NOTHING TO BE SORRY ABOUT.
YOU'RE GOING TO BE FINE. DO YOU HEAR ME? I JUST NEED YOU TO REST...
...COLIN...
YES?
I CAN TELL YOU'RE LYING.
HOW BAD IS IT?
IT'S AN INFECTION.
IF IT'S STAPH, AND SHE DOESN'T GET ANTIBIOTICS SOON, SHE COULD DIE FROM SEPSIS WITHIN DAYS...
THEN I'LL GO. I'LL FIND SOME.
THIS ISN'T SHIT YOU JUST "FIND," MAN. WE'RE NOT TALKING ASPIRIN HERE. SHE NEEDS AN I.V. OF CEFAZOLIN OR, AT THE VERY LEAST, CEPHALEXIN. SHE NEEDS HEMOSTATIC GAUZE...
AND YOU CAN'T EXACTLY WALK INTO AN E.R. WITH A FUCKING SHOPPING LIST. YOUR FACE -- OUR FACE -- IS ON EVERY TV, ON THE FRONT PAGE OF EVERY NEWSPAPER...

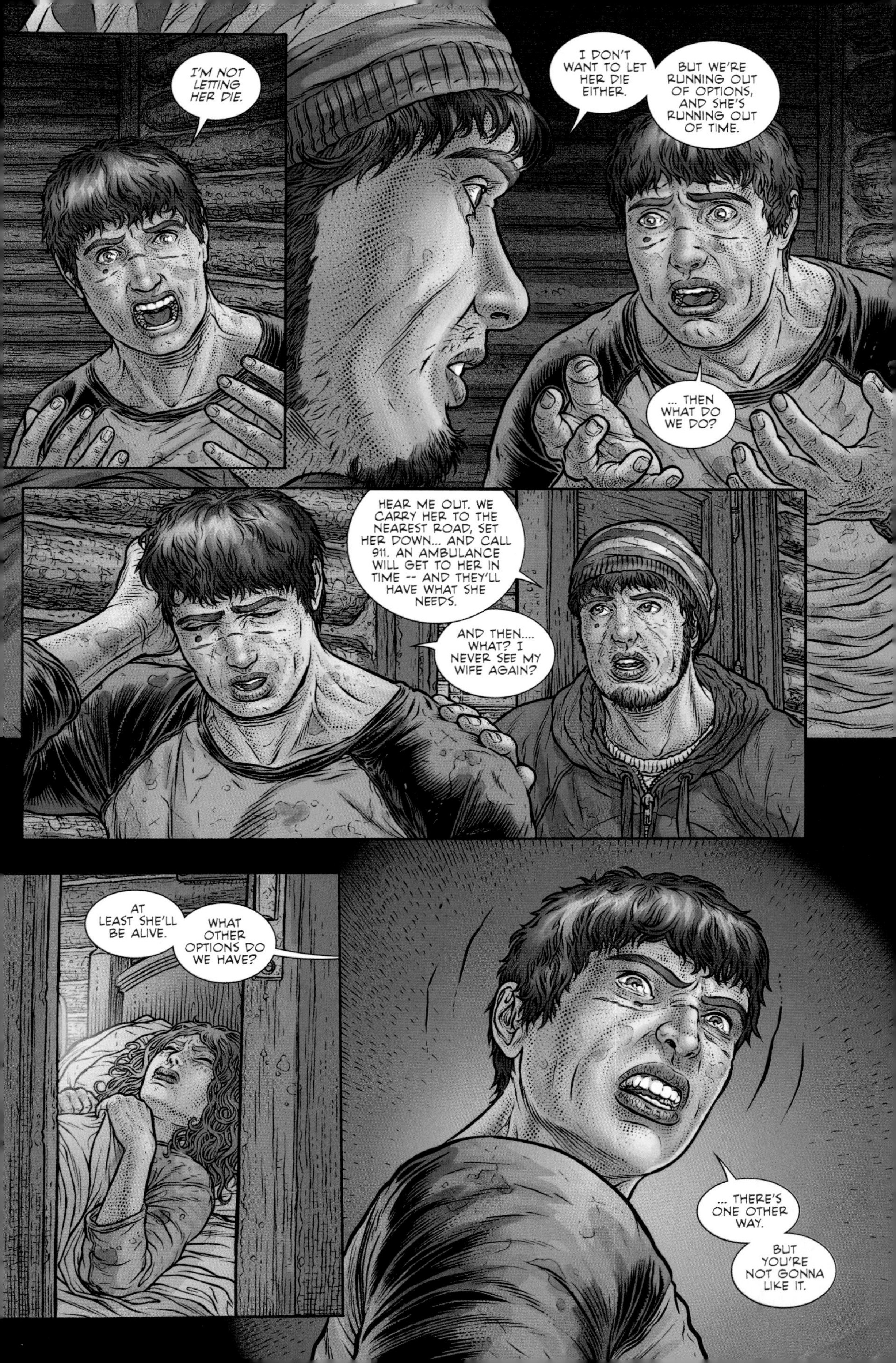
I'M NOT LETTING HER DIE.
I DON'T WANT TO LET HER DIE EITHER.
BUT WE'RE RUNNING OUT OF OPTIONS, AND SHE'S RUNNING OUT OF TIME.
... THEN WHAT DO WE DO?
HEAR ME OUT. WE CARRY HER TO THE NEAREST ROAD, SET HER DOWN... AND CALL 911. AN AMBULANCE WILL GET TO HER IN TIME -- AND THEY'LL HAVE WHAT SHE NEEDS.
AND THEN.... WHAT? I NEVER SEE MY WIFE AGAIN?
AT LEAST SHE'LL BE ALIVE.
WHAT OTHER OPTIONS DO WE HAVE?
... THERE'S ONE OTHER WAY.
BUT YOU'RE NOT GONNA LIKE IT.

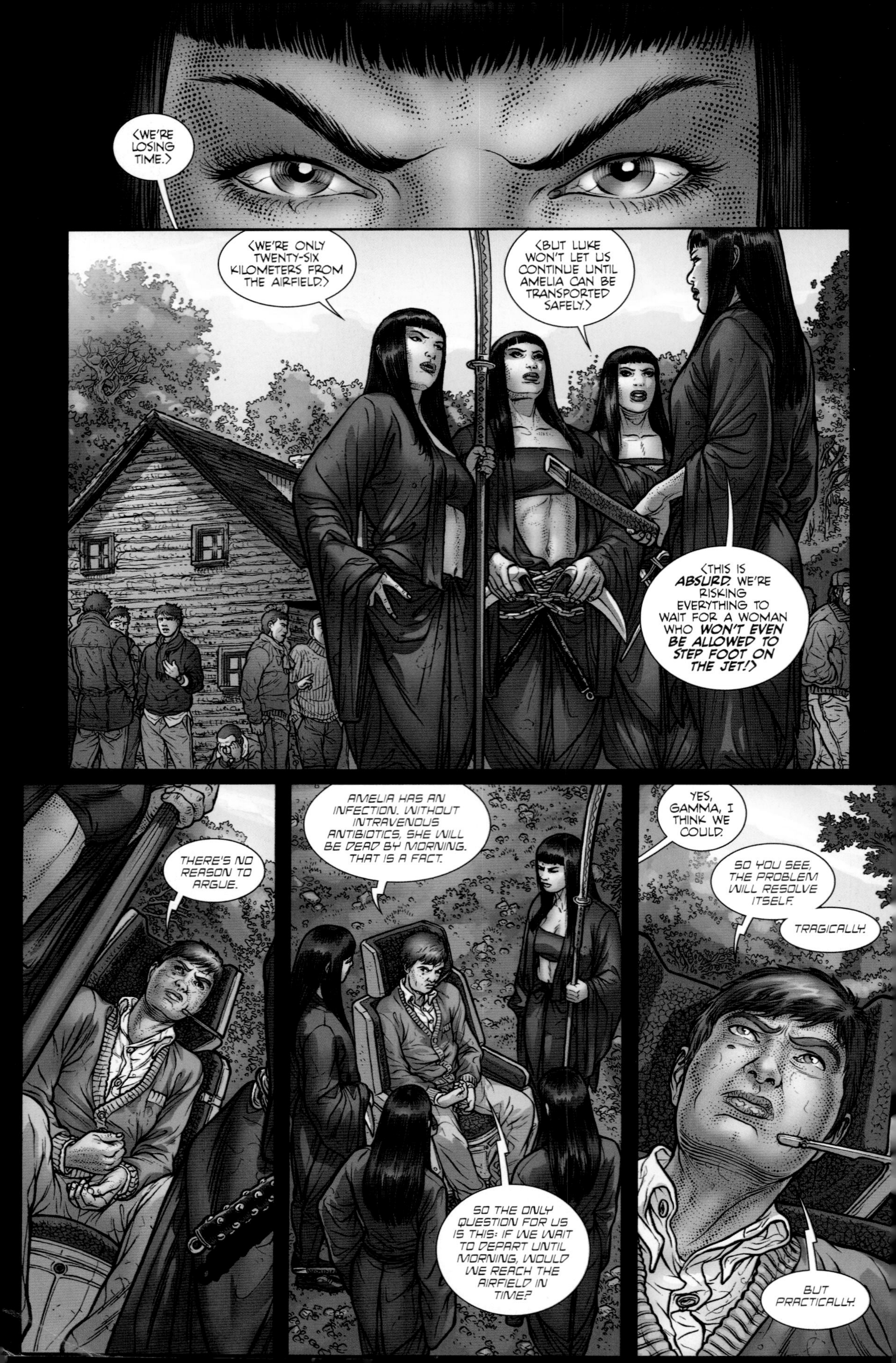
<WE'RE LOSING TIME.>
<WE'RE ONLY TWENTY-SIX KILOMETERS FROM THE AIRFIELD.>
<BUT LUKE WON'T LET US CONTINUE UNTIL AMELIA CAN BE TRANSPORTED SAFELY.>
<THIS IS ABSURD. WE'RE RISKING EVERYTHING TO WAIT FOR A WOMAN WHO WON'T EVEN BE ALLOWED TO STEP FOOT ON THE JET!>
THERE'S NO REASON TO ARGUE.
AMELIA HAS AN INFECTION. WITHOUT INTRAVENOUS ANTIBIOTICS, SHE WILL BE DEAD BY MORNING. THAT IS A FACT.
SO THE ONLY QUESTION FOR US IS THIS: IF WE WAIT TO DEPART UNTIL MORNING, WOULD WE REACH THE AIRFIELD IN TIME?
YES, GAMMA, I THINK WE COULD.
SO YOU SEE, THE PROBLEM WILL RESOLVE ITSELF.
TRAGICALLY.
BUT PRACTICALLY.

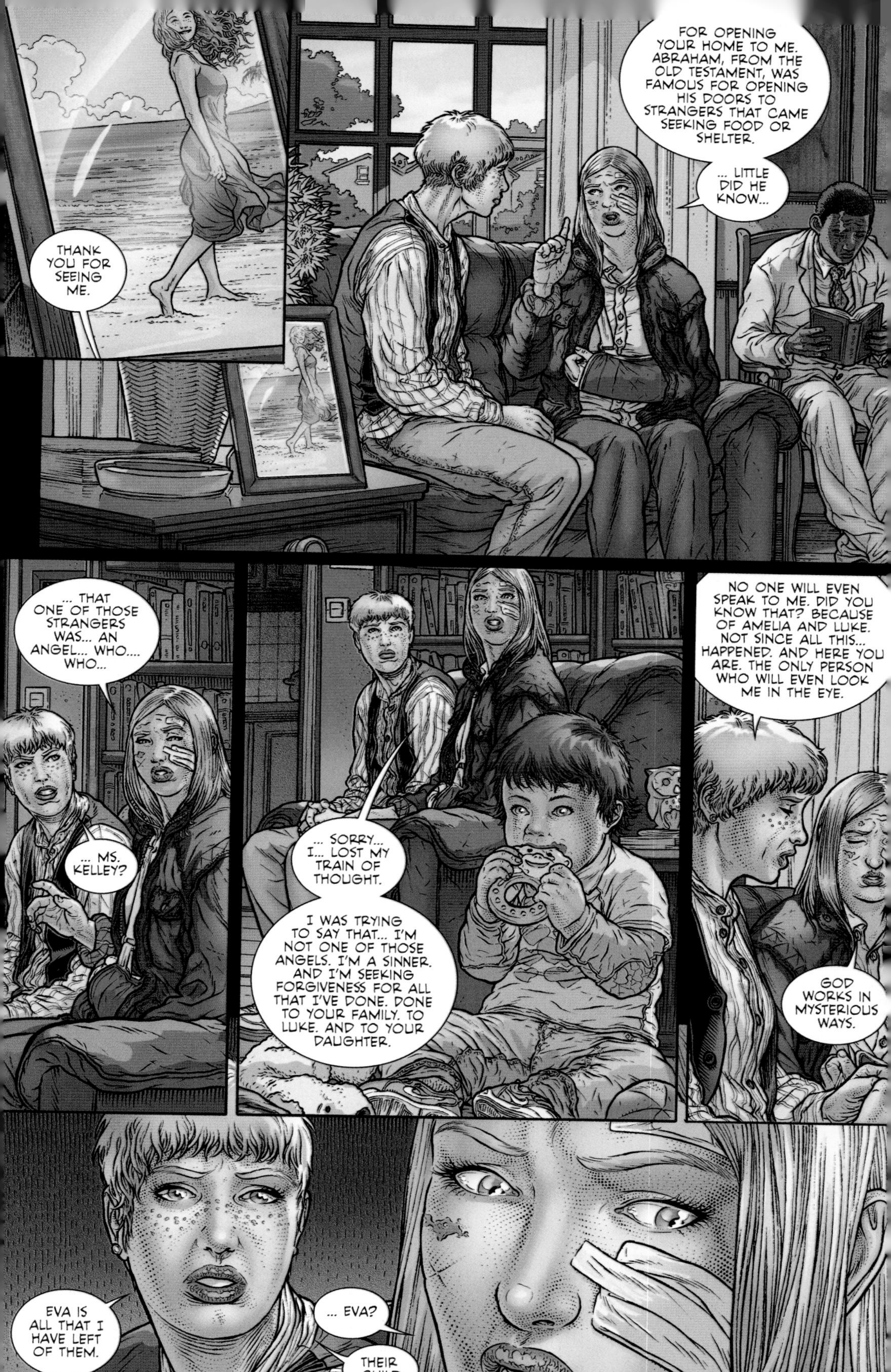
THANK YOU FOR SEEING ME.
FOR OPENING YOUR HOME TO ME. ABRAHAM, FROM THE OLD TESTAMENT, WAS FAMOUS FOR OPENING HIS DOORS TO STRANGERS THAT CAME SEEKING FOOD OR SHELTER.
... LITTLE DID HE KNOW...
... THAT ONE OF THOSE STRANGERS WAS... AN ANGEL... WHO.... WHO...
... MS. KELLEY?
... SORRY... I... LOST MY TRAIN OF THOUGHT.
I WAS TRYING TO SAY THAT... I'M NOT ONE OF THOSE ANGELS. I'M A SINNER. AND I'M SEEKING FORGIVENESS FOR ALL THAT I'VE DONE. DONE TO YOUR FAMILY. TO LUKE. AND TO YOUR DAUGHTER.
NO ONE WILL EVEN SPEAK TO ME. DID YOU KNOW THAT? BECAUSE OF AMELIA AND LUKE. NOT SINCE ALL THIS... HAPPENED. AND HERE YOU ARE. THE ONLY PERSON WHO WILL EVEN LOOK ME IN THE EYE.
GOD WORKS IN MYSTERIOUS WAYS.
EVA IS ALL THAT I HAVE LEFT OF THEM.
... EVA?
THEIR CHILD.

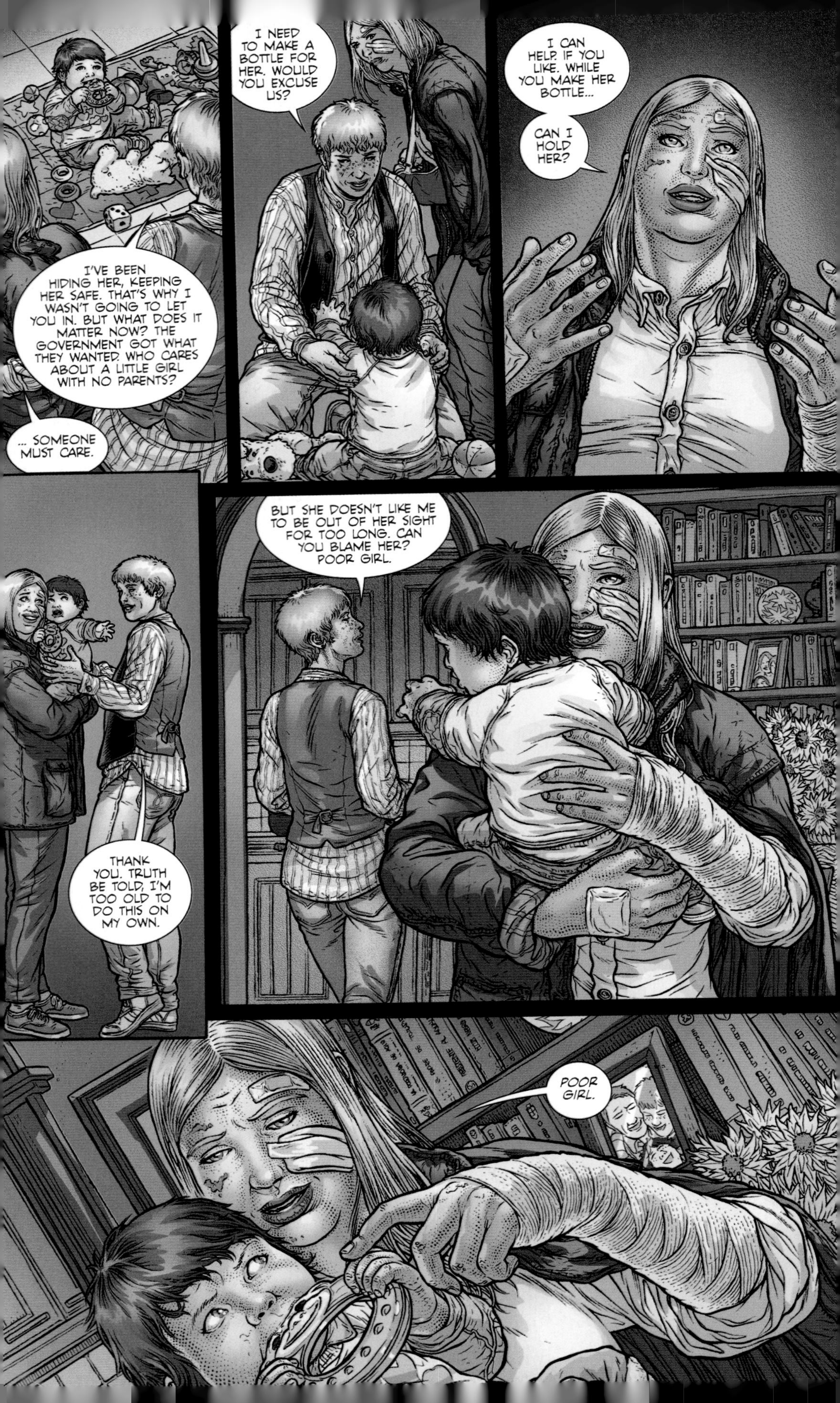

I'VE BEEN HIDING HER, KEEPING HER SAFE. THAT'S WHY I WASN'T GOING TO LET YOU IN. BUT WHAT DOES IT MATTER NOW? THE GOVERNMENT GOT WHAT THEY WANTED. WHO CARES ABOUT A LITTLE GIRL WITH NO PARENTS?
... SOMEONE MUST CARE.
I NEED TO MAKE A BOTTLE FOR HER. WOULD YOU EXCUSE US?
I CAN HELP. IF YOU LIKE. WHILE YOU MAKE HER BOTTLE...
CAN I HOLD HER?
THANK YOU. TRUTH BE TOLD, I'M TOO OLD TO DO THIS ON MY OWN.
BUT SHE DOESN'T LIKE ME TO BE OUT OF HER SIGHT FOR TOO LONG. CAN YOU BLAME HER? POOR GIRL.
POOR GIRL.

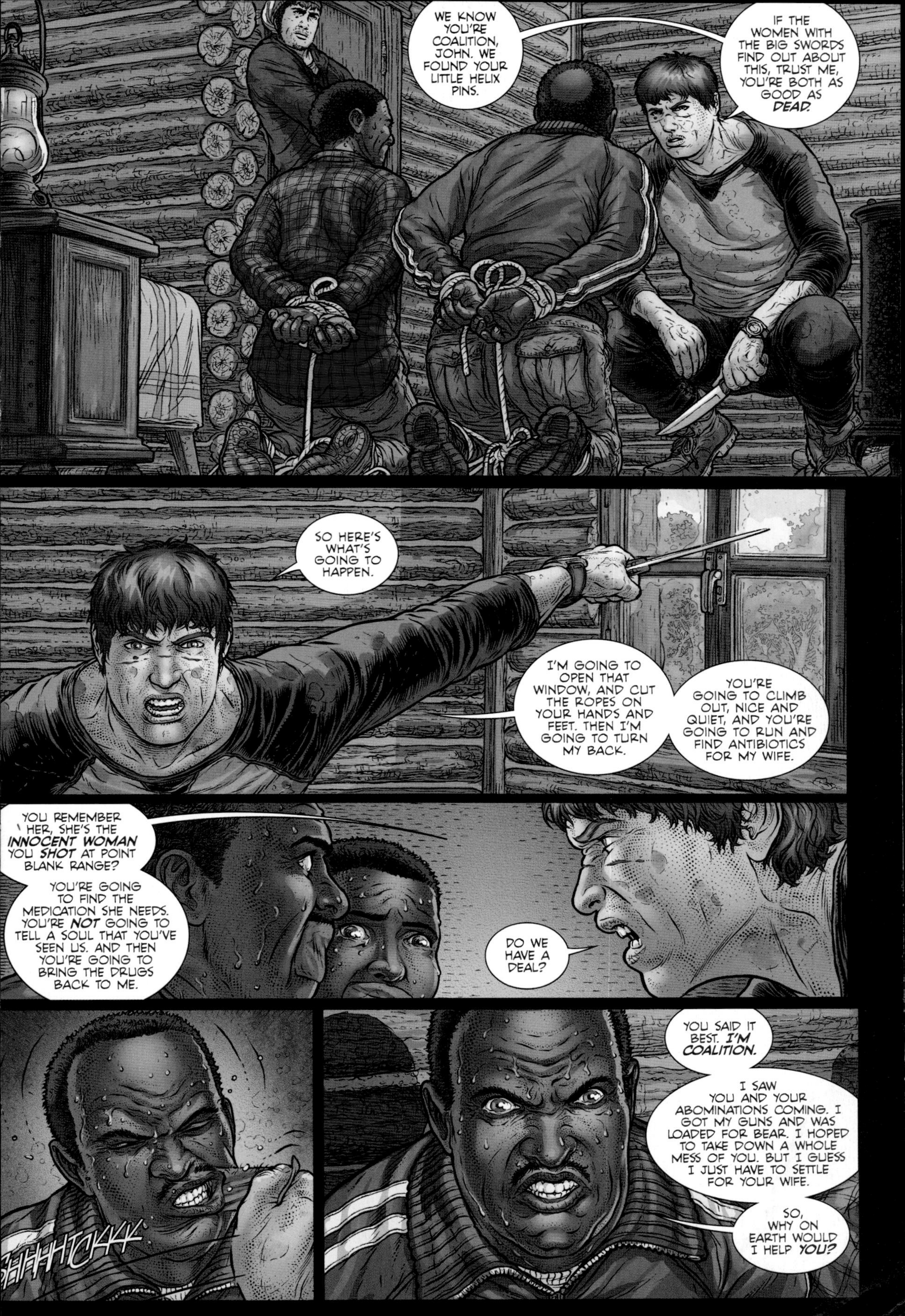
WE KNOW YOU'RE COALITION, JOHN. WE FOUND YOUR LITTLE HELIX PINS.
IF THE WOMEN WITH THE BIG SWORDS FIND OUT ABOUT THIS, TRUST ME, YOU'RE BOTH AS GOOD AS DEAD.
SO HERE'S WHAT'S GOING TO HAPPEN.
I'M GOING TO OPEN THAT WINDOW, AND CUT THE ROPES ON YOUR HANDS AND FEET. THEN I'M GOING TO TURN MY BACK.
YOU'RE GOING TO CLIMB OUT, NICE AND QUIET, AND YOU'RE GOING TO RUN AND FIND ANTIBIOTICS FOR MY WIFE.
YOU REMEMBER HER, SHE'S THE INNOCENT WOMAN YOU SHOT AT POINT BLANK RANGE?
YOU'RE GOING TO FIND THE MEDICATION SHE NEEDS. YOU'RE NOT GOING TO TELL A SOUL THAT YOU'VE SEEN US. AND THEN YOU'RE GOING TO BRING THE DRUGS BACK TO ME.
DO WE HAVE A DEAL?
SHHHHTCKKK
YOU SAID IT BEST. I'M COALITION.
I SAW YOU AND YOUR ABOMINATIONS COMING. I GOT MY GUNS AND WAS LOADED FOR BEAR. I HOPED TO TAKE DOWN A WHOLE MESS OF YOU. BUT I GUESS I JUST HAVE TO SETTLE FOR YOUR WIFE.
SO, WHY ON EARTH WOULD I HELP YOU?

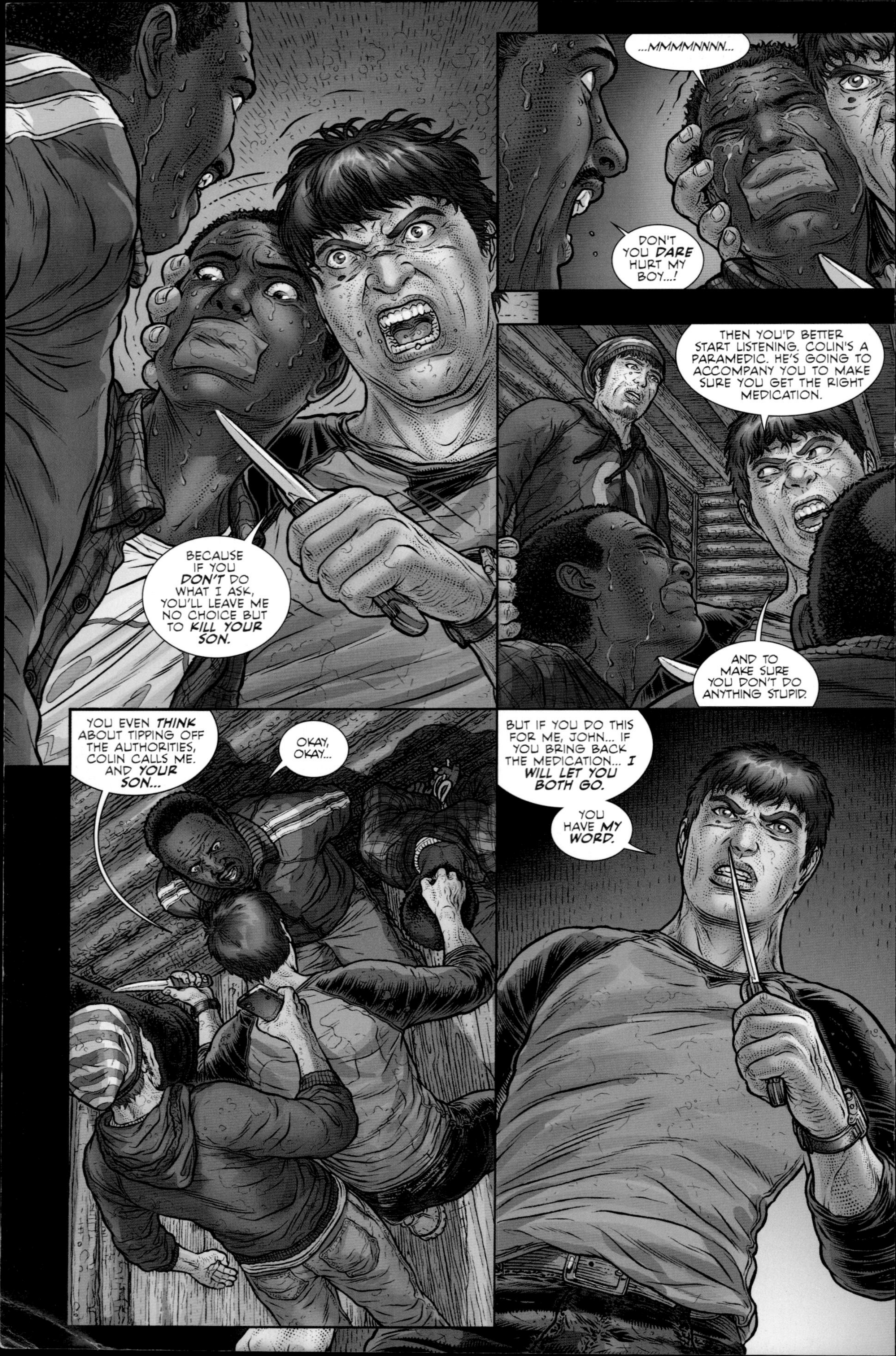
BECAUSE IF YOU DON'T DO WHAT I ASK, YOU'LL LEAVE ME NO CHOICE BUT TO KILL YOUR SON.
...MMMMNNNN...
DON'T YOU DARE HURT MY BOY...!
THEN YOU'D BETTER START LISTENING. COLIN'S A PARAMEDIC. HE'S GOING TO ACCOMPANY YOU TO MAKE SURE YOU GET THE RIGHT MEDICATION.
AND TO MAKE SURE YOU DON'T DO ANYTHING STUPID.
YOU EVEN THINK ABOUT TIPPING OFF THE AUTHORITIES, COLIN CALLS ME. AND YOUR SON...
OKAY, OKAY...
BUT IF YOU DO THIS FOR ME, JOHN... IF YOU BRING BACK THE MEDICATION... I WILL LET YOU BOTH GO.
YOU HAVE MY WORD.

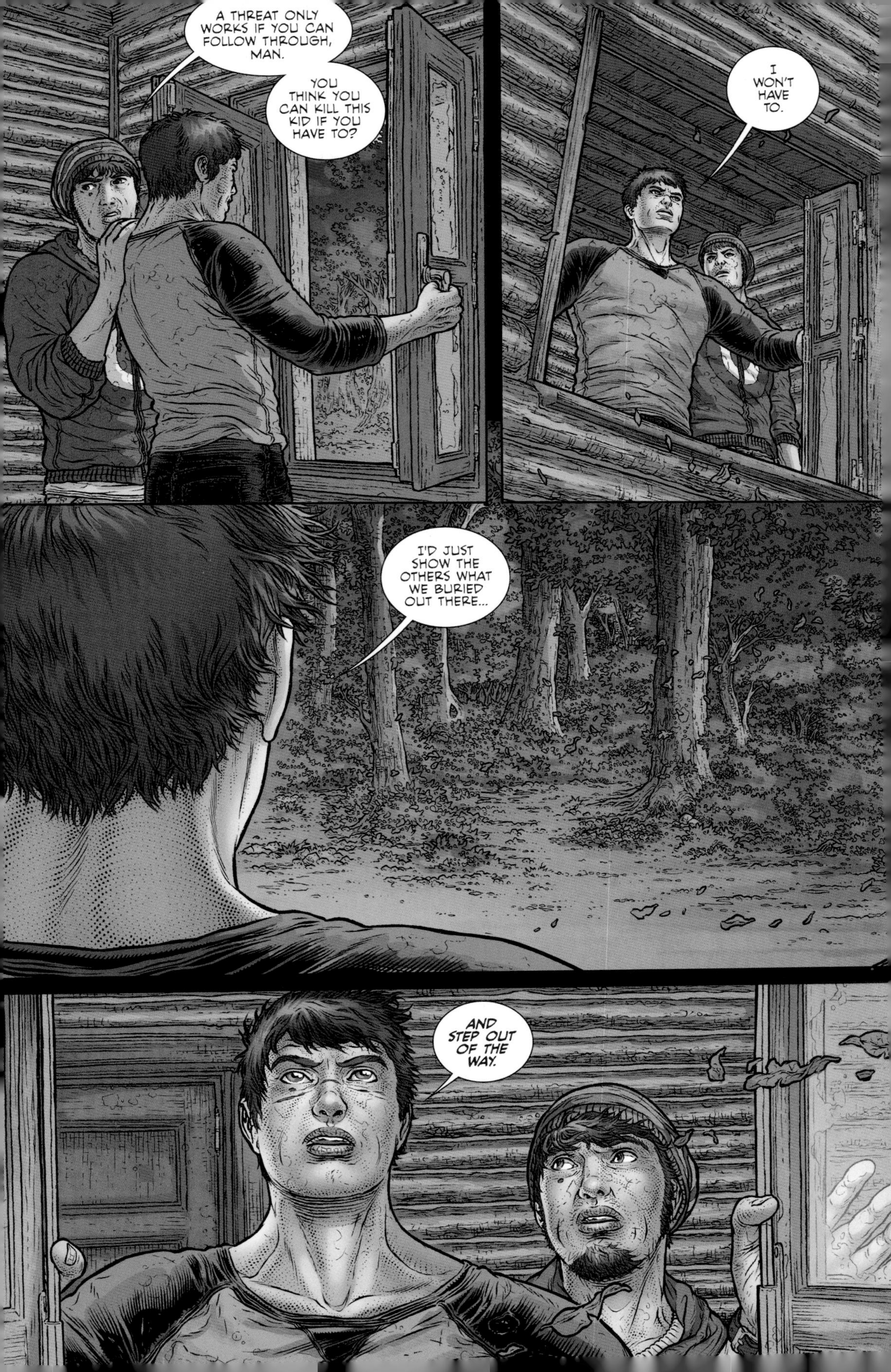
A THREAT ONLY WORKS IF YOU CAN FOLLOW THROUGH, MAN.
YOU THINK YOU CAN KILL THIS KID IF YOU HAVE TO?
I WON'T HAVE TO.
I'D JUST SHOW THE OTHERS WHAT WE BURIED OUT THERE...
AND STEP OUT OF THE WAY.

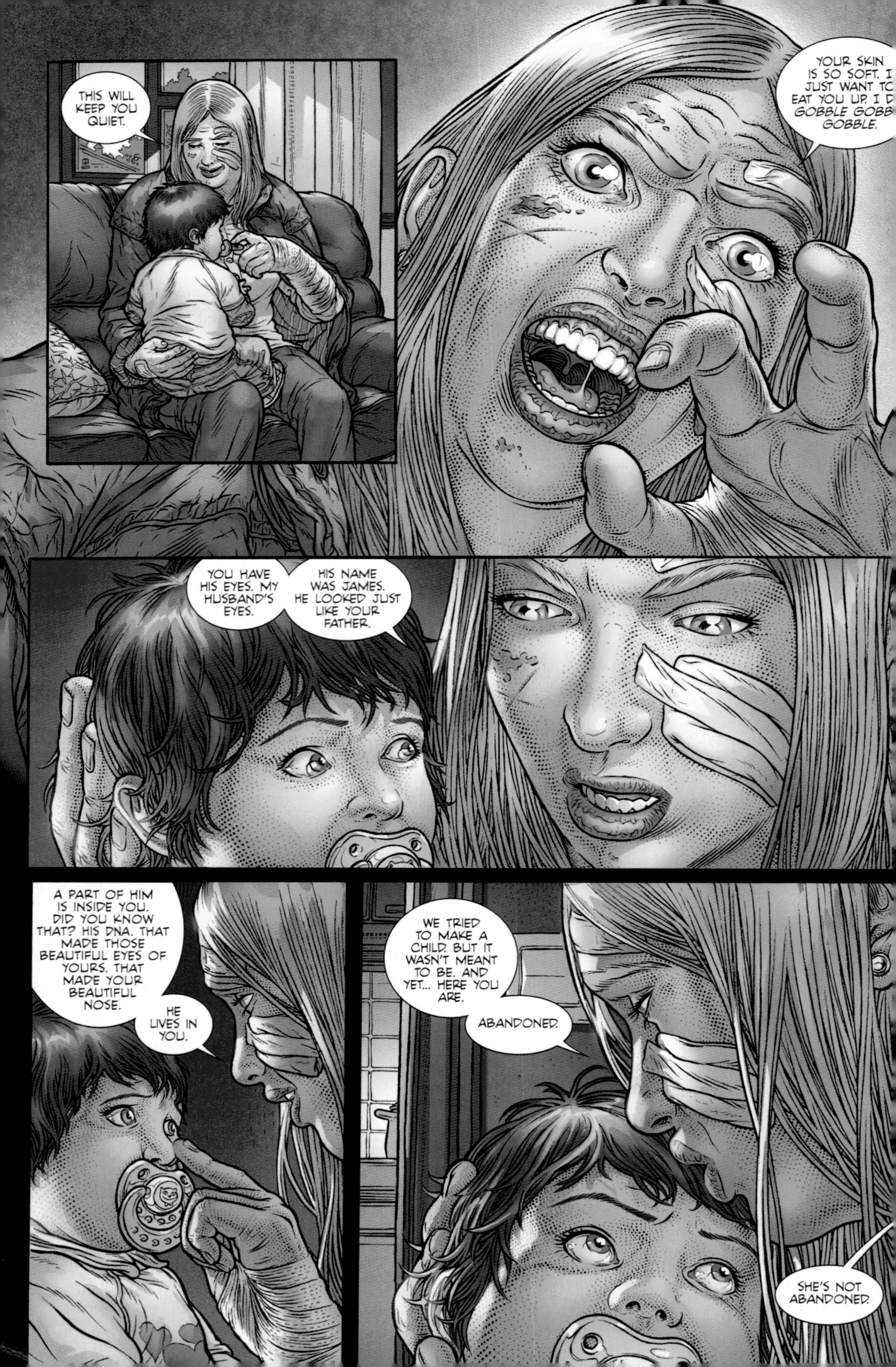
THIS WILL KEEP YOU QUIET.
YOUR SKIN IS SO SOFT. I JUST WANT TO EAT YOU UP. I D GOBBLE GOBB GOBBLE.
YOU HAVE HIS EYES. MY HUSBAND'S EYES.
HIS NAME WAS JAMES. HE LOOKED JUST LIKE YOUR FATHER.
A PART OF HIM IS INSIDE YOU. DID YOU KNOW THAT? HIS DNA. THAT MADE THOSE BEAUTIFUL EYES OF YOURS. THAT MADE YOUR BEAUTIFUL NOSE.
HE LIVES IN YOU.
WE TRIED TO MAKE A CHILD. BUT IT WASN'T MEANT TO BE. AND YET... HERE YOU ARE.
ABANDONED.
SHE'S NOT ABANDONED.

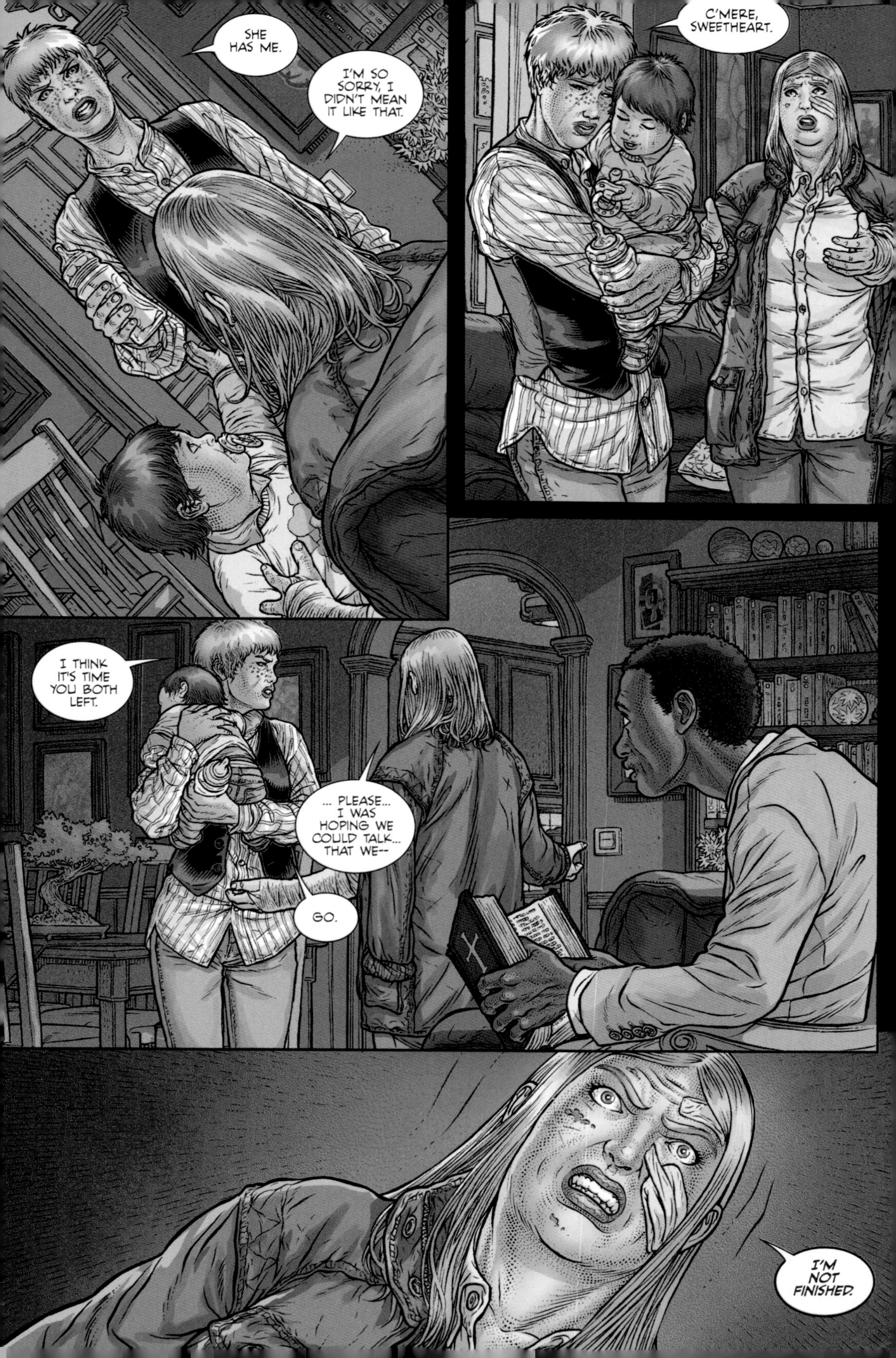
SHE HAS ME.
I'M SO SORRY, I DIDN'T MEAN IT LIKE THAT.
C'MERE, SWEETHEART.
I THINK IT'S TIME YOU BOTH LEFT.
... PLEASE... I WAS HOPING WE COULD TALK... THAT WE--
GO.
I'M NOT FINISHED.

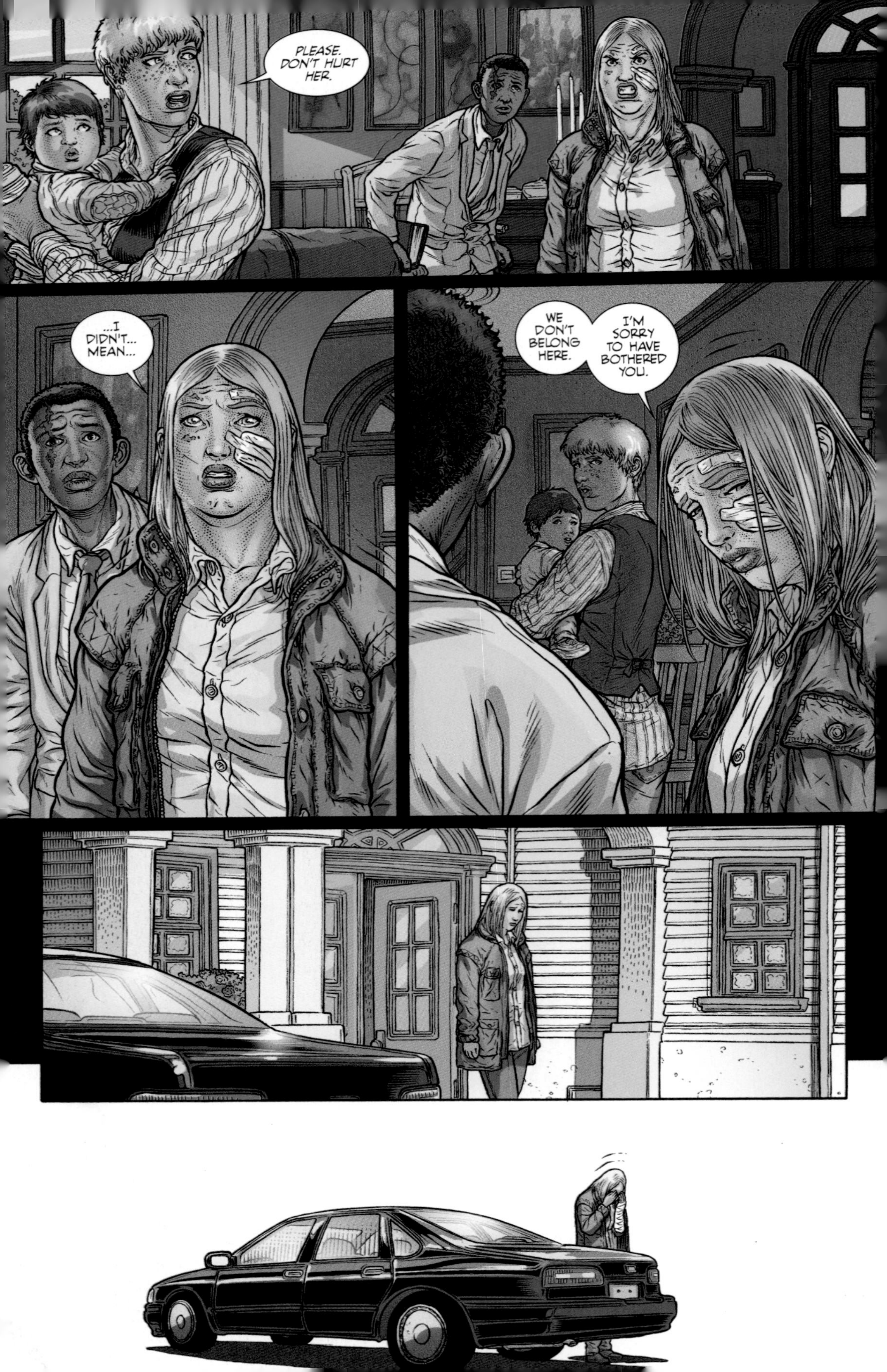
PLEASE. DON'T HURT HER.
...I DIDN'T... MEAN...
WE DON'T BELONG HERE.
I'M SORRY TO HAVE BOTHERED YOU.

THIRSTY?

YOUR FATHER WILL BE BACK, AND THIS WILL ALL BE OVER SOON.

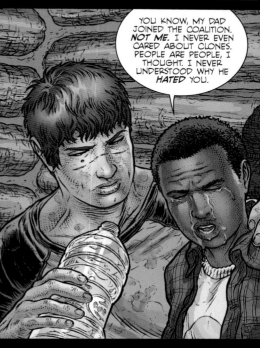

YOU KNOW, MY DAD JOINED THE COALITION. *NOT ME.* I NEVER EVEN CARED ABOUT CLONES. PEOPLE ARE PEOPLE, I THOUGHT. I NEVER UNDERSTOOD WHY HE *HATED* YOU.

NOW I KNOW.

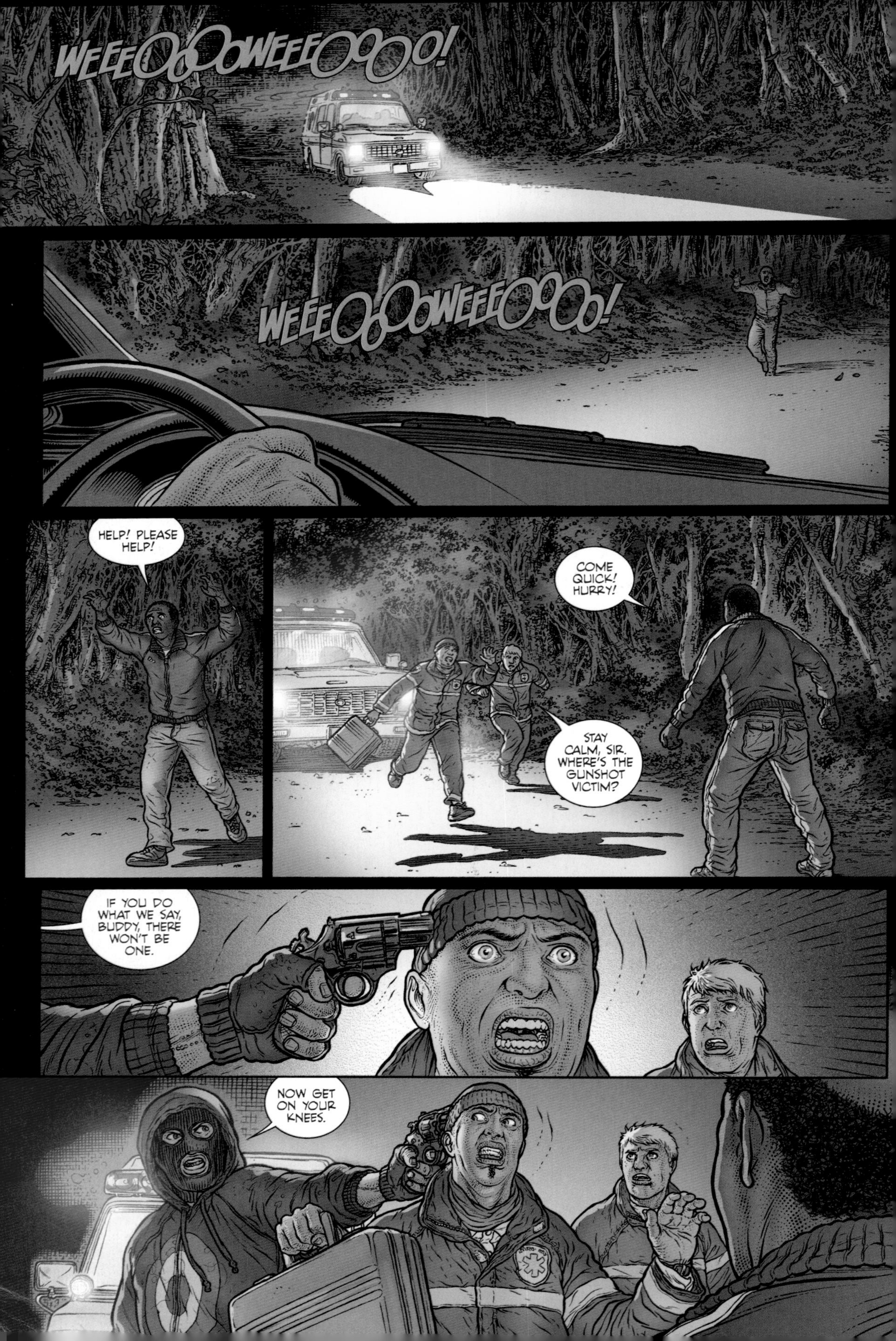
WEEEOOOOWEEEOOOOO!
WEEEOOOOWEEEOOOOO!
HELP! PLEASE HELP!
COME QUICK! HURRY!
STAY CALM, SIR. WHERE'S THE GUNSHOT VICTIM?
IF YOU DO WHAT WE SAY, BUDDY, THERE WON'T BE ONE.
NOW GET ON YOUR KNEES.

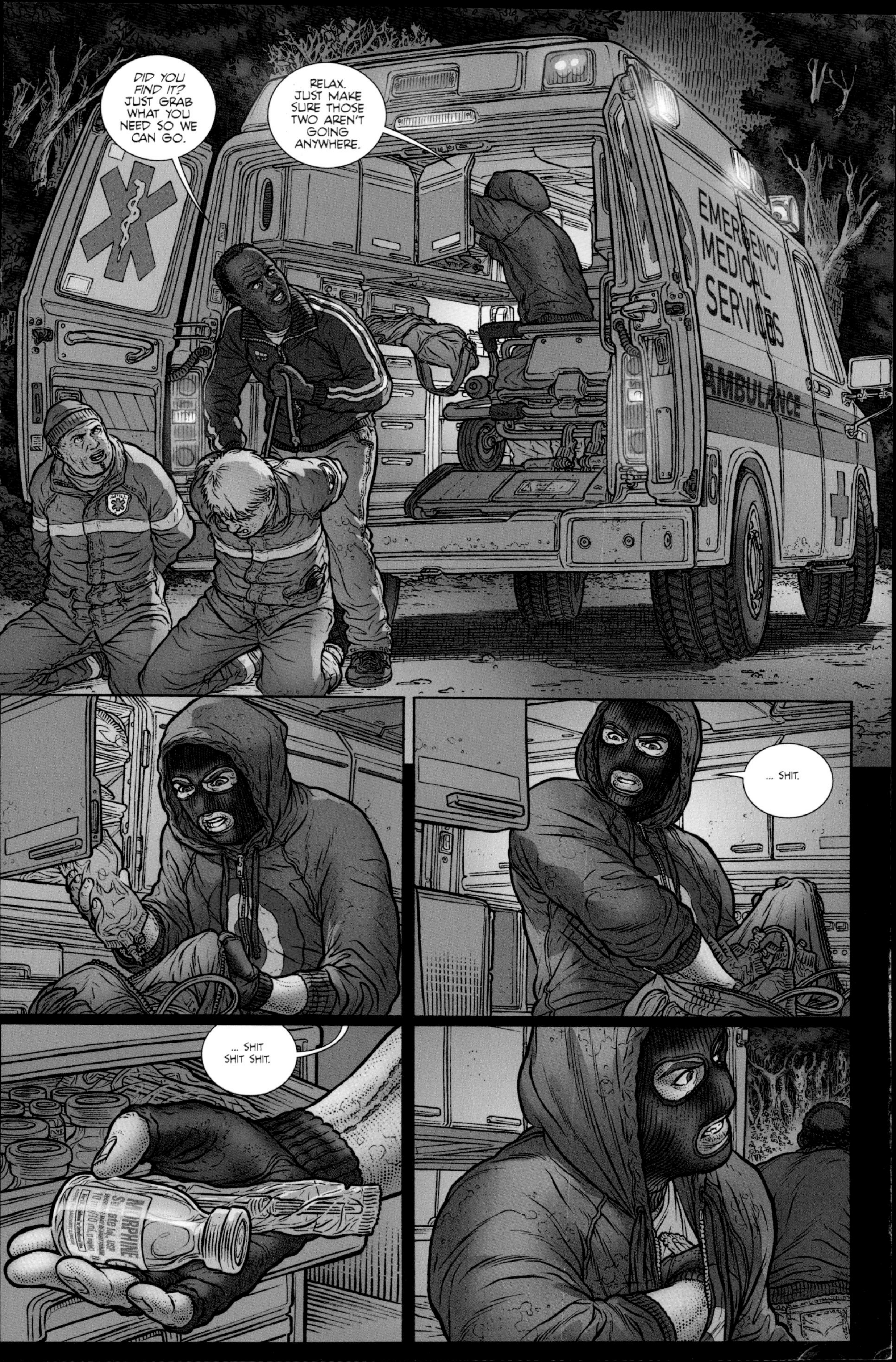
DID YOU FIND IT? JUST GRAB WHAT YOU NEED SO WE CAN GO.
RELAX. JUST MAKE SURE THOSE TWO AREN'T GOING ANYWHERE.
EMERGENCY MEDICAL SERVICES
AMBULANCE
... SHIT.
... SHIT SHIT SHIT.
MORPHINE

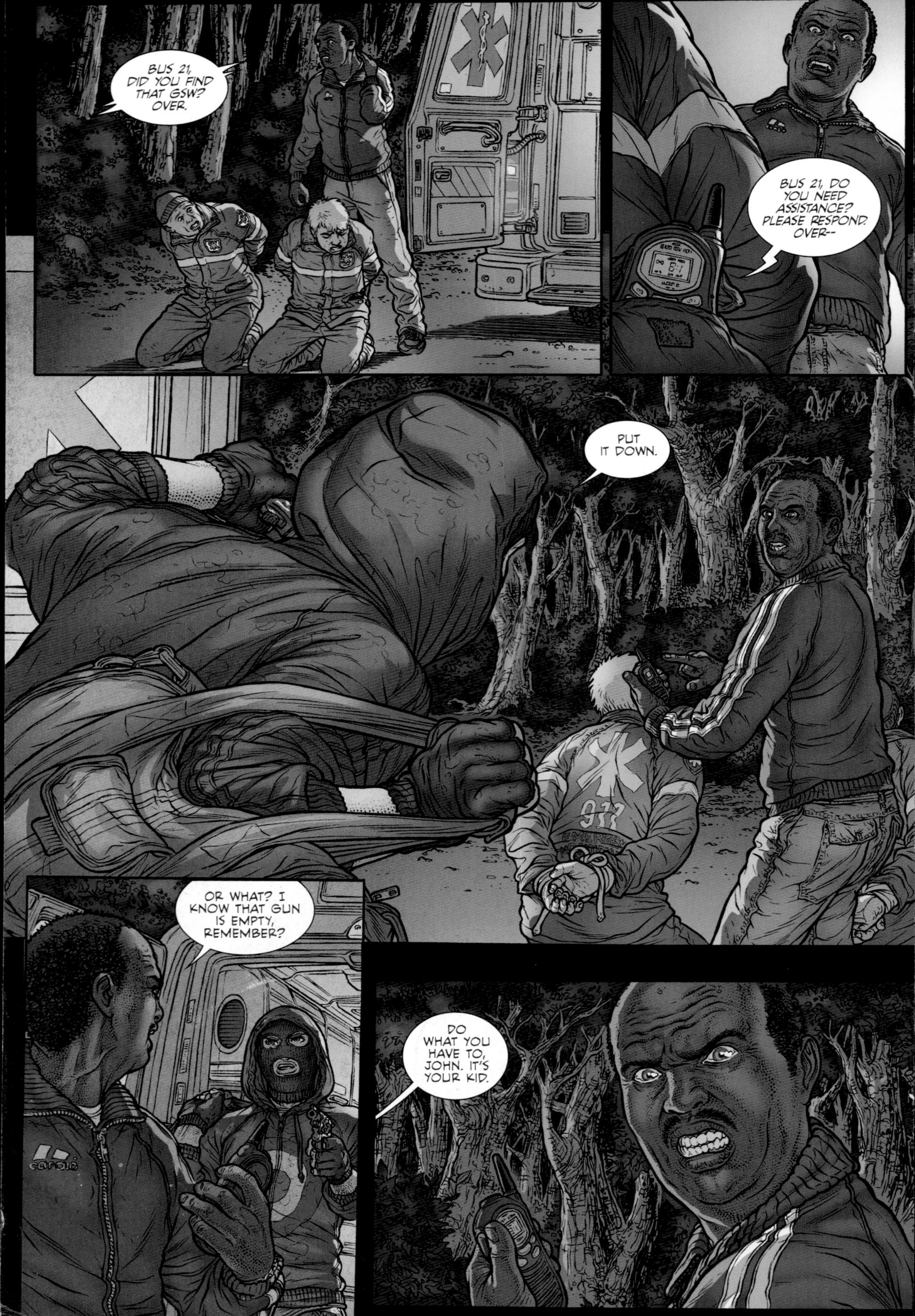
BUS 21, DID YOU FIND THAT GSW? OVER.
BUS 21, DO YOU NEED ASSISTANCE? PLEASE RESPOND. OVER--
PUT IT DOWN.
OR WHAT? I KNOW THAT GUN IS EMPTY, REMEMBER?
DO WHAT YOU HAVE TO, JOHN. IT'S YOUR KID.

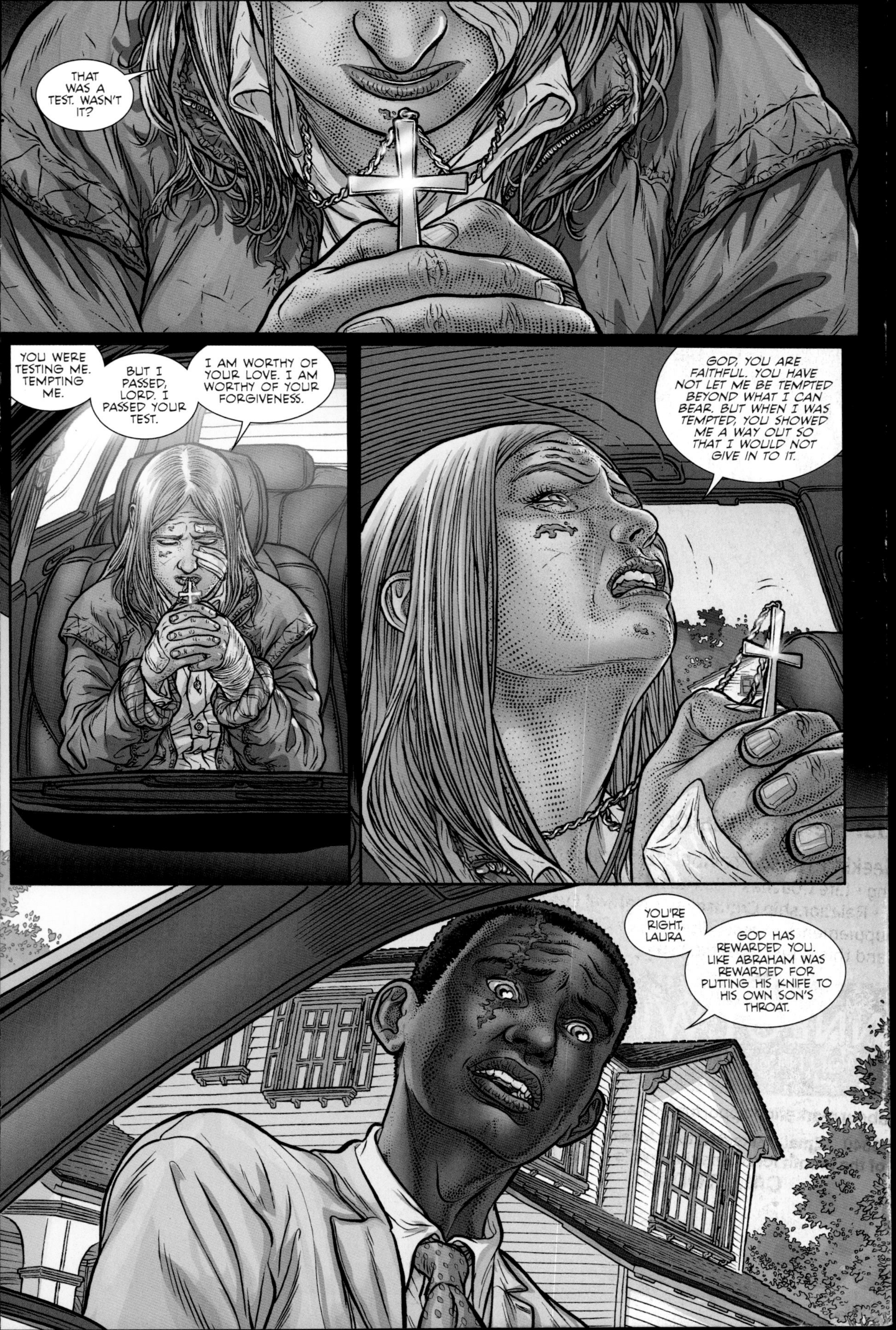
THAT WAS A TEST. WASN'T IT?
YOU WERE TESTING ME. TEMPTING ME.
BUT I PASSED, LORD. I PASSED YOUR TEST.
I AM WORTHY OF YOUR LOVE. I AM WORTHY OF YOUR FORGIVENESS.
GOD, YOU ARE FAITHFUL. YOU HAVE NOT LET ME BE TEMPTED BEYOND WHAT I CAN BEAR. BUT WHEN I WAS TEMPTED, YOU SHOWED ME A WAY OUT SO THAT I WOULD NOT GIVE IN TO IT.
YOU'RE RIGHT, LAURA.
GOD HAS REWARDED YOU. LIKE ABRAHAM WAS REWARDED FOR PUTTING HIS KNIFE TO HIS OWN SON'S THROAT.

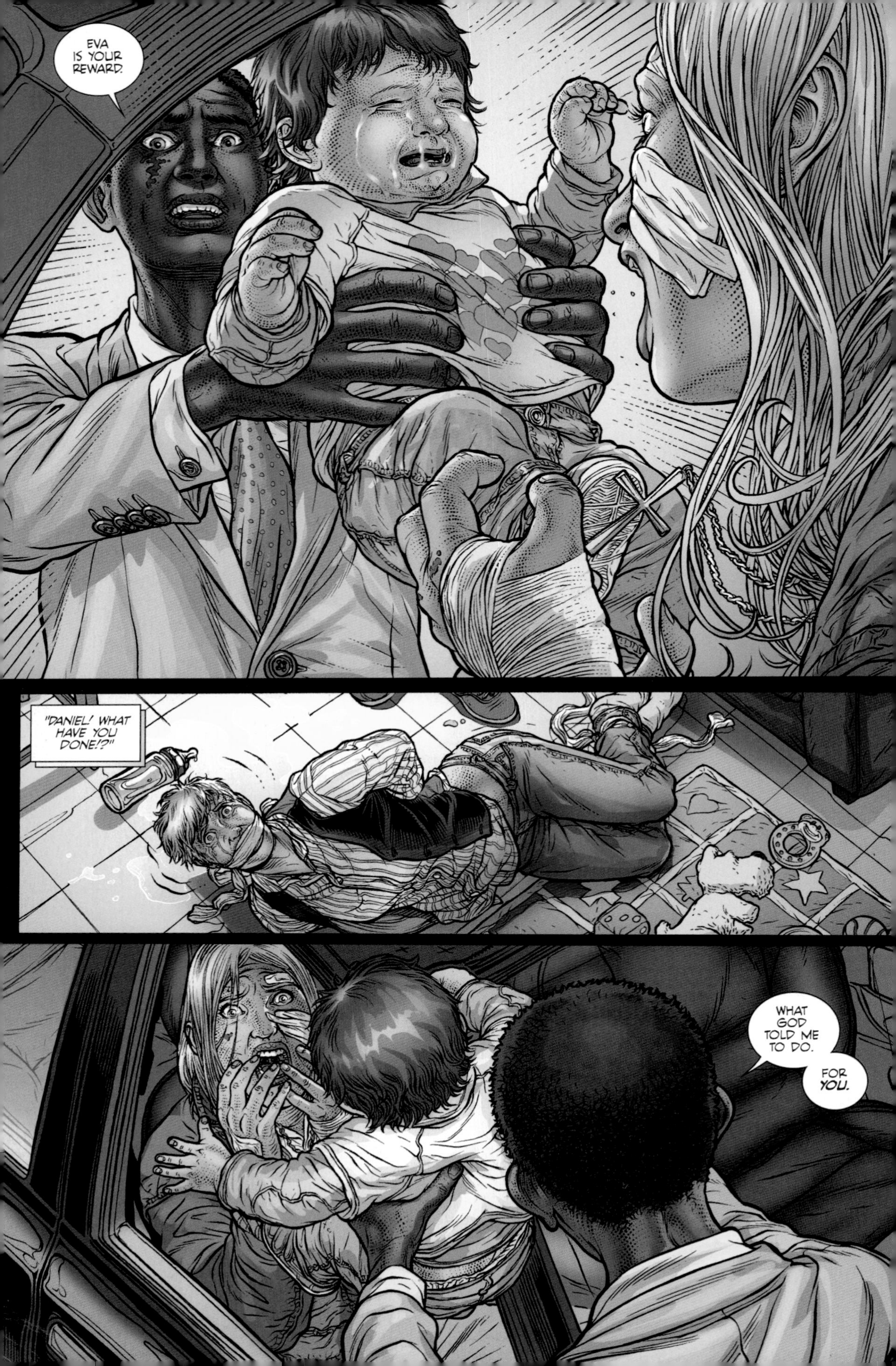
EVA IS YOUR REWARD.
"DANIEL! WHAT HAVE YOU DONE!?"
WHAT GOD TOLD ME TO DO.
FOR YOU.

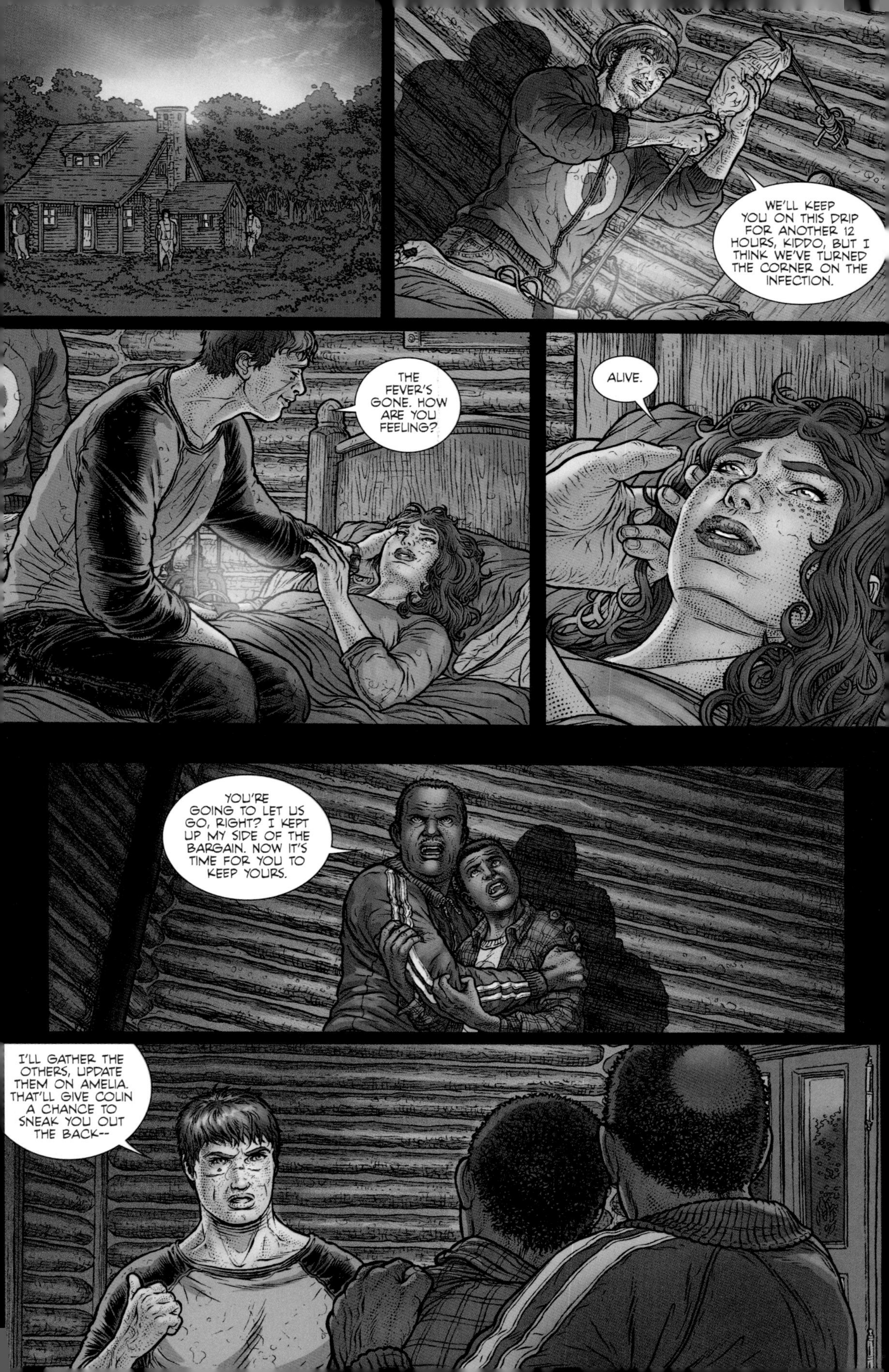
WE'LL KEEP YOU ON THIS DRIP FOR ANOTHER 12 HOURS, KIDDO, BUT I THINK WE'VE TURNED THE CORNER ON THE INFECTION.
THE FEVER'S GONE. HOW ARE YOU FEELING?
ALIVE.
YOU'RE GOING TO LET US GO, RIGHT? I KEPT UP MY SIDE OF THE BARGAIN. NOW IT'S TIME FOR YOU TO KEEP YOURS.
I'LL GATHER THE OTHERS, UPDATE THEM ON AMELIA. THAT'LL GIVE COLIN A CHANCE TO SNEAK YOU OUT THE BACK--

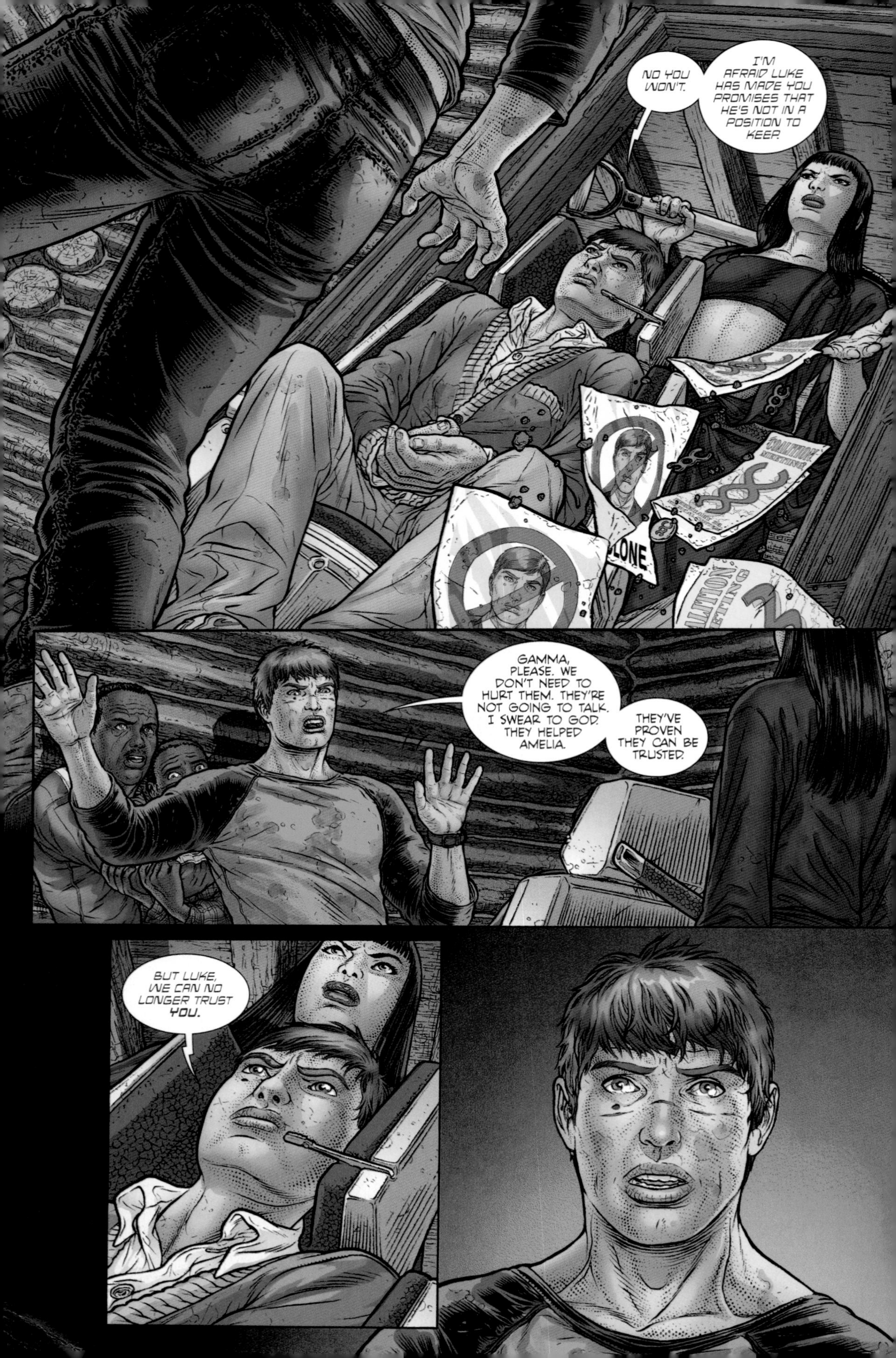
NO YOU WON'T.
I'M AFRAID LUKE HAS MADE YOU PROMISES THAT HE'S NOT IN A POSITION TO KEEP.
CLONE
GAMMA, PLEASE. WE DON'T NEED TO HURT THEM. THEY'RE NOT GOING TO TALK. I SWEAR TO GOD. THEY HELPED AMELIA.
THEY'VE PROVEN THEY CAN BE TRUSTED.
BUT LUKE, WE CAN NO LONGER TRUST YOU.

CHAPTER 19

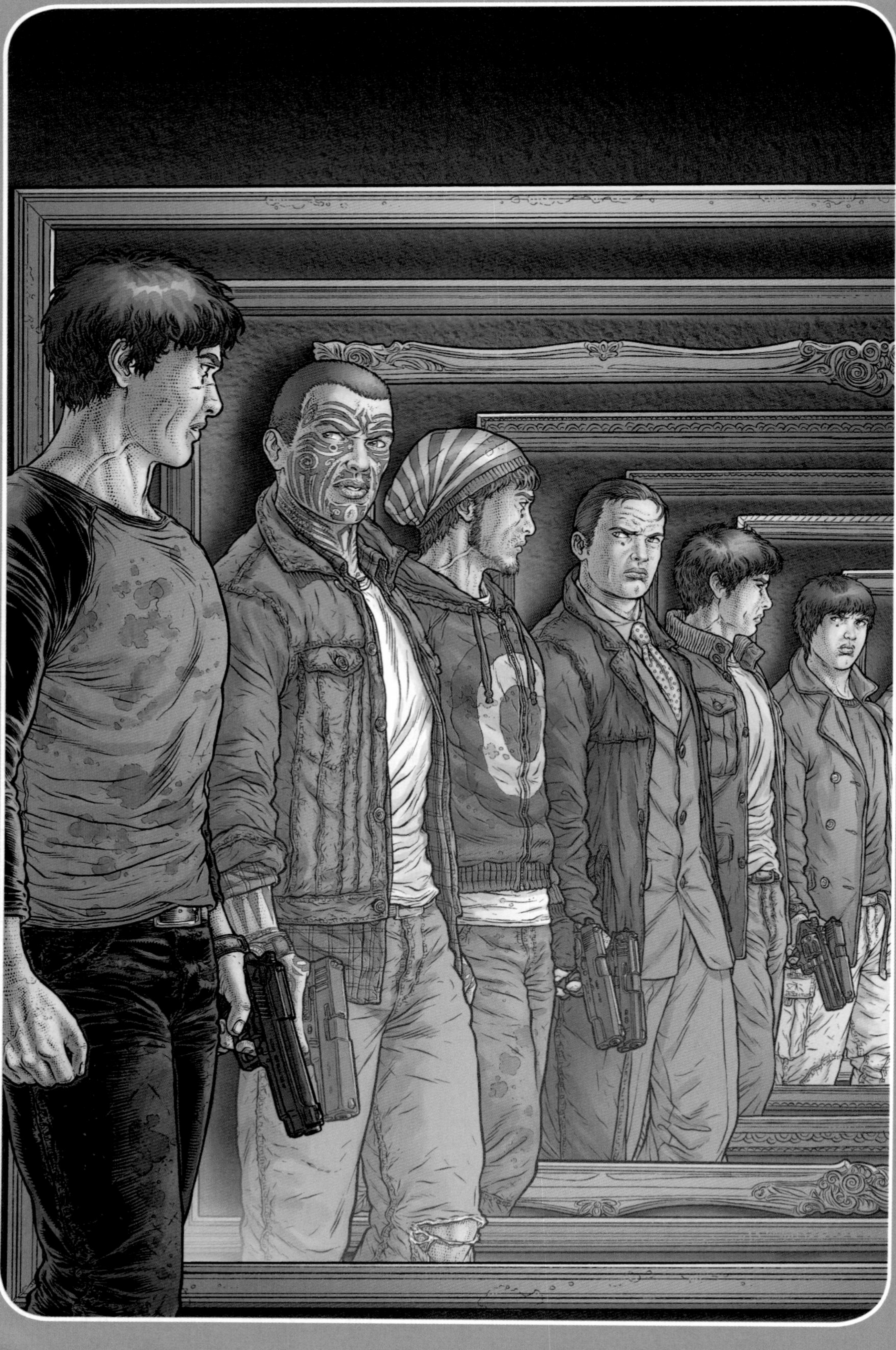

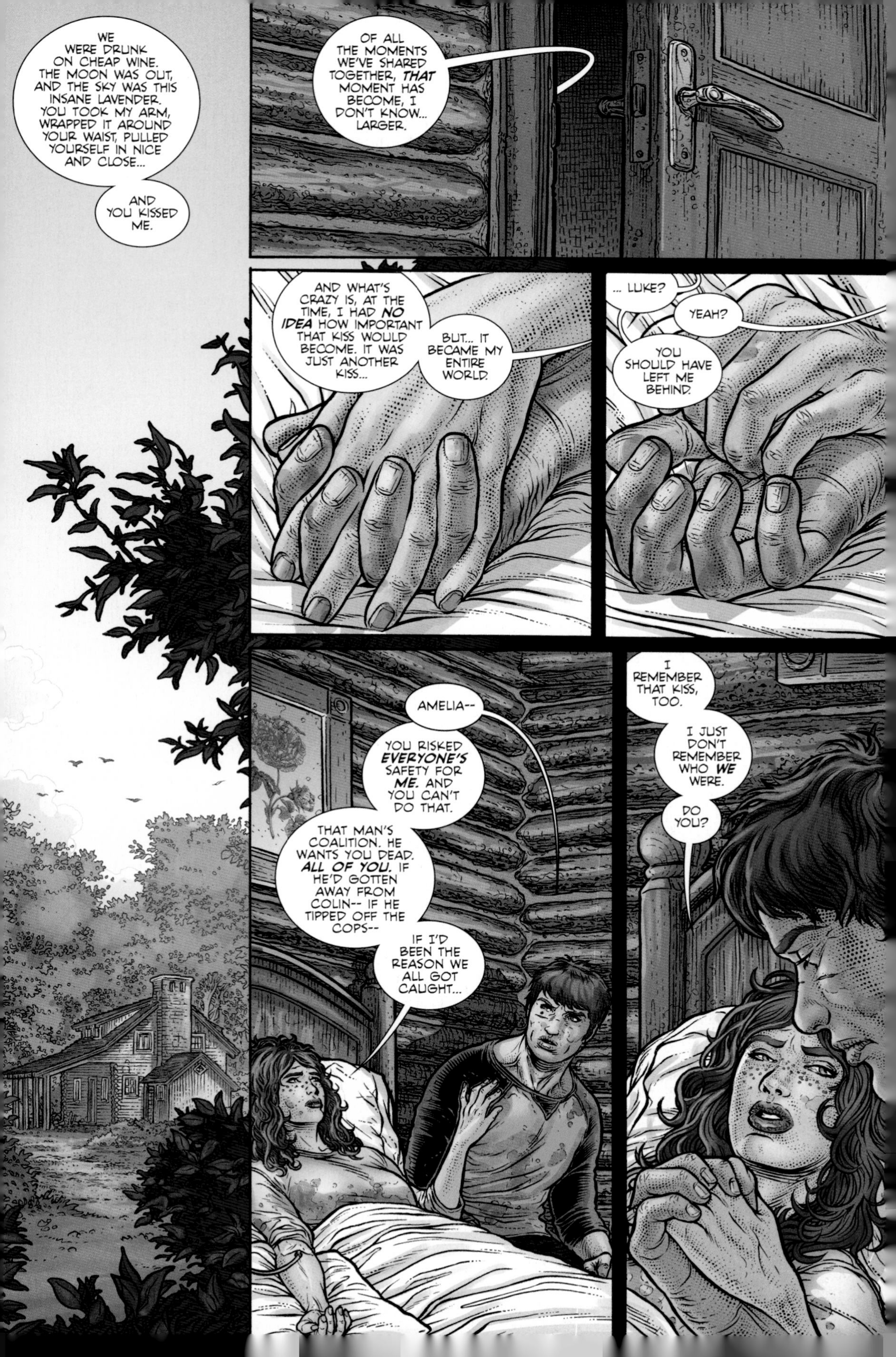
WE WERE DRUNK ON CHEAP WINE. THE MOON WAS OUT, AND THE SKY WAS THIS INSANE LAVENDER. YOU TOOK MY ARM, WRAPPED IT AROUND YOUR WAIST, PULLED YOURSELF IN NICE AND CLOSE...
AND YOU KISSED ME.
OF ALL THE MOMENTS WE'VE SHARED TOGETHER, *THAT* MOMENT HAS BECOME, I DON'T KNOW... LARGER.
AND WHAT'S CRAZY IS, AT THE TIME, I HAD ***NO IDEA*** HOW IMPORTANT THAT KISS WOULD BECOME. IT WAS JUST ANOTHER KISS...
BUT... IT BECAME MY ENTIRE WORLD.
... LUKE?
YEAH?
YOU SHOULD HAVE LEFT ME BEHIND.
AMELIA--
YOU RISKED ***EVERYONE'S*** SAFETY FOR ***ME.*** AND YOU CAN'T DO THAT.
THAT MAN'S COALITION. HE WANTS YOU DEAD. ***ALL OF YOU.*** IF HE'D GOTTEN AWAY FROM COLIN-- IF HE TIPPED OFF THE COPS--
IF I'D BEEN THE REASON WE ALL GOT CAUGHT...
I REMEMBER THAT KISS, TOO.
I JUST DON'T REMEMBER WHO ***WE*** WERE.
DO YOU?

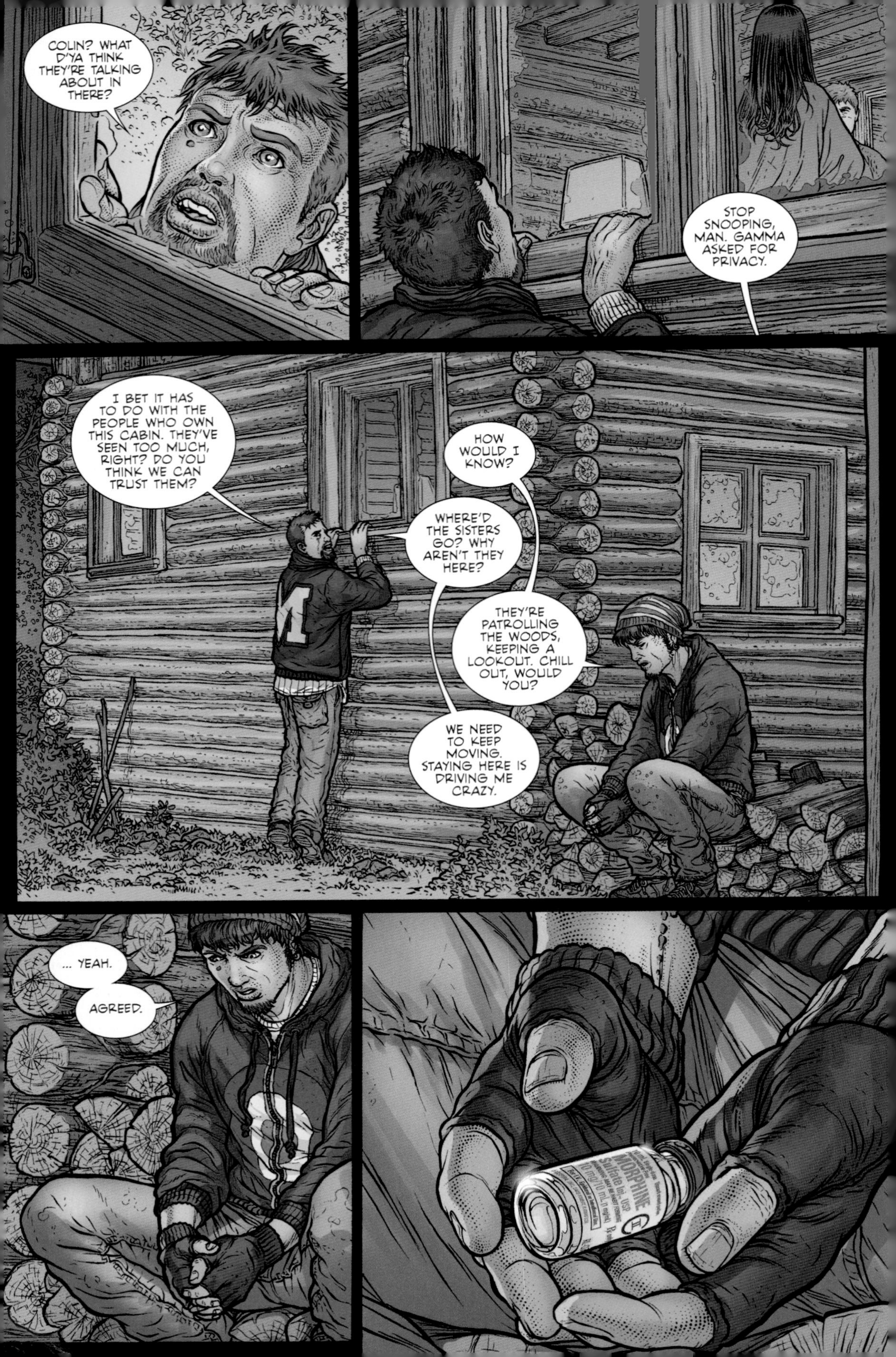
COLIN? WHAT D'YA THINK THEY'RE TALKING ABOUT IN THERE?
STOP SNOOPING, MAN. GAMMA ASKED FOR PRIVACY.
I BET IT HAS TO DO WITH THE PEOPLE WHO OWN THIS CABIN. THEY'VE SEEN TOO MUCH, RIGHT? DO YOU THINK WE CAN TRUST THEM?
HOW WOULD I KNOW?
WHERE'D THE SISTERS GO? WHY AREN'T THEY HERE?
THEY'RE PATROLLING THE WOODS, KEEPING A LOOKOUT. CHILL OUT, WOULD YOU?
WE NEED TO KEEP MOVING. STAYING HERE IS DRIVING ME CRAZY.
... YEAH.
AGREED.
MORPHINE

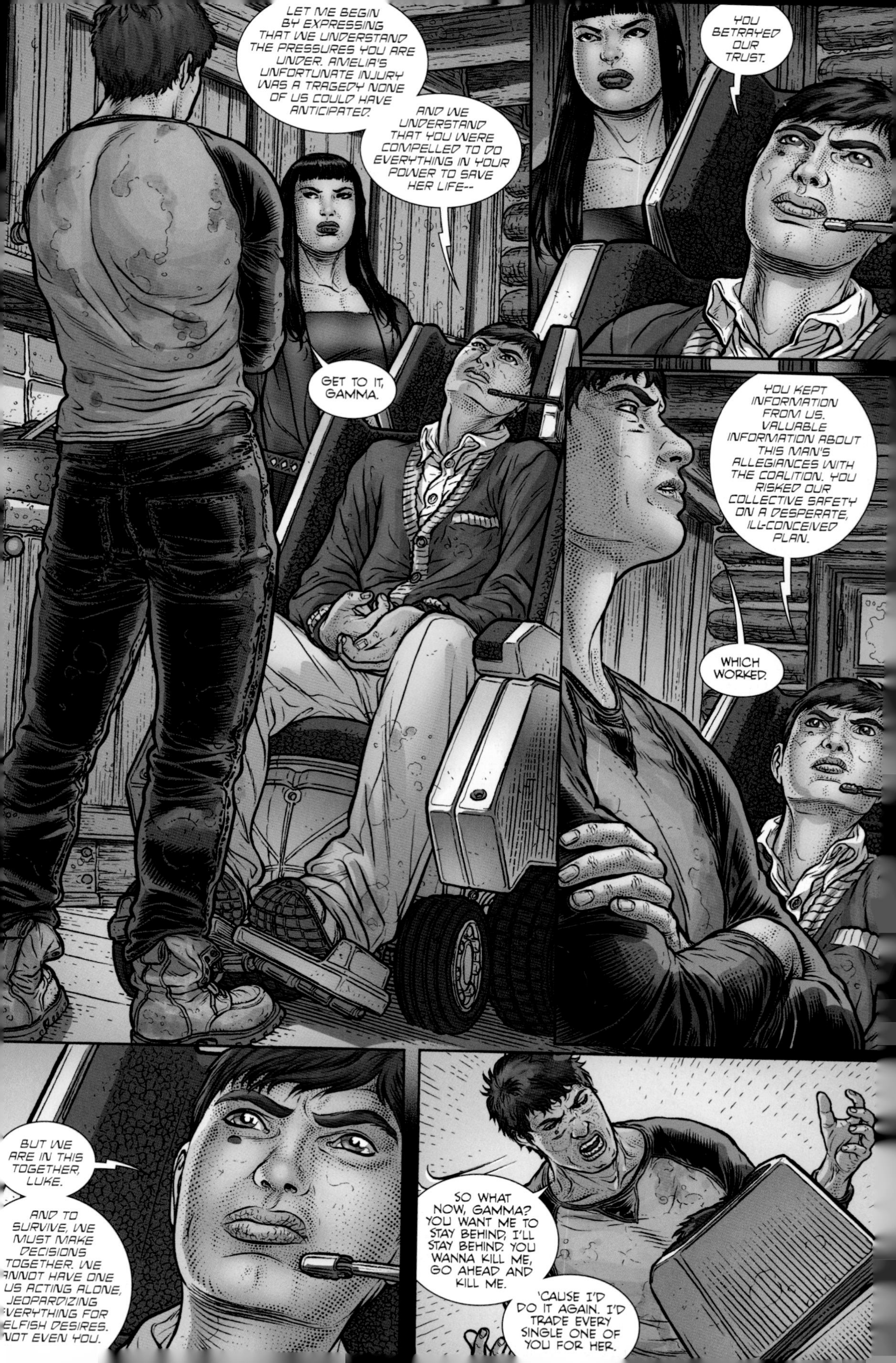
LET ME BEGIN BY EXPRESSING THAT WE UNDERSTAND THE PRESSURES YOU ARE UNDER. AMELIA'S UNFORTUNATE INJURY WAS A TRAGEDY NONE OF US COULD HAVE ANTICIPATED.
AND WE UNDERSTAND THAT YOU WERE COMPELLED TO DO EVERYTHING IN YOUR POWER TO SAVE HER LIFE--
GET TO IT, GAMMA.
YOU BETRAYED OUR TRUST.
YOU KEPT INFORMATION FROM US. VALUABLE INFORMATION ABOUT THIS MAN'S ALLEGIANCES WITH THE COALITION. YOU RISKED OUR COLLECTIVE SAFETY ON A DESPERATE, ILL-CONCEIVED PLAN.
WHICH WORKED.
BUT WE ARE IN THIS TOGETHER, LUKE.
AND TO SURVIVE, WE MUST MAKE DECISIONS TOGETHER. WE ANNOT HAVE ONE US ACTING ALONE, JEOPARDIZING EVERYTHING FOR ELFISH DESIRES. NOT EVEN YOU.
SO WHAT NOW, GAMMA? YOU WANT ME TO STAY BEHIND, I'LL STAY BEHIND. YOU WANNA KILL ME, GO AHEAD AND KILL ME.
'CAUSE I'D DO IT AGAIN. I'D TRADE EVERY SINGLE ONE OF YOU FOR HER.

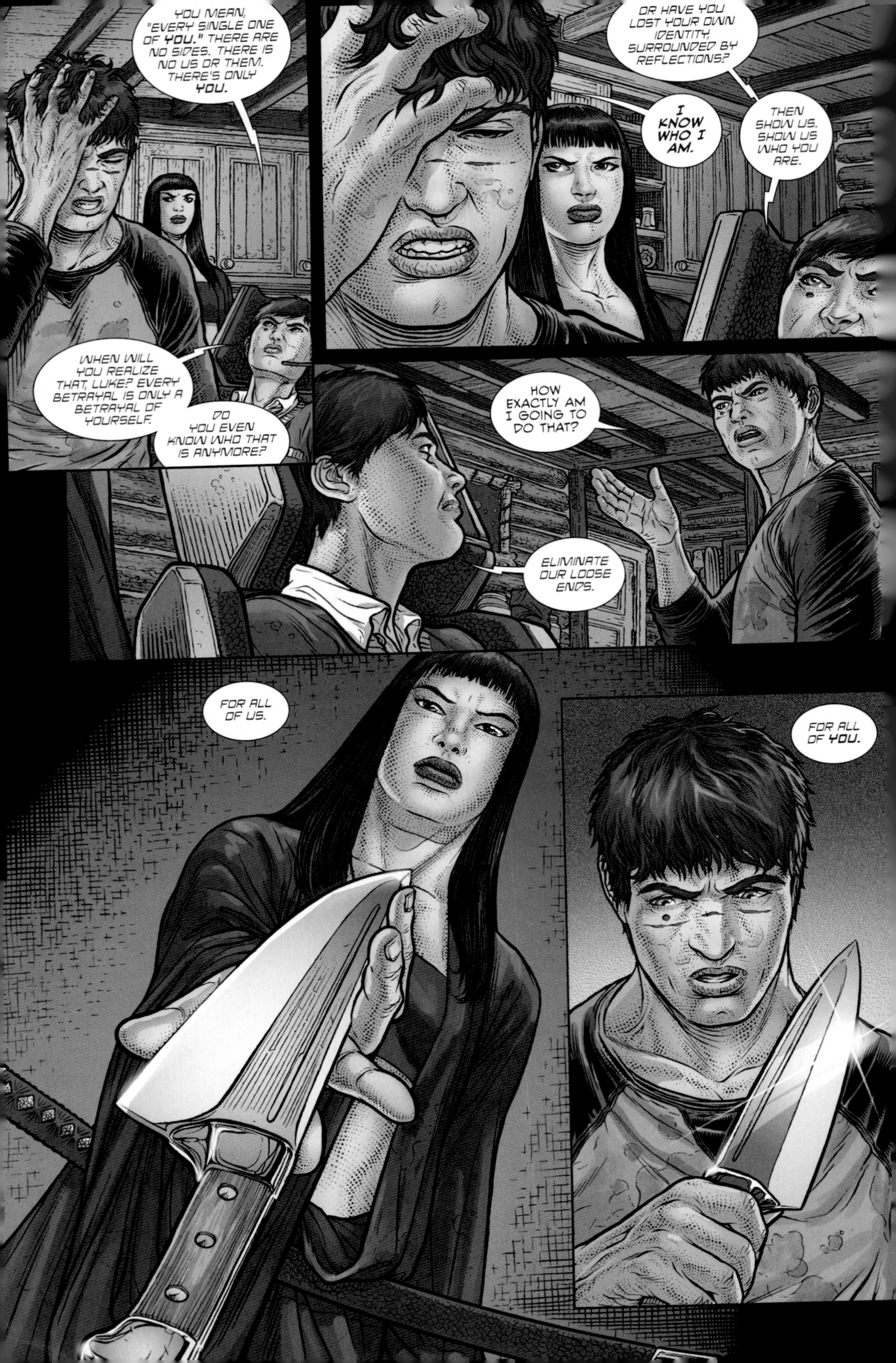
YOU MEAN, "EVERY SINGLE ONE OF **YOU.**" THERE ARE NO SIDES. THERE IS NO US OR THEM. THERE'S ONLY **YOU.**
WHEN WILL YOU REALIZE THAT, LUKE? EVERY BETRAYAL IS ONLY A BETRAYAL OF YOURSELF.
DO YOU EVEN KNOW WHO THAT IS ANYMORE?
OR HAVE YOU LOST YOUR OWN IDENTITY, SURROUNDED BY REFLECTIONS?
I KNOW WHO I AM.
THEN SHOW US. SHOW US WHO YOU ARE.
HOW EXACTLY AM I GOING TO DO THAT?
ELIMINATE OUR LOOSE ENDS.
FOR ALL OF US.
FOR ALL OF **YOU.**

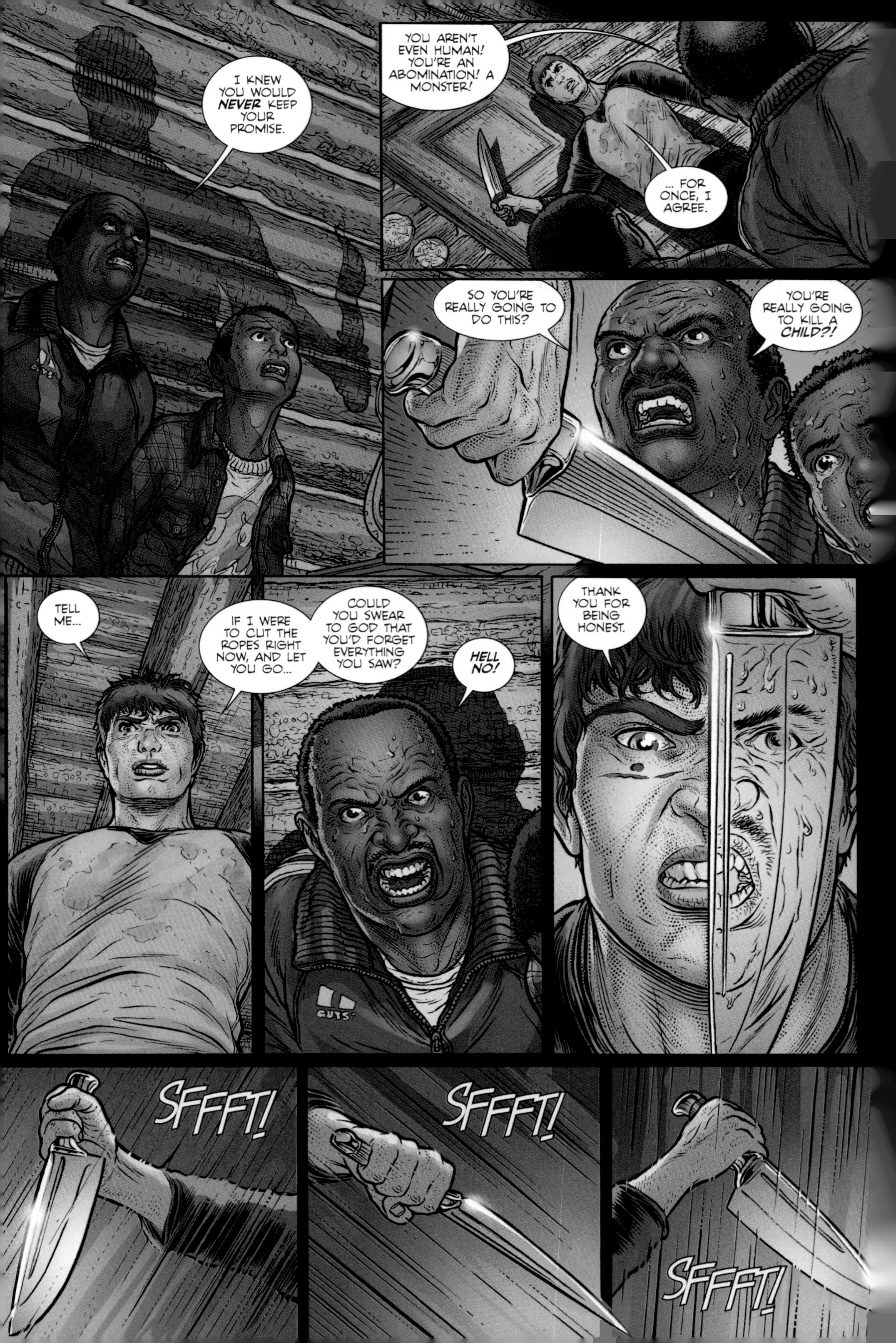
I KNEW YOU WOULD NEVER KEEP YOUR PROMISE.
YOU AREN'T EVEN HUMAN! YOU'RE AN ABOMINATION! A MONSTER!
... FOR ONCE, I AGREE.
SO YOU'RE REALLY GOING TO DO THIS?
YOU'RE REALLY GOING TO KILL A CHILD?!
TELL ME...
IF I WERE TO CUT THE ROPES RIGHT NOW, AND LET YOU GO...
COULD YOU SWEAR TO GOD THAT YOU'D FORGET EVERYTHING YOU SAW?
HELL NO!
THANK YOU FOR BEING HONEST.
SFFFT!
SFFFT!
SFFFT!

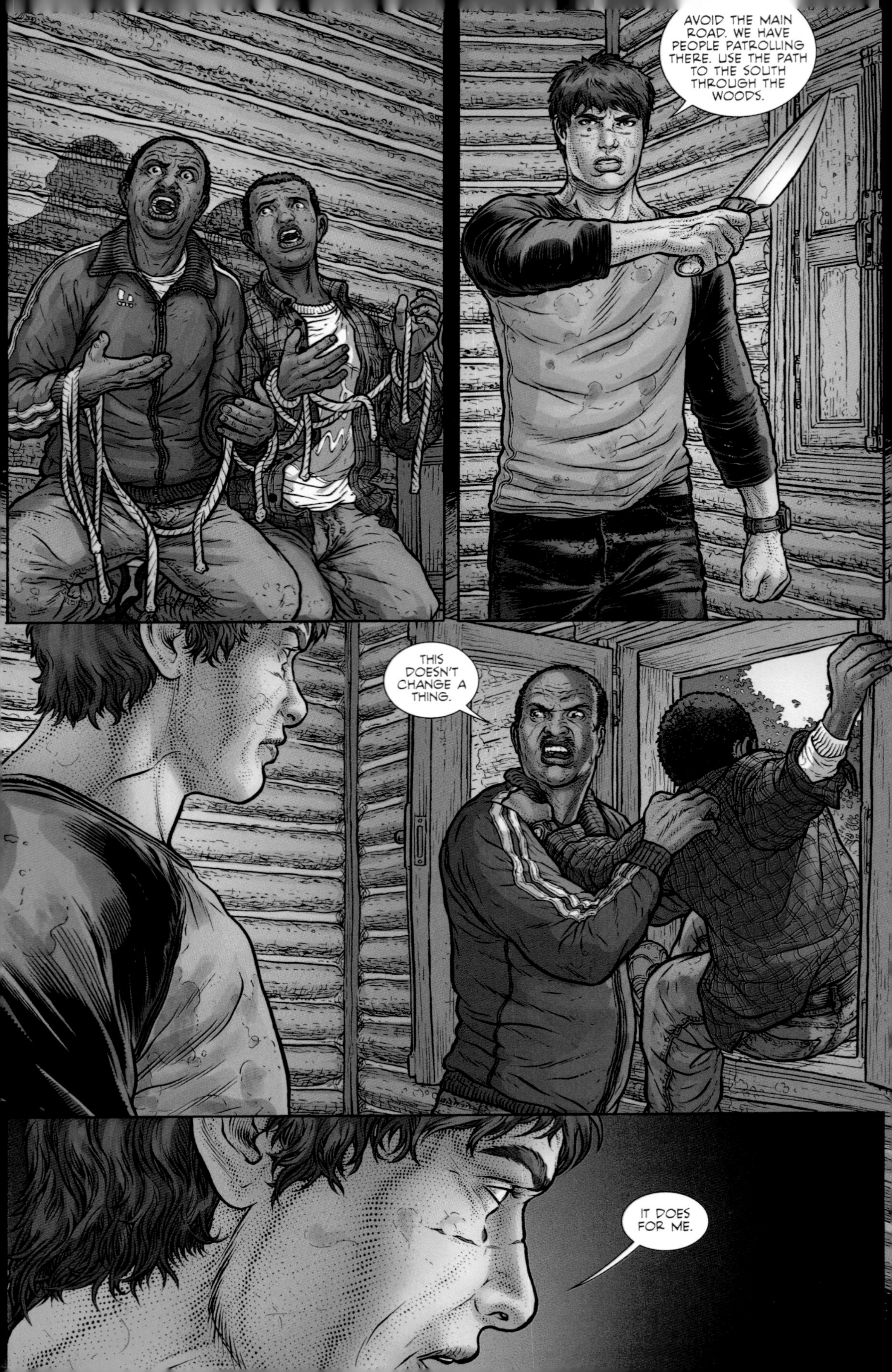
AVOID THE MAIN ROAD. WE HAVE PEOPLE PATROLLING THERE. USE THE PATH TO THE SOUTH THROUGH THE WOODS.
THIS DOESN'T CHANGE A THING.
IT DOES FOR ME.

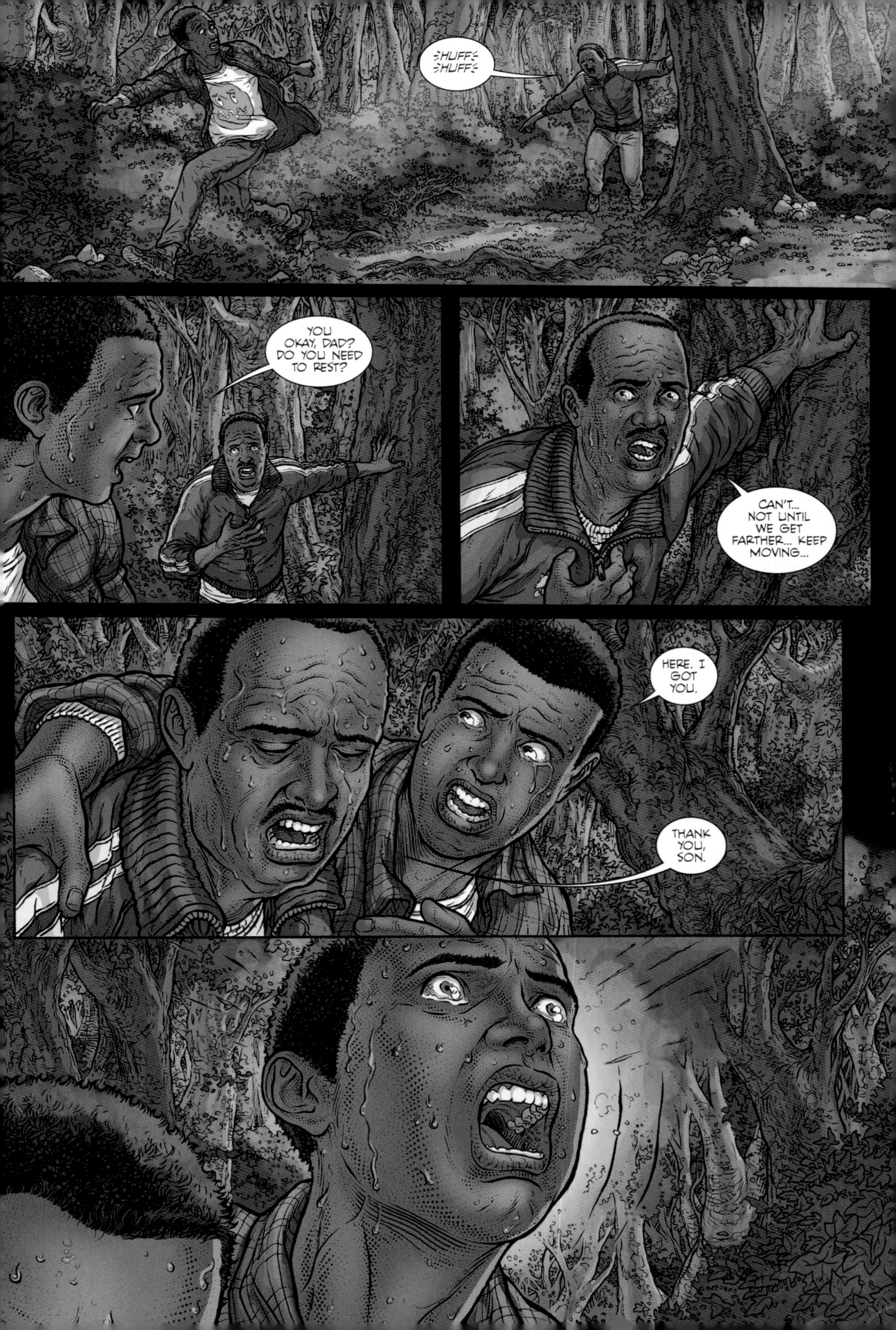
HUFF HUFF
YOU OKAY, DAD? DO YOU NEED TO REST?
CAN'T... NOT UNTIL WE GET FARTHER... KEEP MOVING...
HERE. I GOT YOU.
THANK YOU, SON.

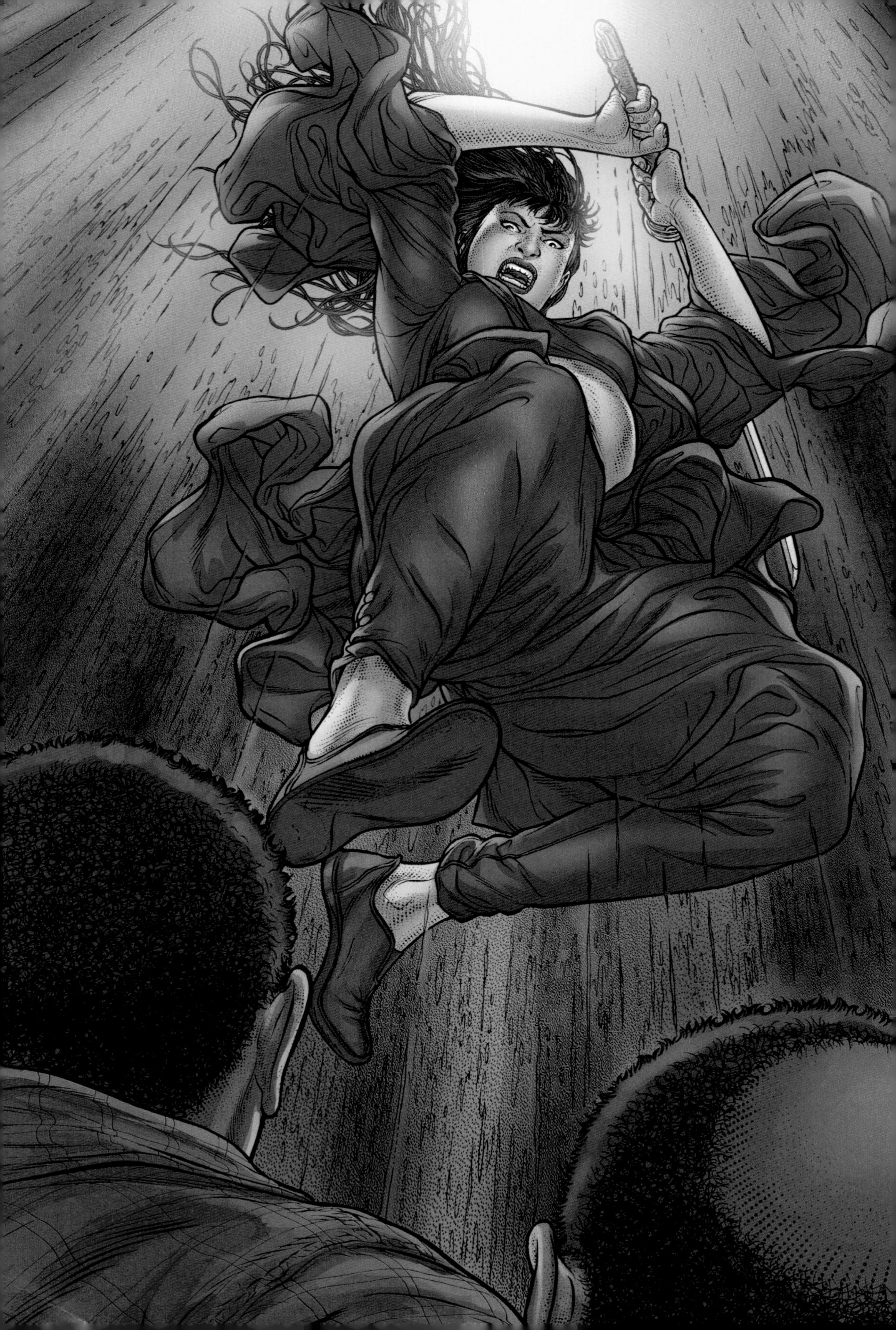

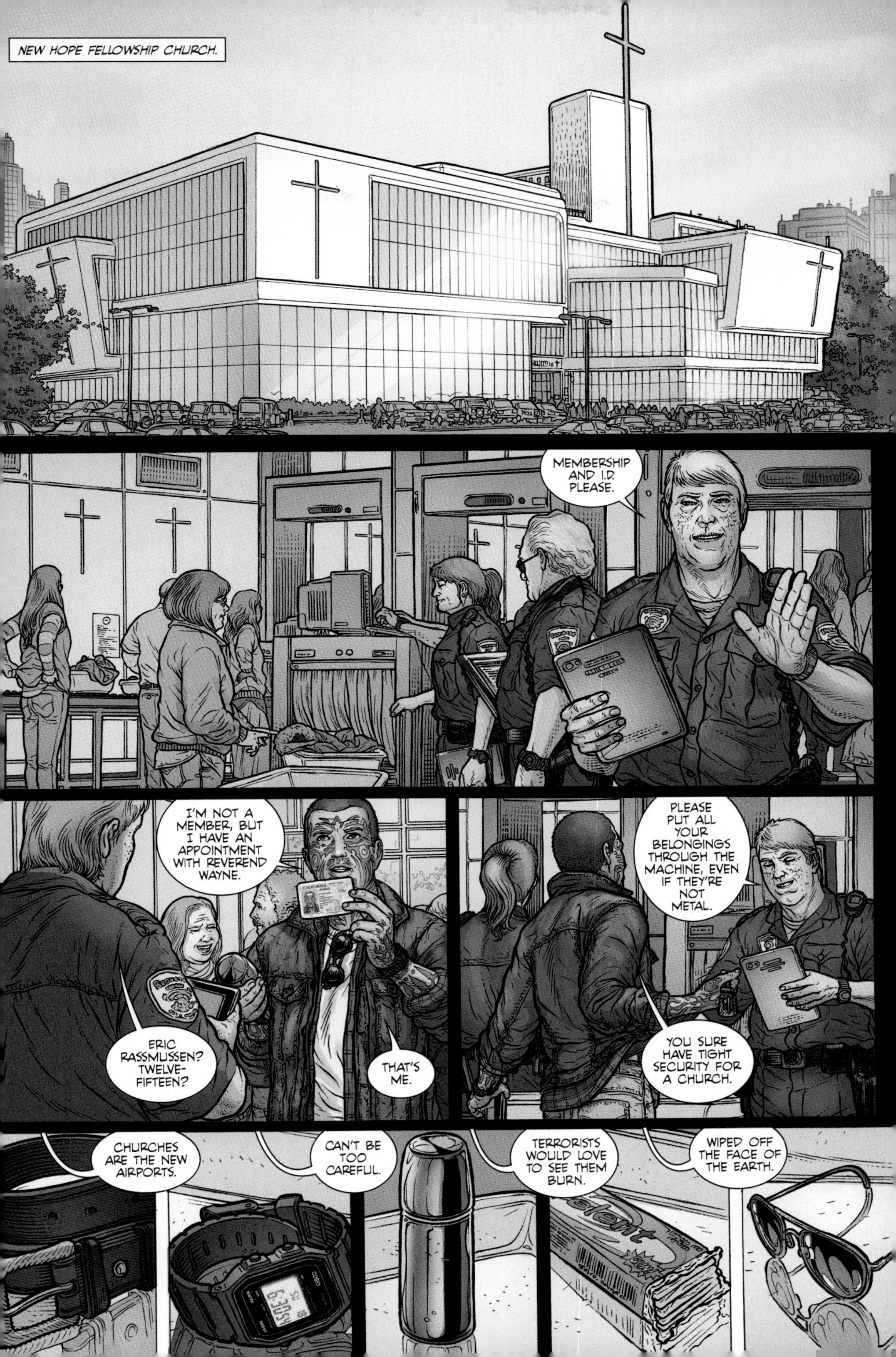
NEW HOPE FELLOWSHIP CHURCH.
MEMBERSHIP AND I.D. PLEASE.
I'M NOT A MEMBER, BUT I HAVE AN APPOINTMENT WITH REVEREND WAYNE.
ERIC RASSMUSSEN? TWELVE-FIFTEEN?
THAT'S ME.
PLEASE PUT ALL YOUR BELONGINGS THROUGH THE MACHINE, EVEN IF THEY'RE NOT METAL.
YOU SURE HAVE TIGHT SECURITY FOR A CHURCH.
CHURCHES ARE THE NEW AIRPORTS.
CAN'T BE TOO CAREFUL.
TERRORISTS WOULD LOVE TO SEE THEM BURN.
WIPED OFF THE FACE OF THE EARTH.

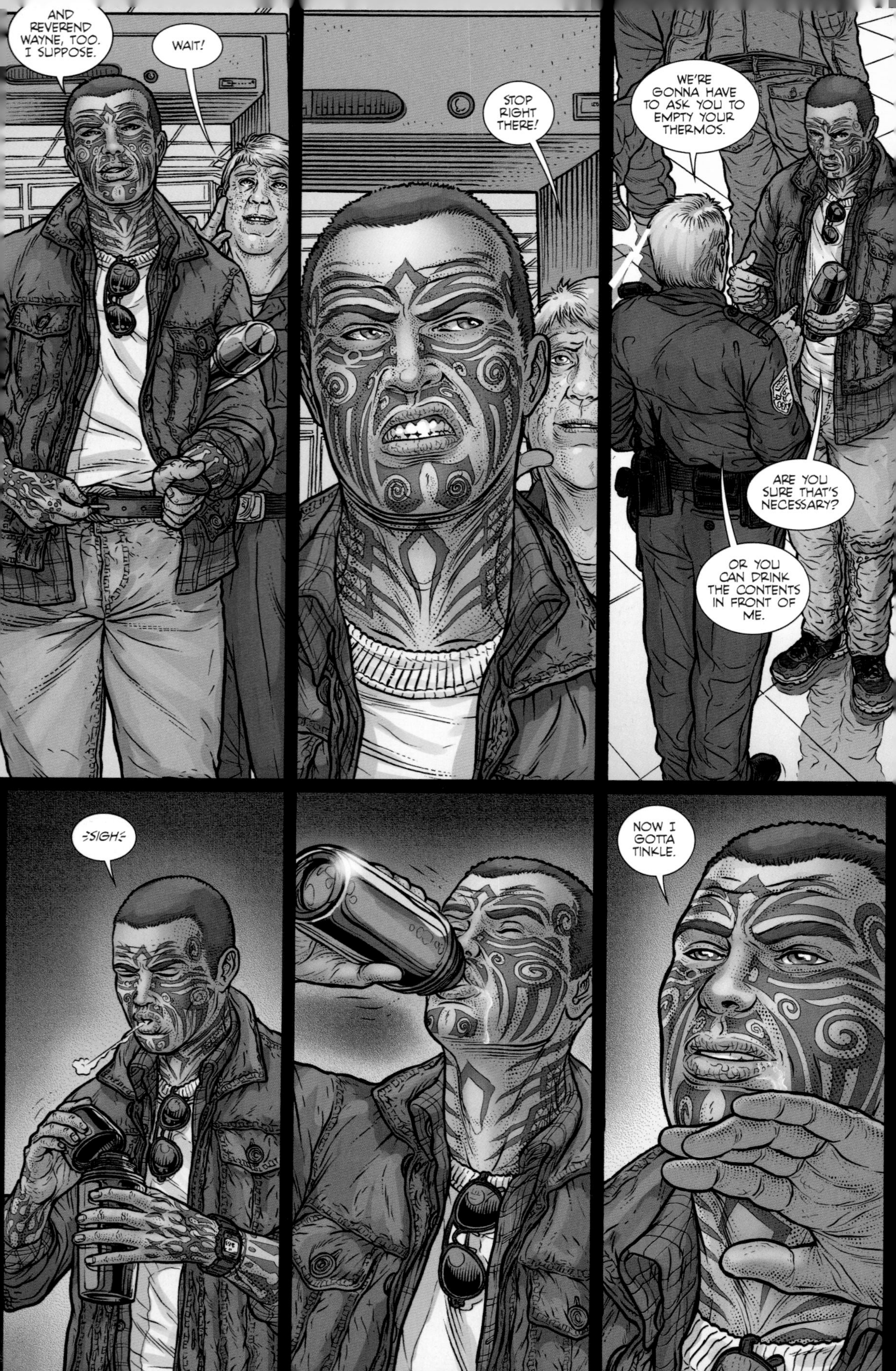
AND REVEREND WAYNE, TOO. I SUPPOSE.
WAIT!
STOP RIGHT THERE!
WE'RE GONNA HAVE TO ASK YOU TO EMPTY YOUR THERMOS.
ARE YOU SURE THAT'S NECESSARY?
OR YOU CAN DRINK THE CONTENTS IN FRONT OF ME.
=SIGH=
NOW I GOTTA TINKLE.

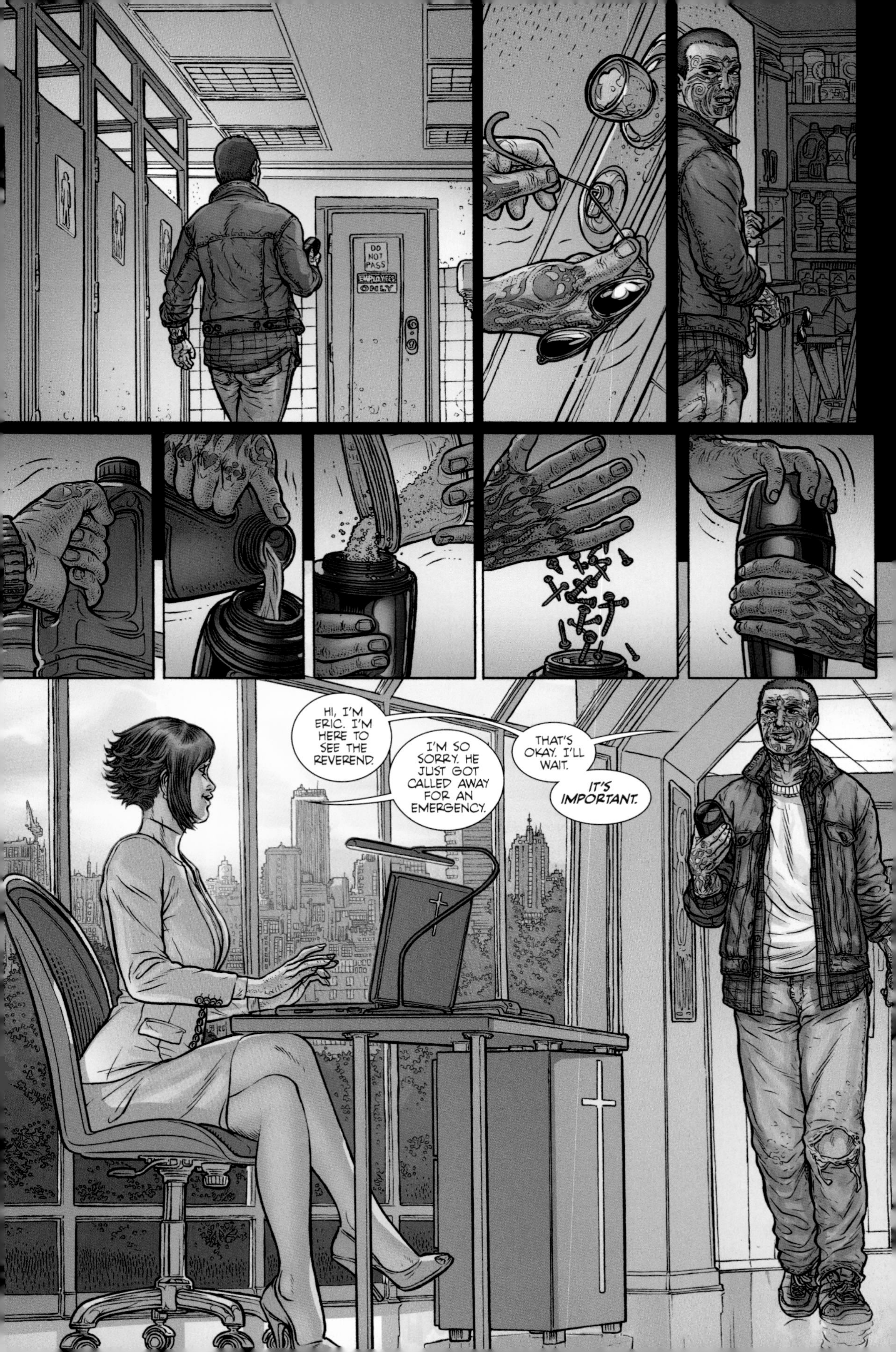
DO NOT PASS
EMPLOYEES ONLY
HI, I'M ERIC. I'M HERE TO SEE THE REVEREND.
I'M SO SORRY. HE JUST GOT CALLED AWAY FOR AN EMERGENCY.
THAT'S OKAY. I'LL WAIT.
IT'S IMPORTANT.

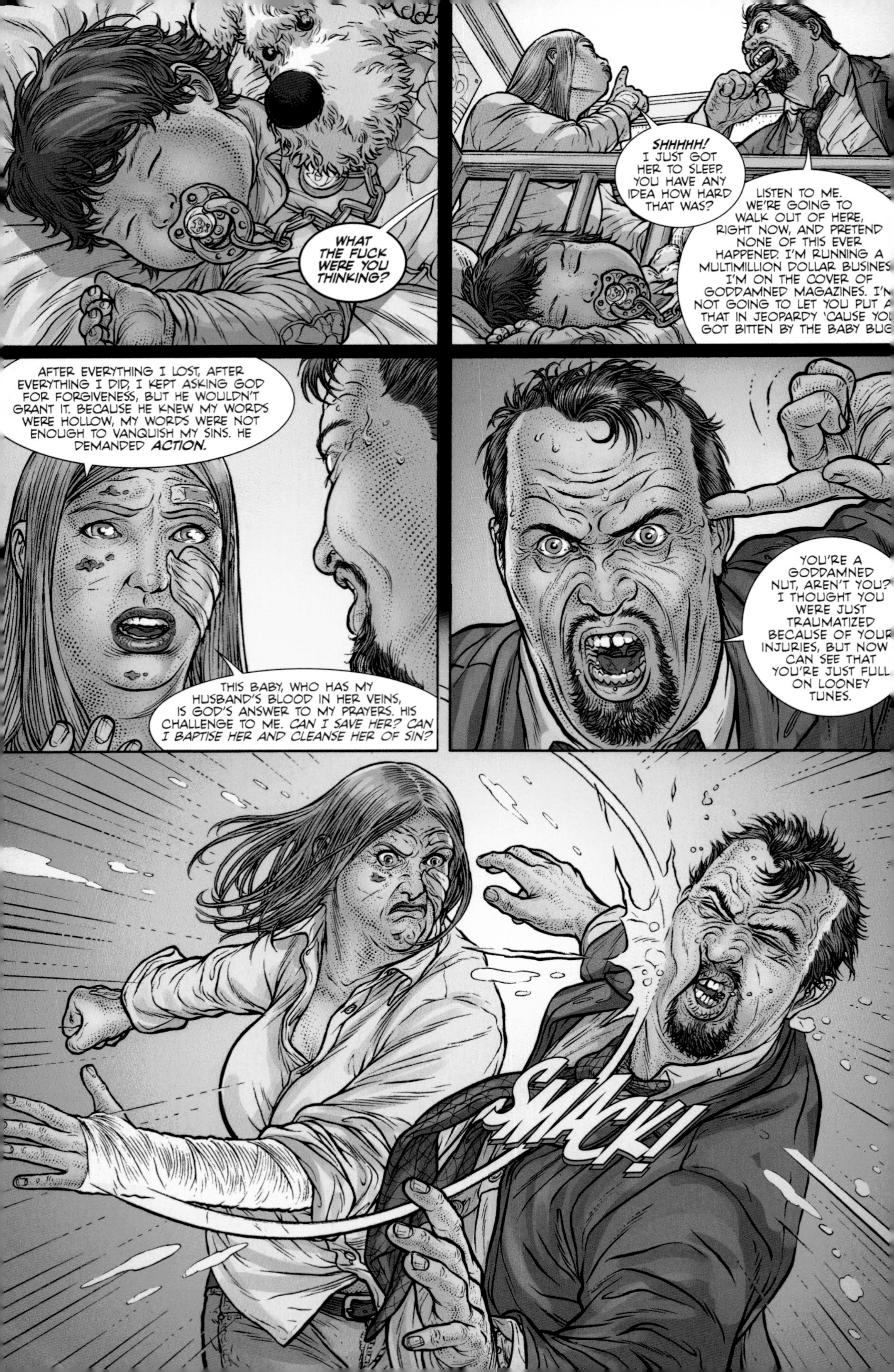
WHAT THE FUCK WERE YOU THINKING?
SHHHHH! I JUST GOT HER TO SLEEP. YOU HAVE ANY IDEA HOW HARD THAT WAS?
LISTEN TO ME. WE'RE GOING TO WALK OUT OF HERE, RIGHT NOW, AND PRETEND NONE OF THIS EVER HAPPENED. I'M RUNNING A MULTIMILLION DOLLAR BUSINES I'M ON THE COVER OF GODDAMNED MAGAZINES. I'N NOT GOING TO LET YOU PUT A THAT IN JEOPARDY 'CAUSE YO GOT BITTEN BY THE BABY BUG
AFTER EVERYTHING I LOST, AFTER EVERYTHING I DID, I KEPT ASKING GOD FOR FORGIVENESS, BUT HE WOULDN'T GRANT IT. BECAUSE HE KNEW MY WORDS WERE HOLLOW, MY WORDS WERE NOT ENOUGH TO VANQUISH MY SINS. HE DEMANDED ACTION.
THIS BABY, WHO HAS MY HUSBAND'S BLOOD IN HER VEINS, IS GOD'S ANSWER TO MY PRAYERS. HIS CHALLENGE TO ME. CAN I SAVE HER? CAN I BAPTISE HER AND CLEANSE HER OF SIN?
YOU'RE A GODDAMNED NUT, AREN'T YOU? I THOUGHT YOU WERE JUST TRAUMATIZED BECAUSE OF YOUR INJURIES, BUT NOW CAN SEE THAT YOU'RE JUST FULL ON LOONEY TUNES.
SMACK!

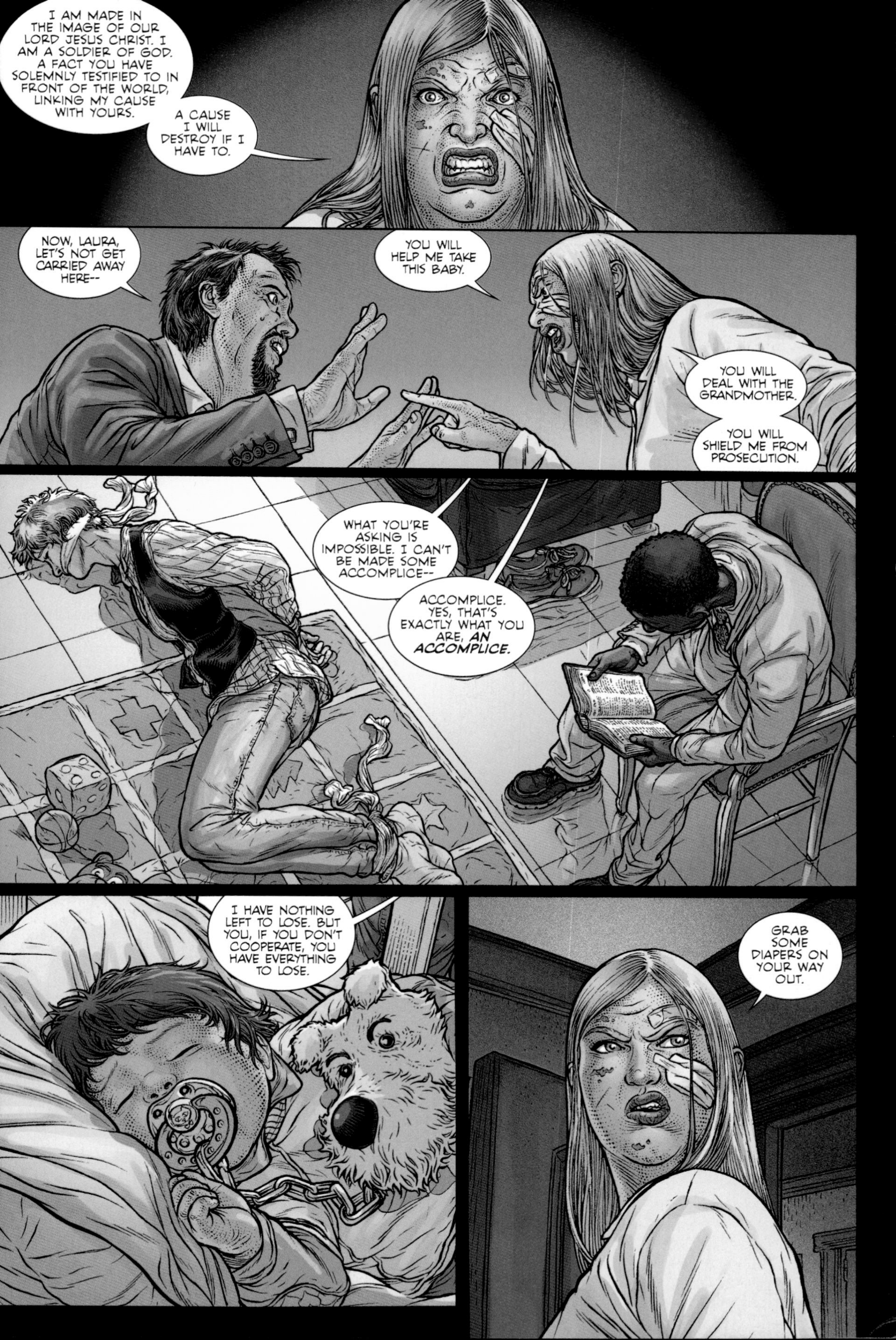
I AM MADE IN THE IMAGE OF OUR LORD JESUS CHRIST. I AM A SOLDIER OF GOD. A FACT YOU HAVE SOLEMNLY TESTIFIED TO IN FRONT OF THE WORLD, LINKING MY CAUSE WITH YOURS.
A CAUSE I WILL DESTROY IF I HAVE TO.
NOW, LAURA, LET'S NOT GET CARRIED AWAY HERE--
YOU WILL HELP ME TAKE THIS BABY.
YOU WILL DEAL WITH THE GRANDMOTHER.
YOU WILL SHIELD ME FROM PROSECUTION.
WHAT YOU'RE ASKING IS IMPOSSIBLE. I CAN'T BE MADE SOME ACCOMPLICE--
ACCOMPLICE. YES, THAT'S EXACTLY WHAT YOU ARE, *AN ACCOMPLICE.*
I HAVE NOTHING LEFT TO LOSE. BUT YOU, IF YOU DON'T COOPERATE, YOU HAVE EVERYTHING TO LOSE.
GRAB SOME DIAPERS ON YOUR WAY OUT.

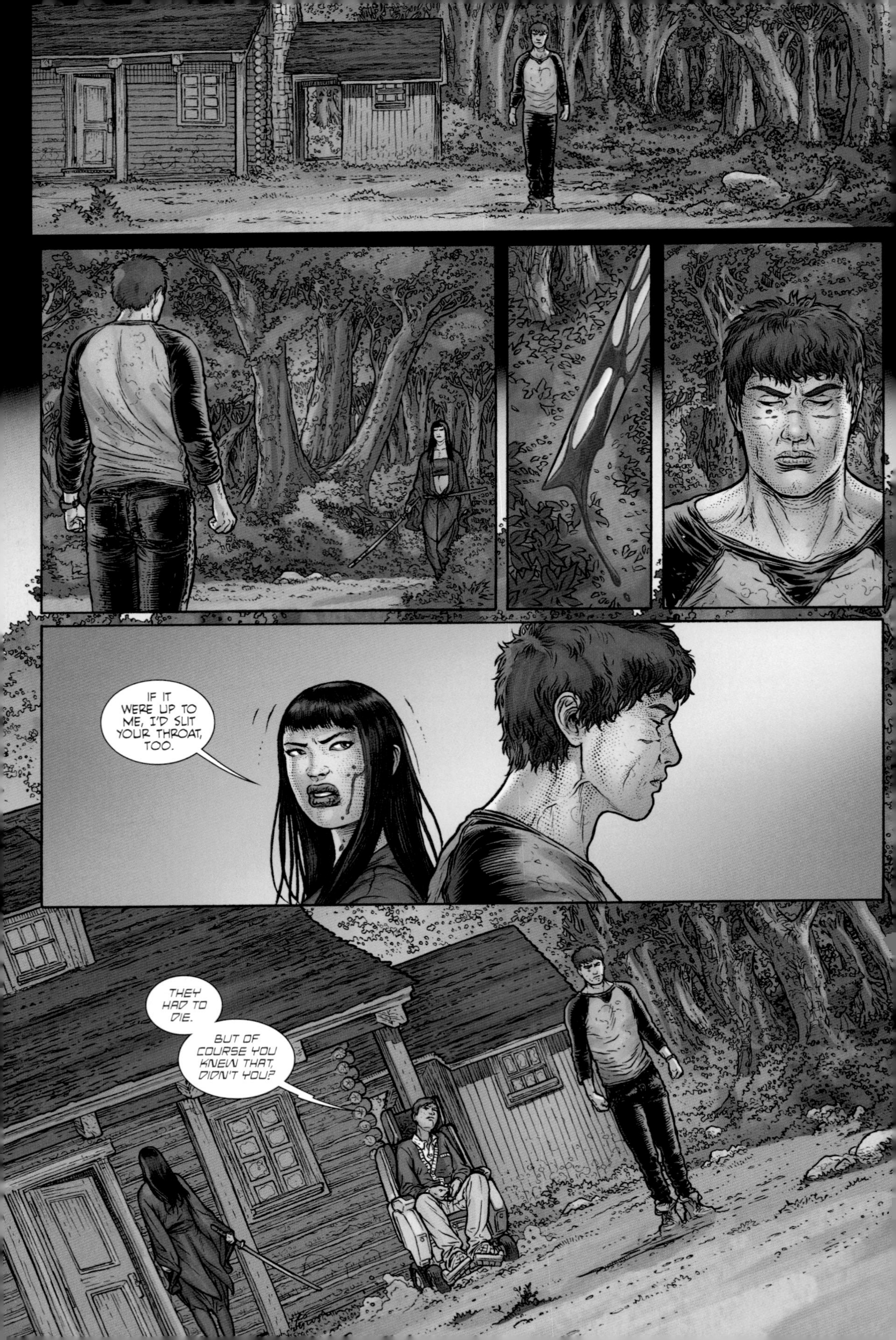
IF IT WERE UP TO ME, I'D SLIT YOUR THROAT, TOO.
THEY HAD TO DIE.
BUT OF COURSE YOU KNEW THAT, DIDN'T YOU?

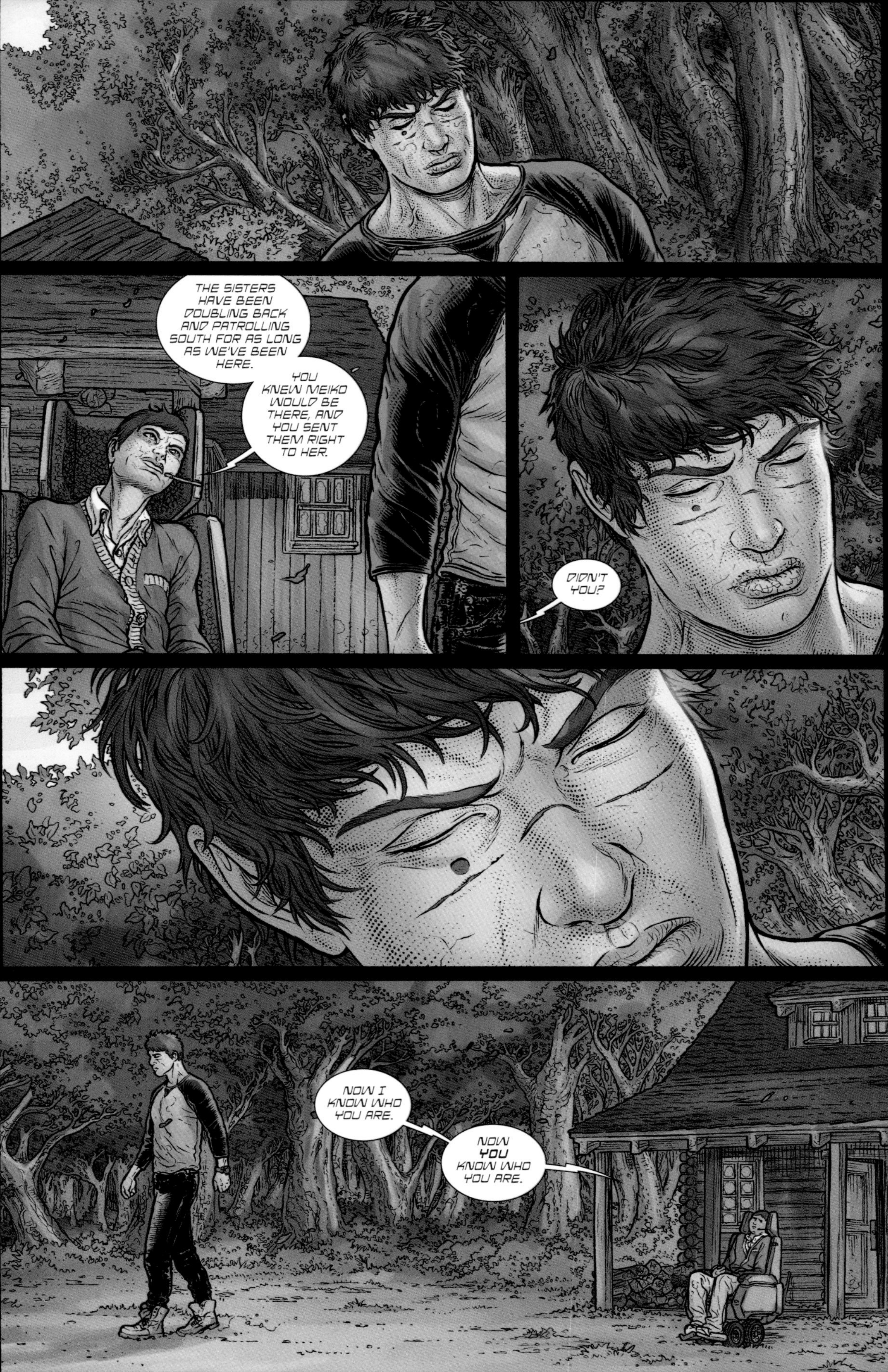
THE SISTERS HAVE BEEN DOUBLING BACK AND PATROLLING SOUTH FOR AS LONG AS WE'VE BEEN HERE.
YOU KNEW MEIKO WOULD BE THERE, AND YOU SENT THEM RIGHT TO HER.
DIDN'T YOU?
NOW I KNOW WHO YOU ARE.
NOW YOU KNOW WHO YOU ARE.

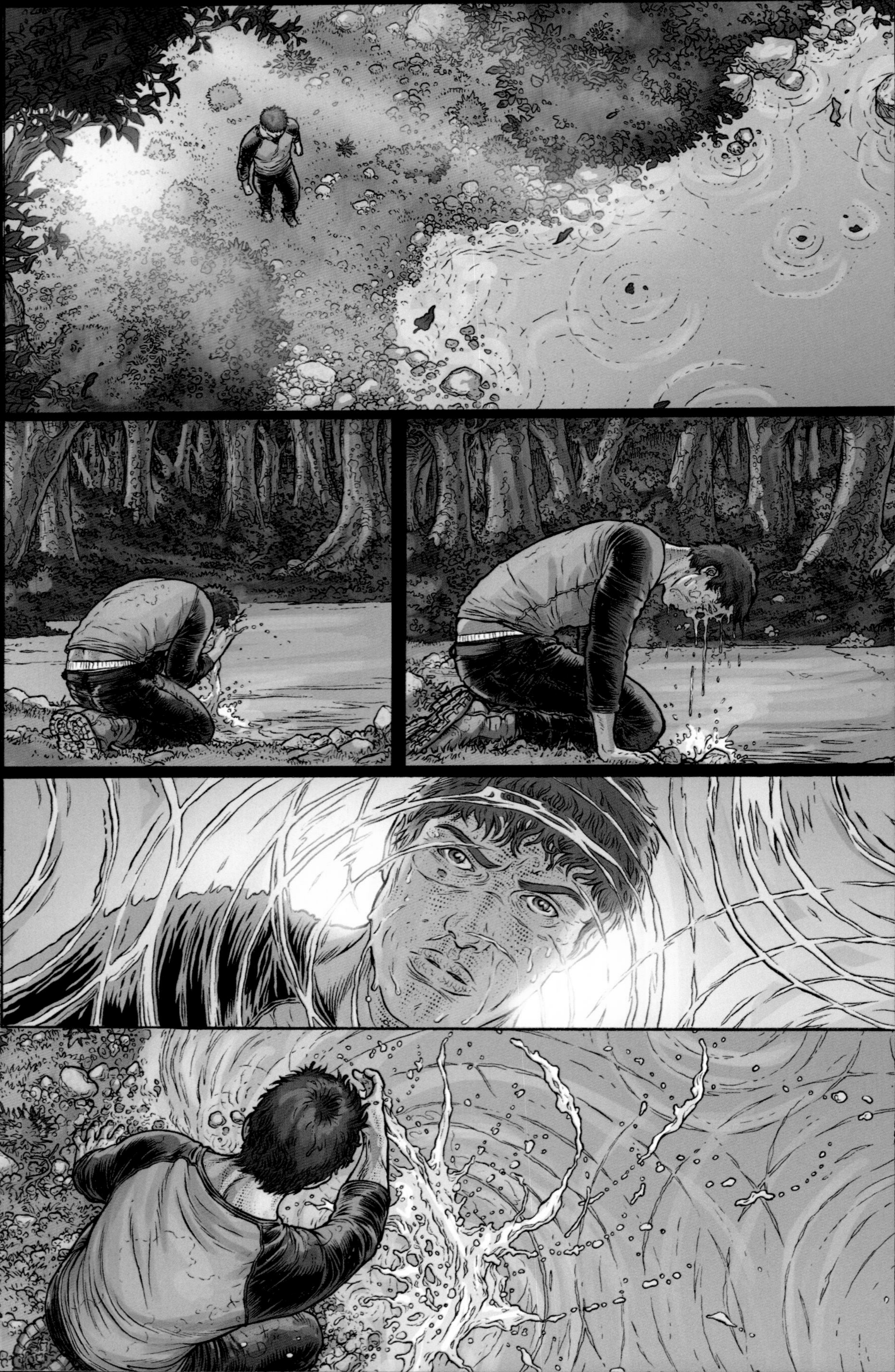

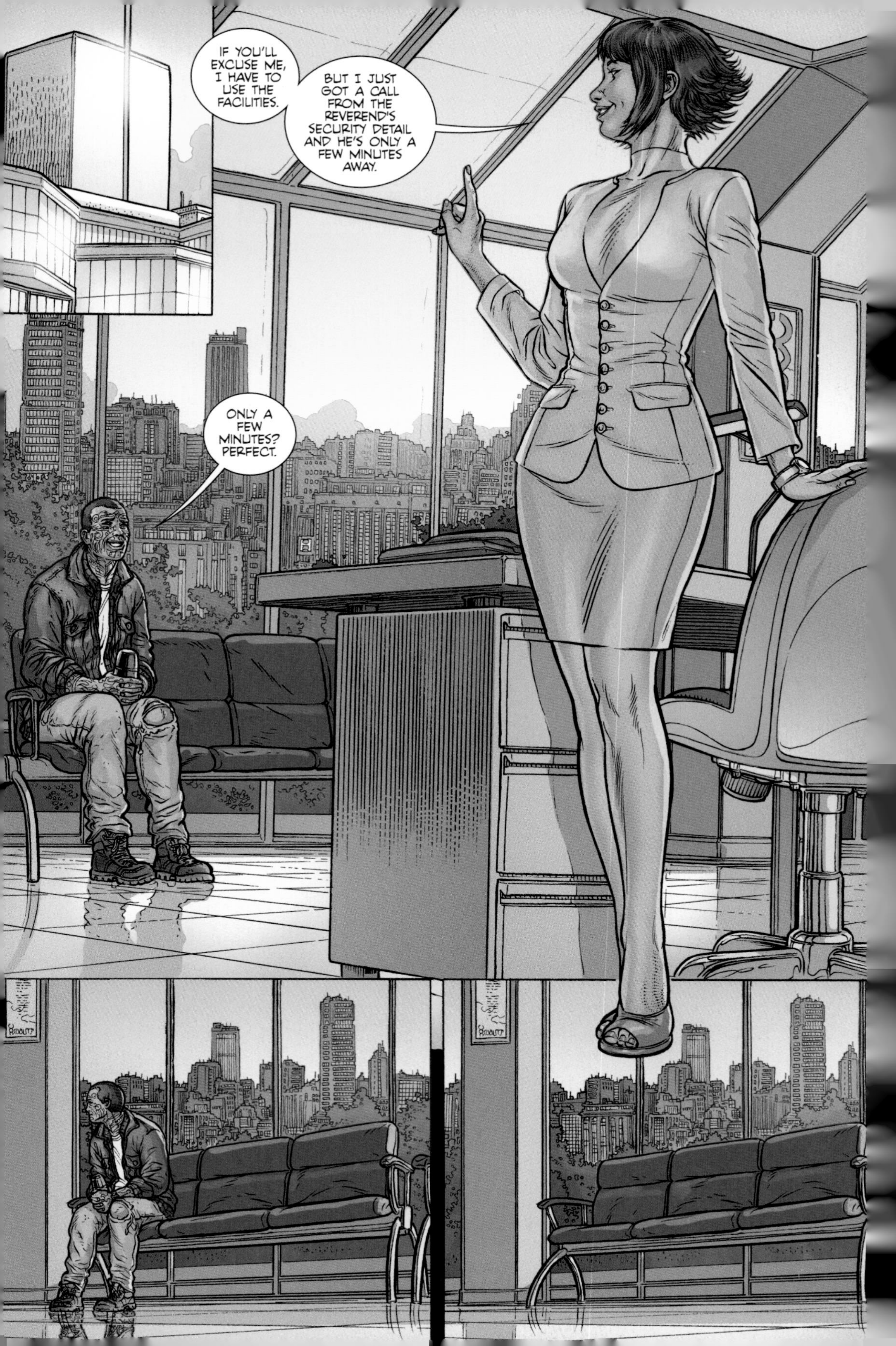
IF YOU'LL EXCUSE ME, I HAVE TO USE THE FACILITIES.
BUT I JUST GOT A CALL FROM THE REVEREND'S SECURITY DETAIL AND HE'S ONLY A FEW MINUTES AWAY.
ONLY A FEW MINUTES? PERFECT.

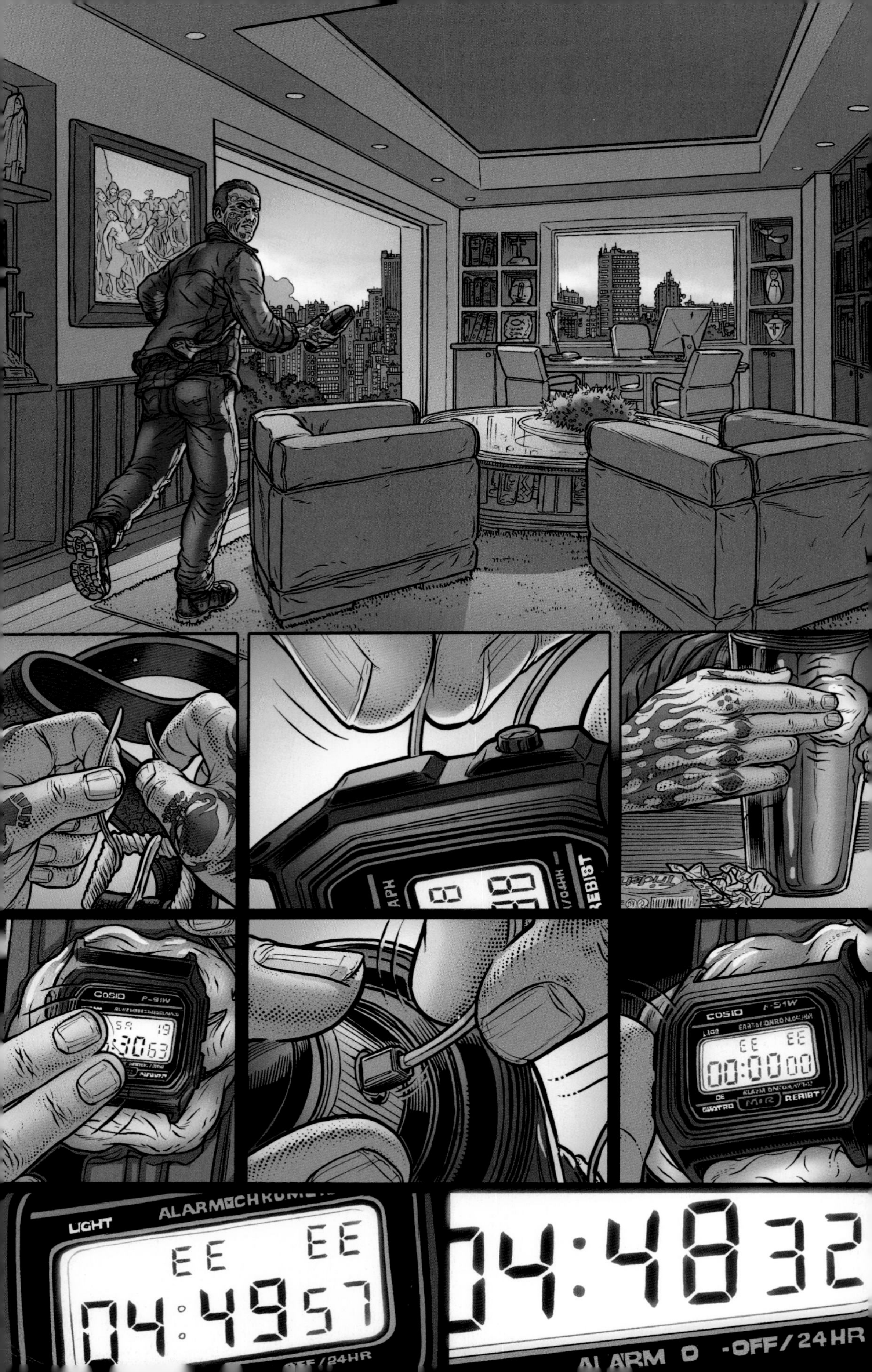
CASIO F-91W
LIGHT
EE EE
04:4957
-OFF/24HR
04:4832
ALARM
-OFF/24HR

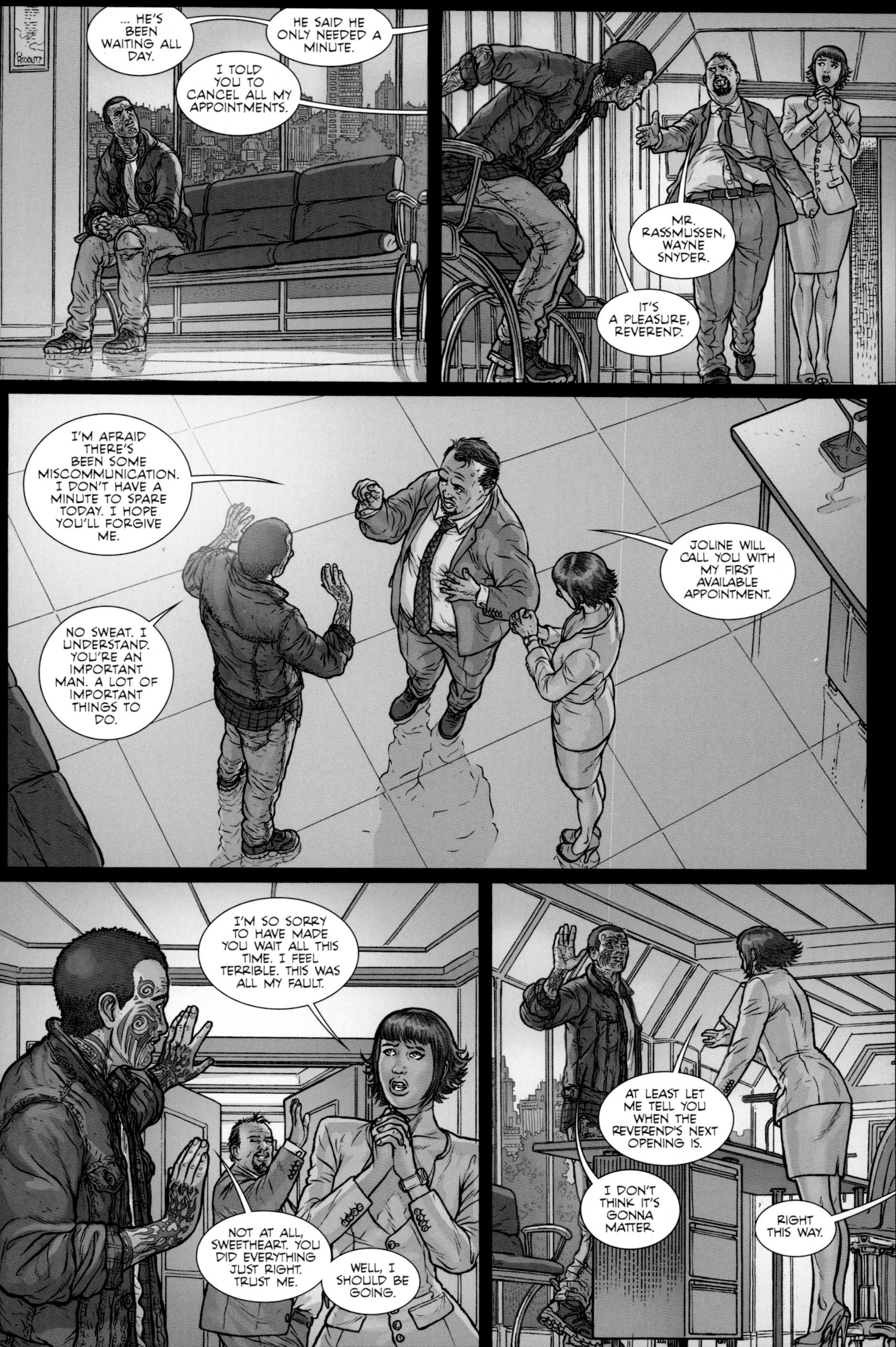
... HE'S BEEN WAITING ALL DAY.
HE SAID HE ONLY NEEDED A MINUTE.
I TOLD YOU TO CANCEL ALL MY APPOINTMENTS.
MR. RASSMUSSEN, WAYNE SNYDER.
IT'S A PLEASURE, REVEREND.
I'M AFRAID THERE'S BEEN SOME MISCOMMUNICATION. I DON'T HAVE A MINUTE TO SPARE TODAY. I HOPE YOU'LL FORGIVE ME.
JOLINE WILL CALL YOU WITH MY FIRST AVAILABLE APPOINTMENT.
NO SWEAT. I UNDERSTAND. YOU'RE AN IMPORTANT MAN. A LOT OF IMPORTANT THINGS TO DO.
I'M SO SORRY TO HAVE MADE YOU WAIT ALL THIS TIME. I FEEL TERRIBLE. THIS WAS ALL MY FAULT.
NOT AT ALL, SWEETHEART. YOU DID EVERYTHING JUST RIGHT. TRUST ME.
WELL, I SHOULD BE GOING.
AT LEAST LET ME TELL YOU WHEN THE REVEREND'S NEXT OPENING IS.
I DON'T THINK IT'S GONNA MATTER.
RIGHT THIS WAY.

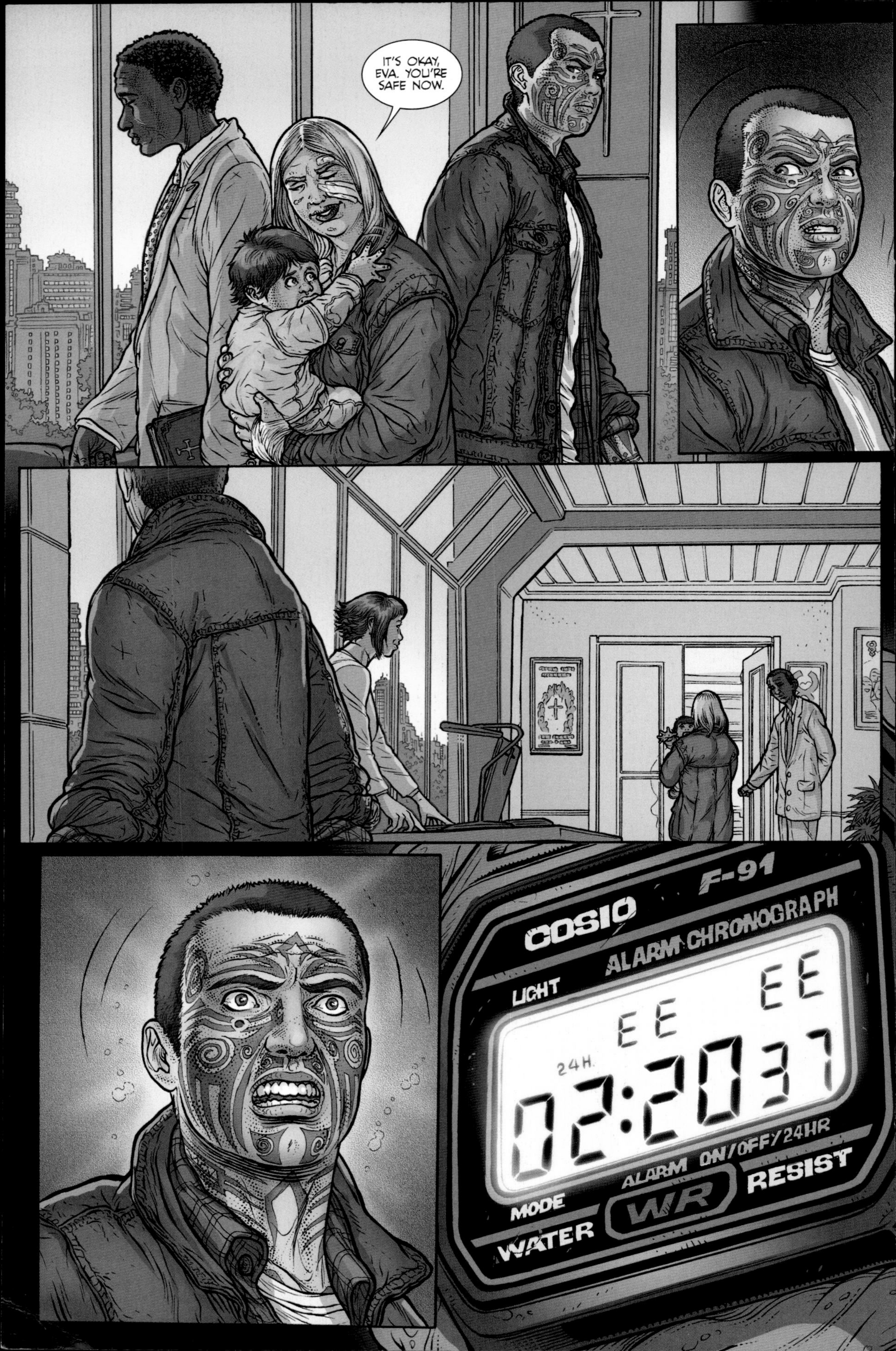
IT'S OKAY, EVA. YOU'RE SAFE NOW.
COSIO
F-91
ALARM CHRONOGRAPH
LIGHT
24H.
02:20 37
ALARM ON/OFF/24HR
MODE
WR
WATER
RESIST

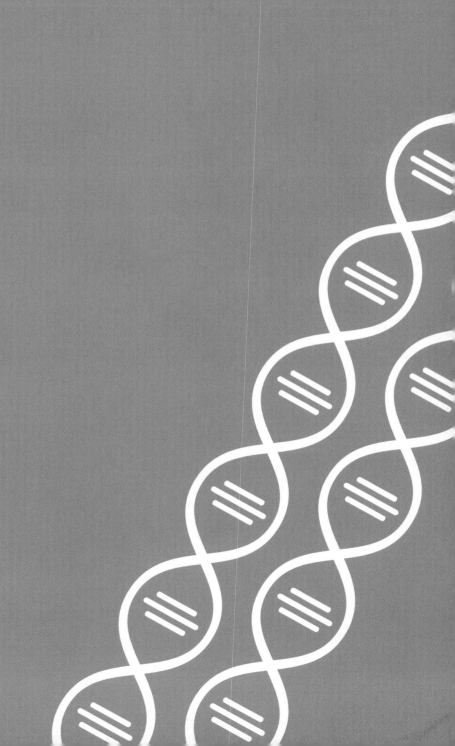

CHAPTER 20

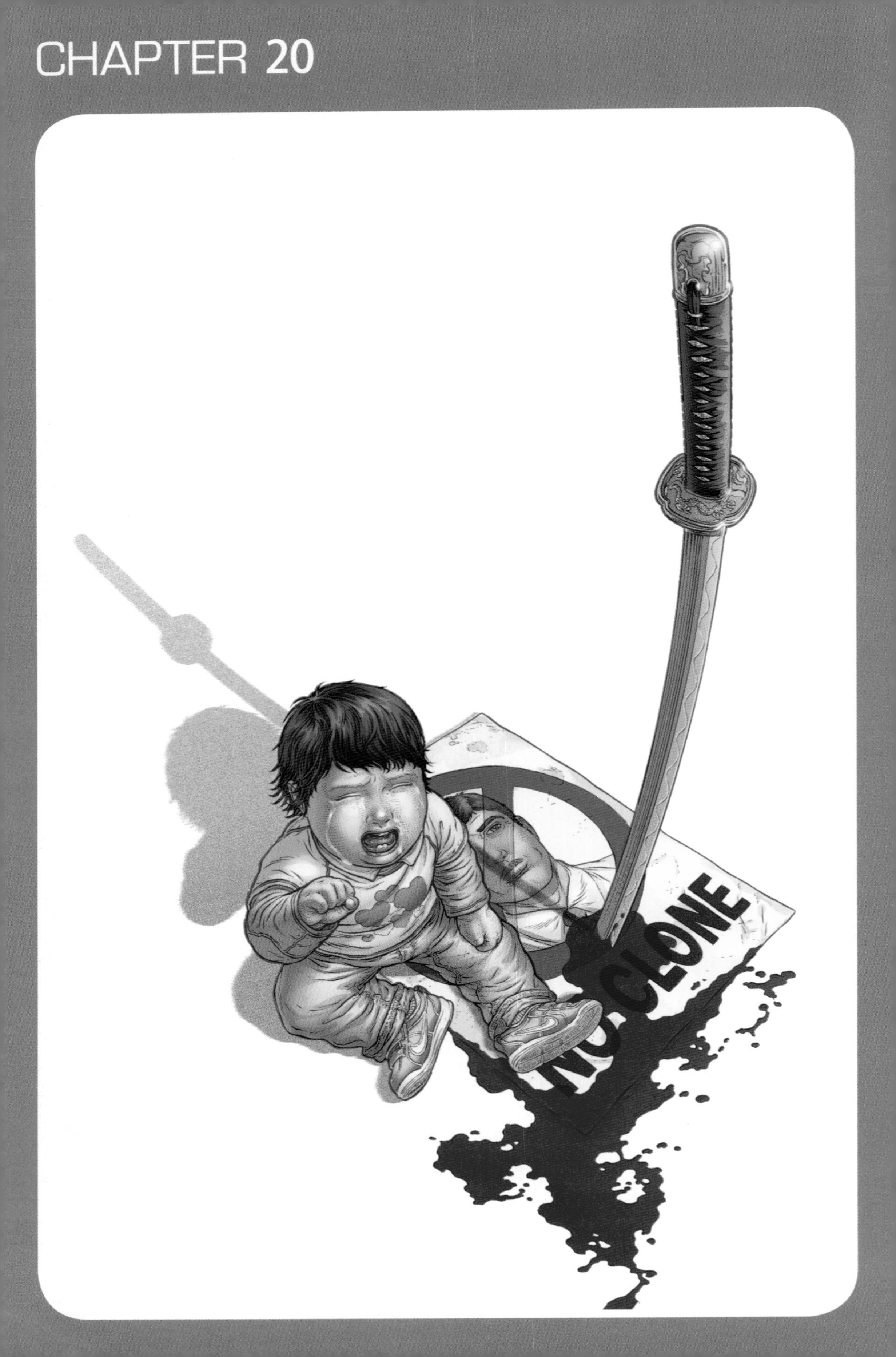
NO CLONE

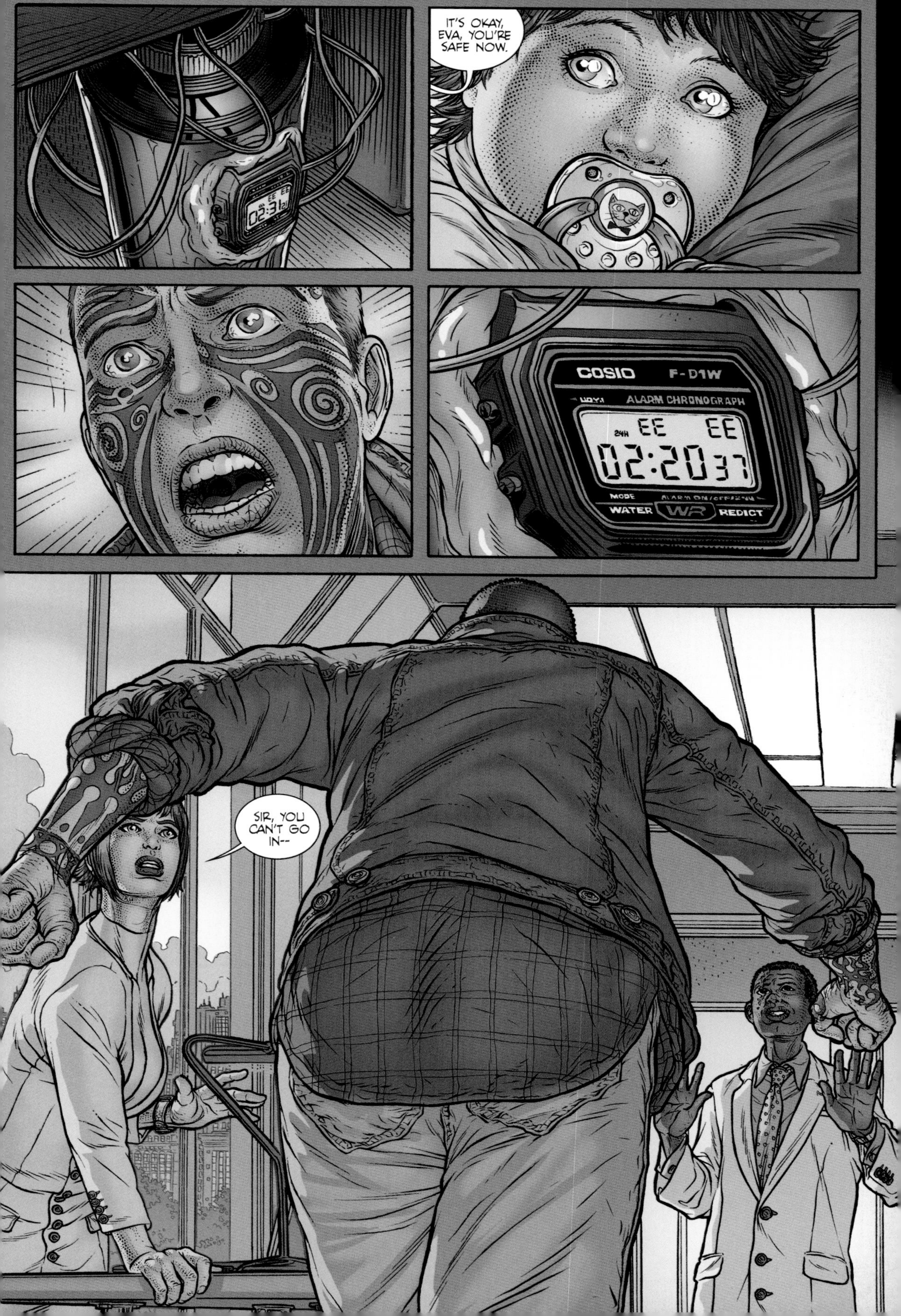
02:31
IT'S OKAY, EVA, YOU'RE SAFE NOW.
COSIO
F-D1W
ALARM CHRONOGRAPH
EE EE
24H
02:20 37
MODE
WATER
WR
REDICT
SIR, YOU CAN'T GO IN--

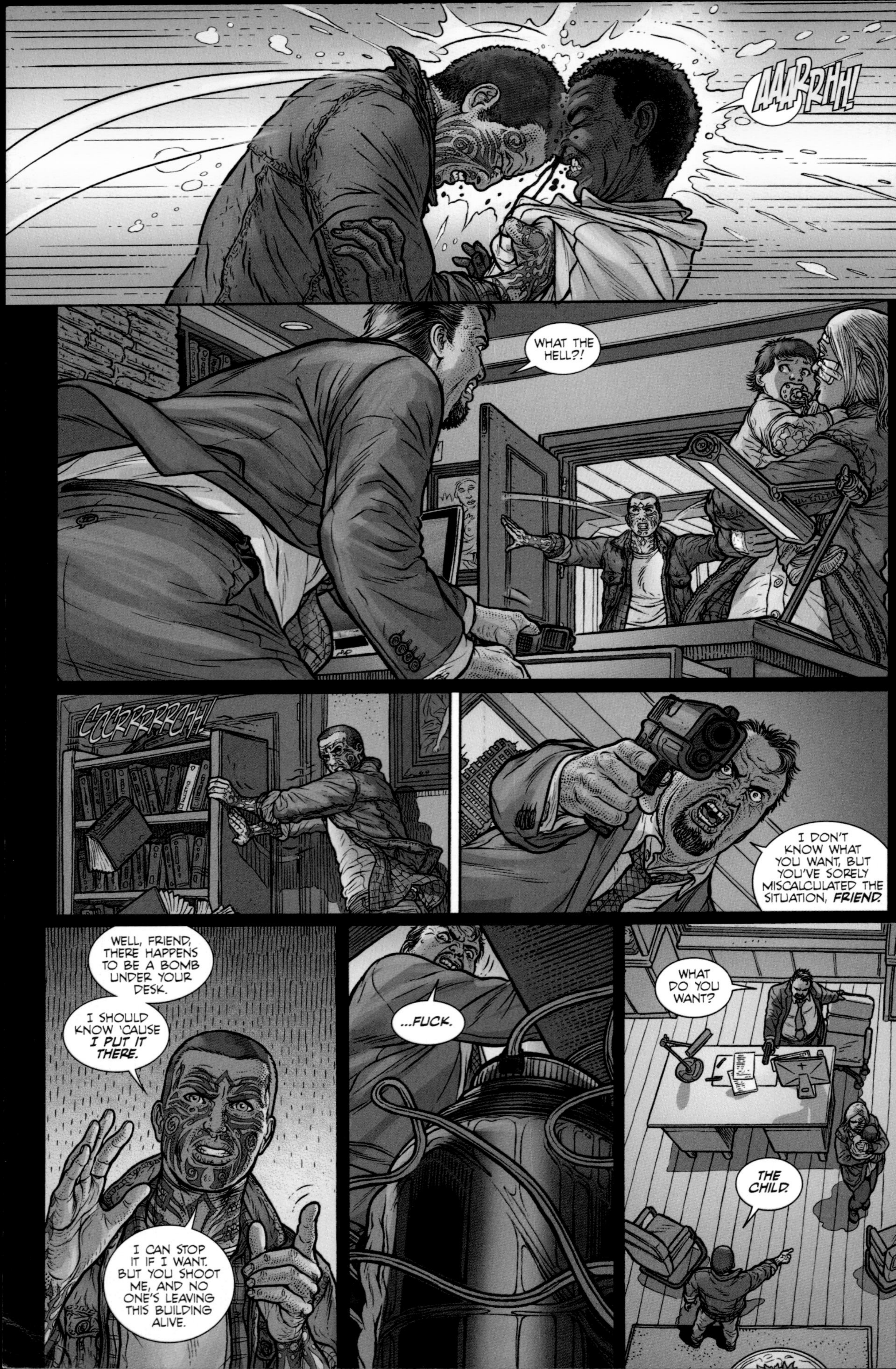
AAARRHH!
WHAT THE HELL?!
CCCRRRRRCHH!
I DON'T KNOW WHAT YOU WANT, BUT YOU'VE SORELY MISCALCULATED THE SITUATION, FRIEND.
WELL, FRIEND, THERE HAPPENS TO BE A BOMB UNDER YOUR DESK.
I SHOULD KNOW 'CAUSE I PUT IT THERE.
I CAN STOP IT IF I WANT. BUT YOU SHOOT ME, AND NO ONE'S LEAVING THIS BUILDING ALIVE.
...FUCK.
WHAT DO YOU WANT?
THE CHILD.

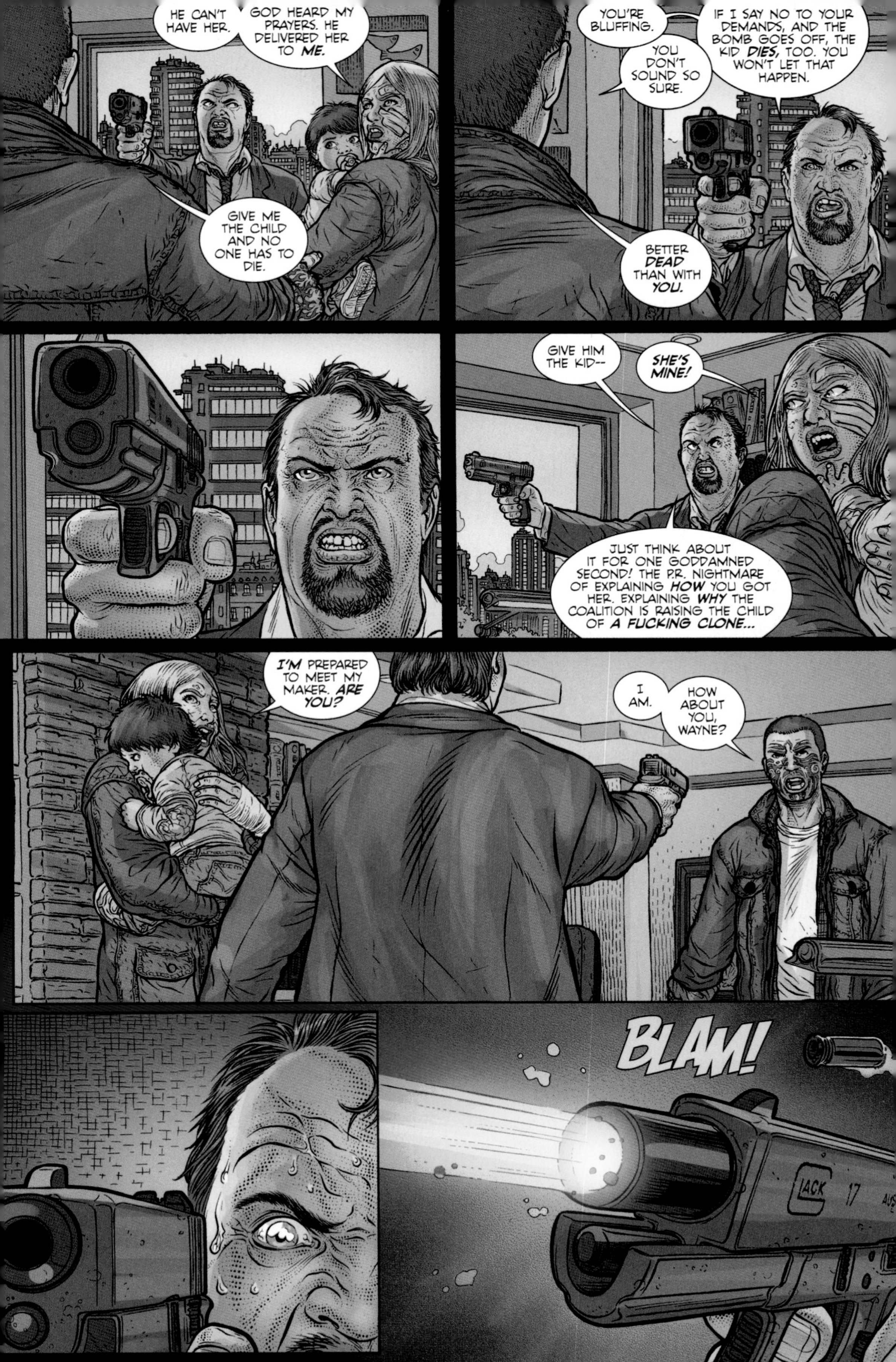
HE CAN'T HAVE HER.
GOD HEARD MY PRAYERS. HE DELIVERED HER TO ME.
GIVE ME THE CHILD AND NO ONE HAS TO DIE.
YOU'RE BLUFFING.
IF I SAY NO TO YOUR DEMANDS, AND THE BOMB GOES OFF, THE KID DIES, TOO. YOU WON'T LET THAT HAPPEN.
YOU DON'T SOUND SO SURE.
BETTER DEAD THAN WITH YOU.
GIVE HIM THE KID--
SHE'S MINE!
JUST THINK ABOUT IT FOR ONE GODDAMNED SECOND! THE P.R. NIGHTMARE OF EXPLAINING HOW YOU GOT HER. EXPLAINING WHY THE COALITION IS RAISING THE CHILD OF A FUCKING CLONE...
I'M PREPARED TO MEET MY MAKER. ARE YOU?
I AM.
HOW ABOUT YOU, WAYNE?
BLAM!
17

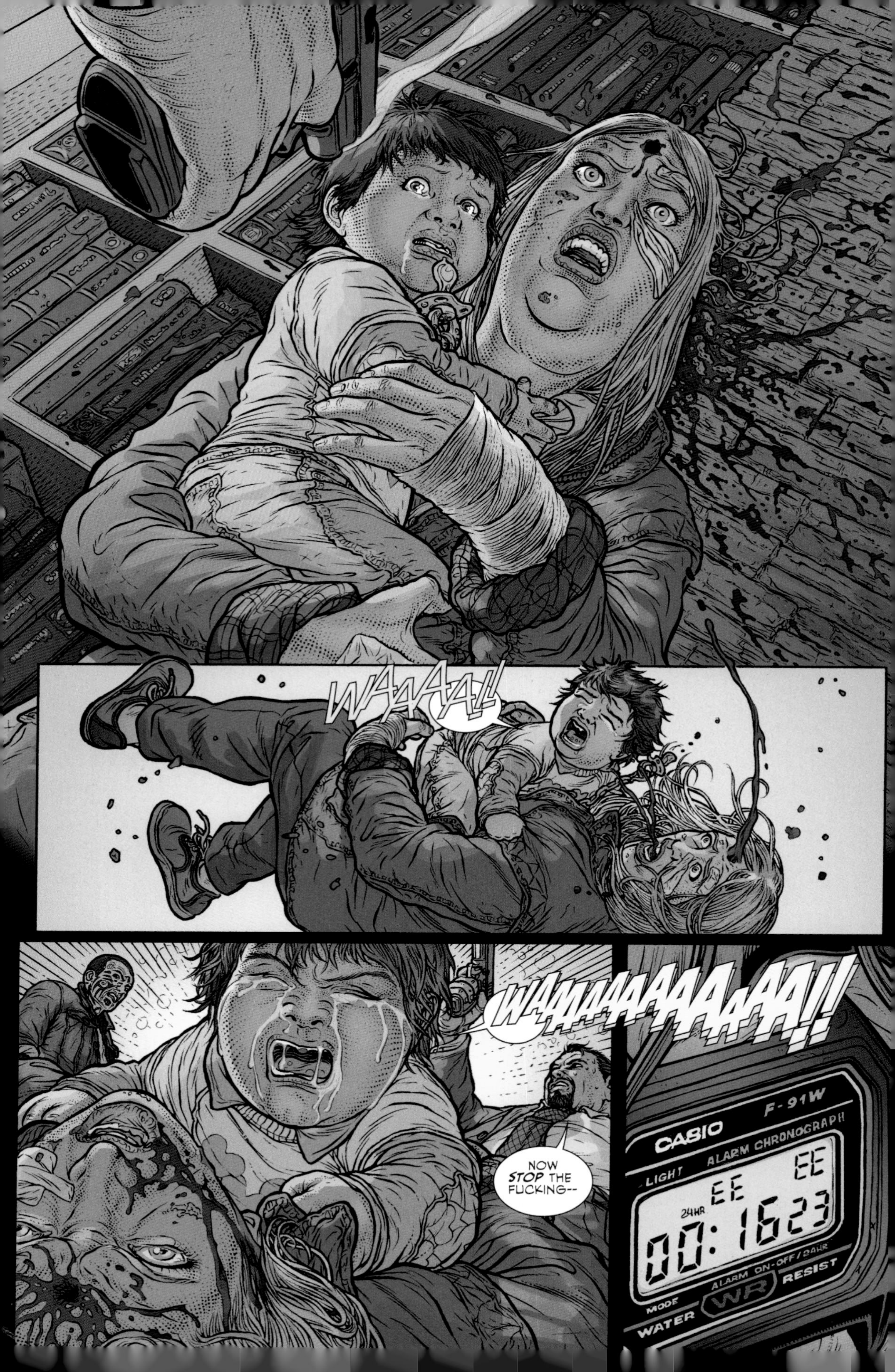
WAAAAA!!
WAAAAAAAAAAAA!!
NOW STOP THE FUCKING--
CASIO
F-91W
LIGHT ALARM CHRONOGRAPH
24HR
00:16 23
ALARM ON-OFF/24HR
MODE
WATER WR RESIST

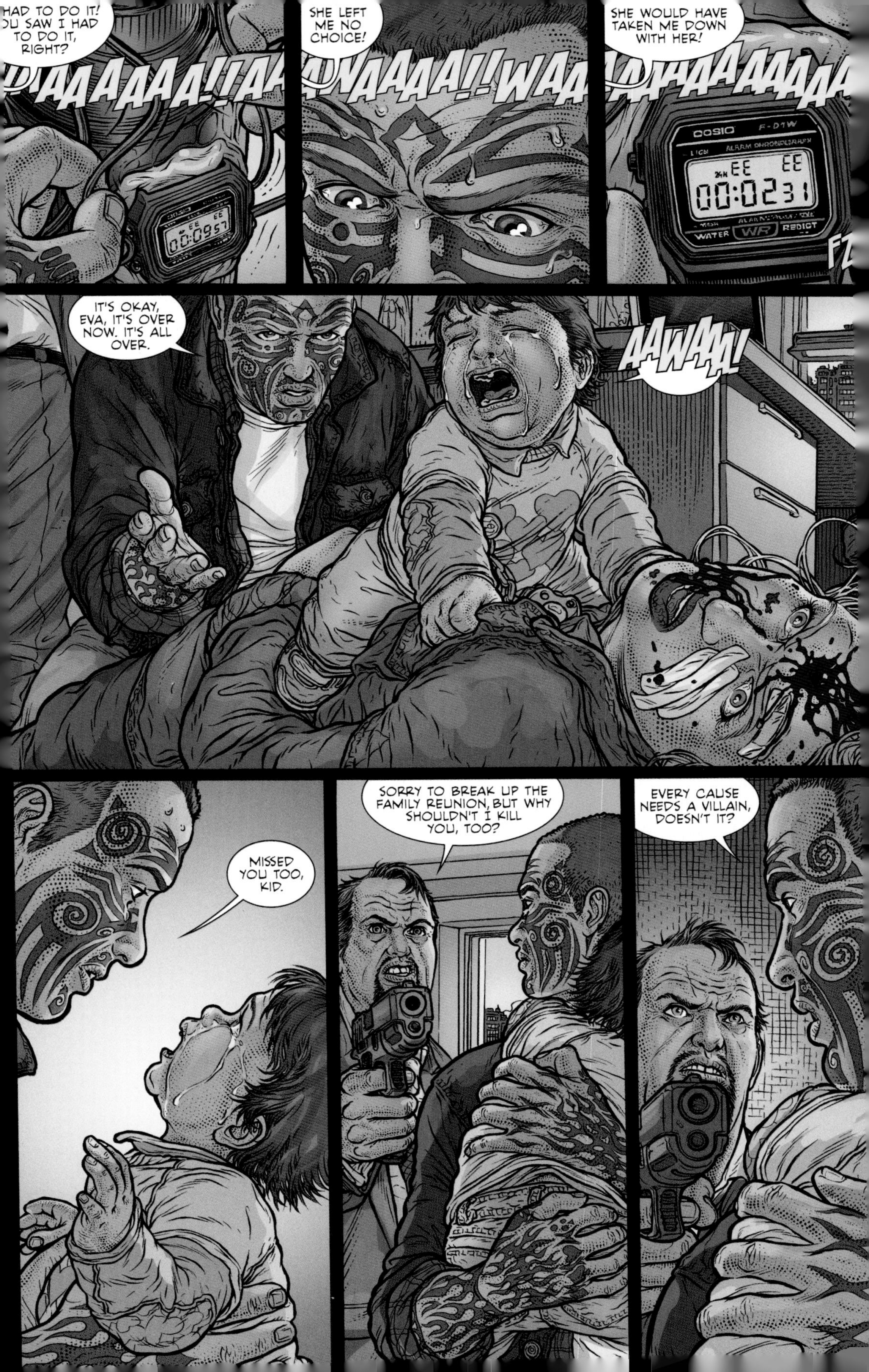
I HAD TO DO IT! YOU SAW I HAD TO DO IT, RIGHT?
AAAAAA!!AA
SHE LEFT ME NO CHOICE!
NAAAAA!!WAA
SHE WOULD HAVE TAKEN ME DOWN WITH HER!
AAAAAAAAAA
CASIO F-91W
00:02 31
WATER WR RESIST
IT'S OKAY, EVA, IT'S OVER NOW. IT'S ALL OVER.
AAWAAA!
MISSED YOU TOO, KID.
SORRY TO BREAK UP THE FAMILY REUNION, BUT WHY SHOULDN'T I KILL YOU, TOO?
EVERY CAUSE NEEDS A VILLAIN, DOESN'T IT?

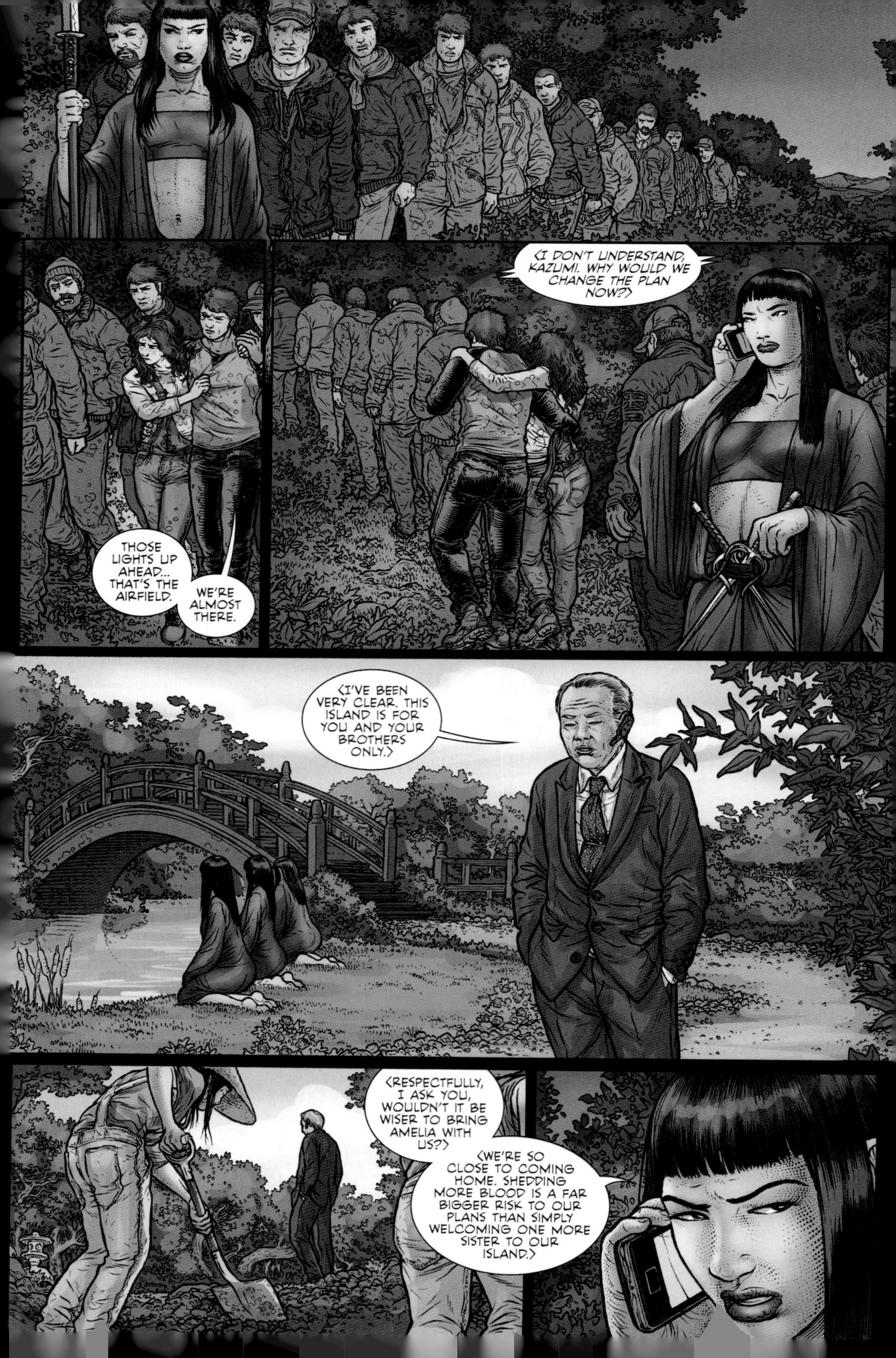
THOSE LIGHTS UP AHEAD... THAT'S THE AIRFIELD.
WE'RE ALMOST THERE.
<I DON'T UNDERSTAND, KAZUMI. WHY WOULD WE CHANGE THE PLAN NOW?>
<I'VE BEEN VERY CLEAR. THIS ISLAND IS FOR YOU AND YOUR BROTHERS ONLY.>
<RESPECTFULLY, I ASK YOU, WOULDN'T IT BE WISER TO BRING AMELIA WITH US?>
<WE'RE SO CLOSE TO COMING HOME. SHEDDING MORE BLOOD IS A FAR BIGGER RISK TO OUR PLANS THAN SIMPLY WELCOMING ONE MORE SISTER TO OUR ISLAND.>

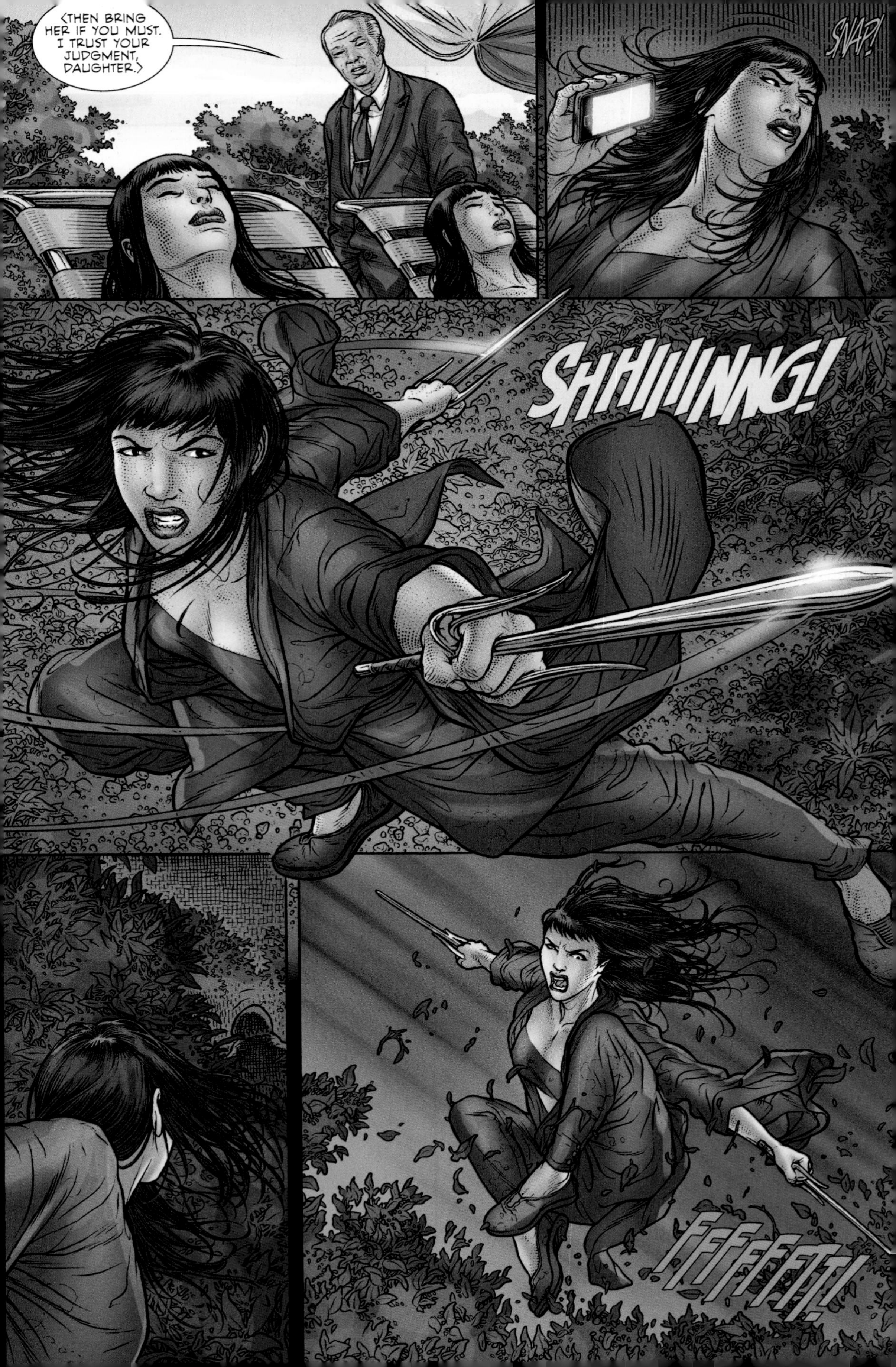
<THEN BRING HER IF YOU MUST. I TRUST YOUR JUDGMENT, DAUGHTER.>
SNAP!
SHHIIIINNG!
FFFFFT!

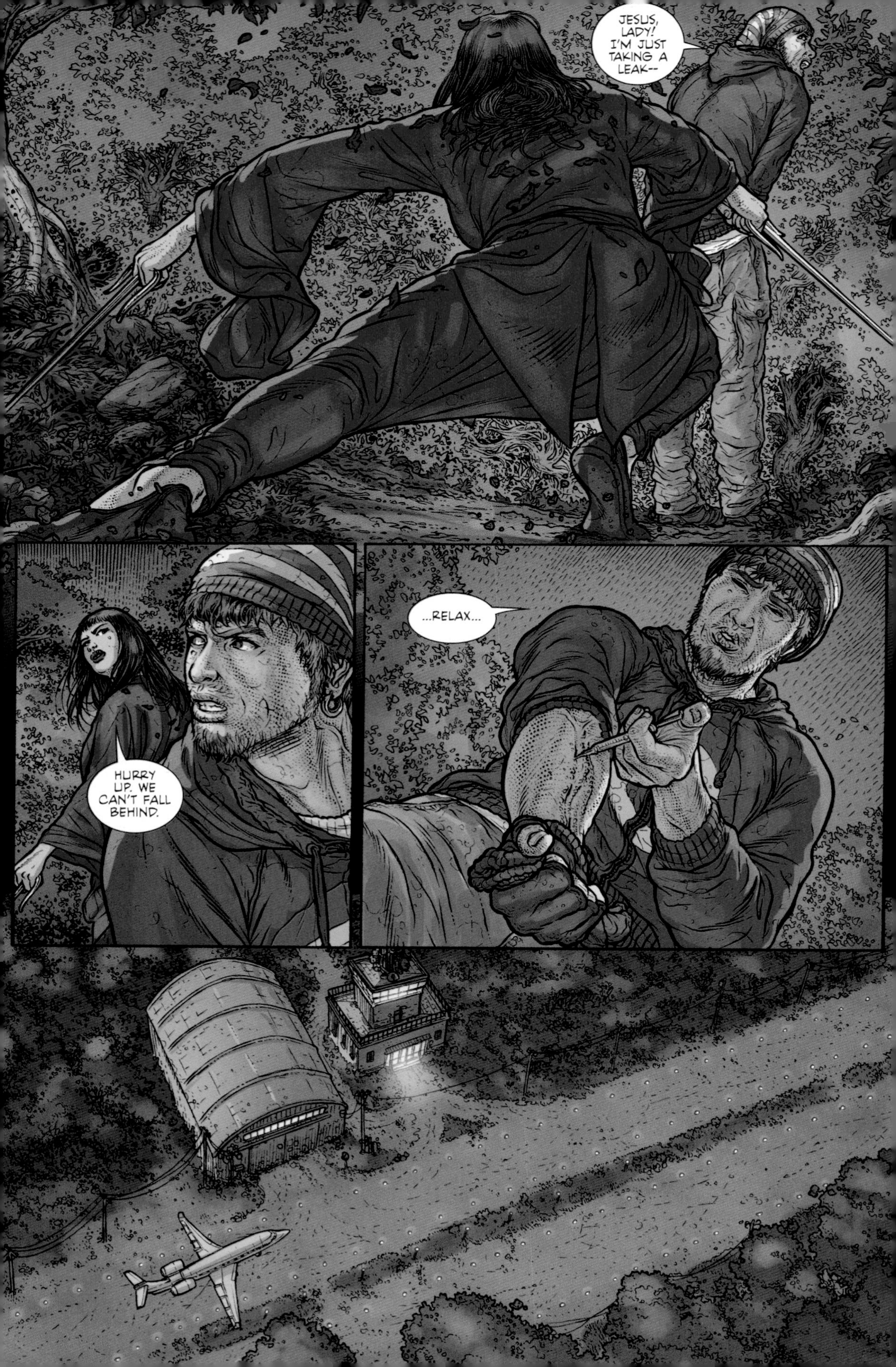
JESUS, LADY! I'M JUST TAKING A LEAK--
HURRY UP. WE CAN'T FALL BEHIND.
...RELAX...

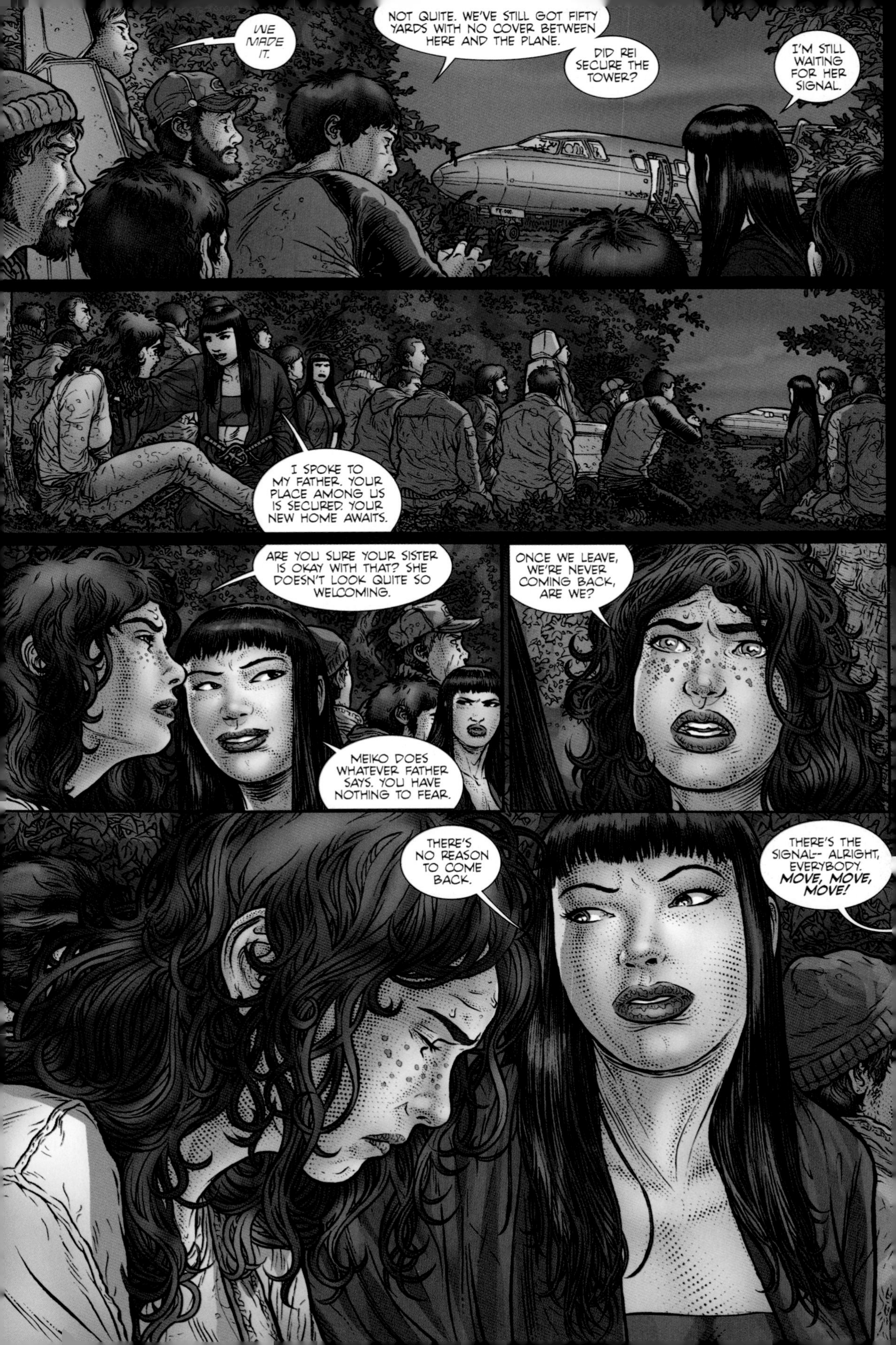
WE MADE IT.
NOT QUITE. WE'VE STILL GOT FIFTY YARDS WITH NO COVER BETWEEN HERE AND THE PLANE.
DID REI SECURE THE TOWER?
I'M STILL WAITING FOR HER SIGNAL.
I SPOKE TO MY FATHER. YOUR PLACE AMONG US IS SECURED. YOUR NEW HOME AWAITS.
ARE YOU SURE YOUR SISTER IS OKAY WITH THAT? SHE DOESN'T LOOK QUITE SO WELCOMING.
MEIKO DOES WHATEVER FATHER SAYS. YOU HAVE NOTHING TO FEAR.
ONCE WE LEAVE, WE'RE NEVER COMING BACK, ARE WE?
THERE'S NO REASON TO COME BACK.
THERE'S THE SIGNAL-- ALRIGHT, EVERYBODY. ***MOVE, MOVE, MOVE!***

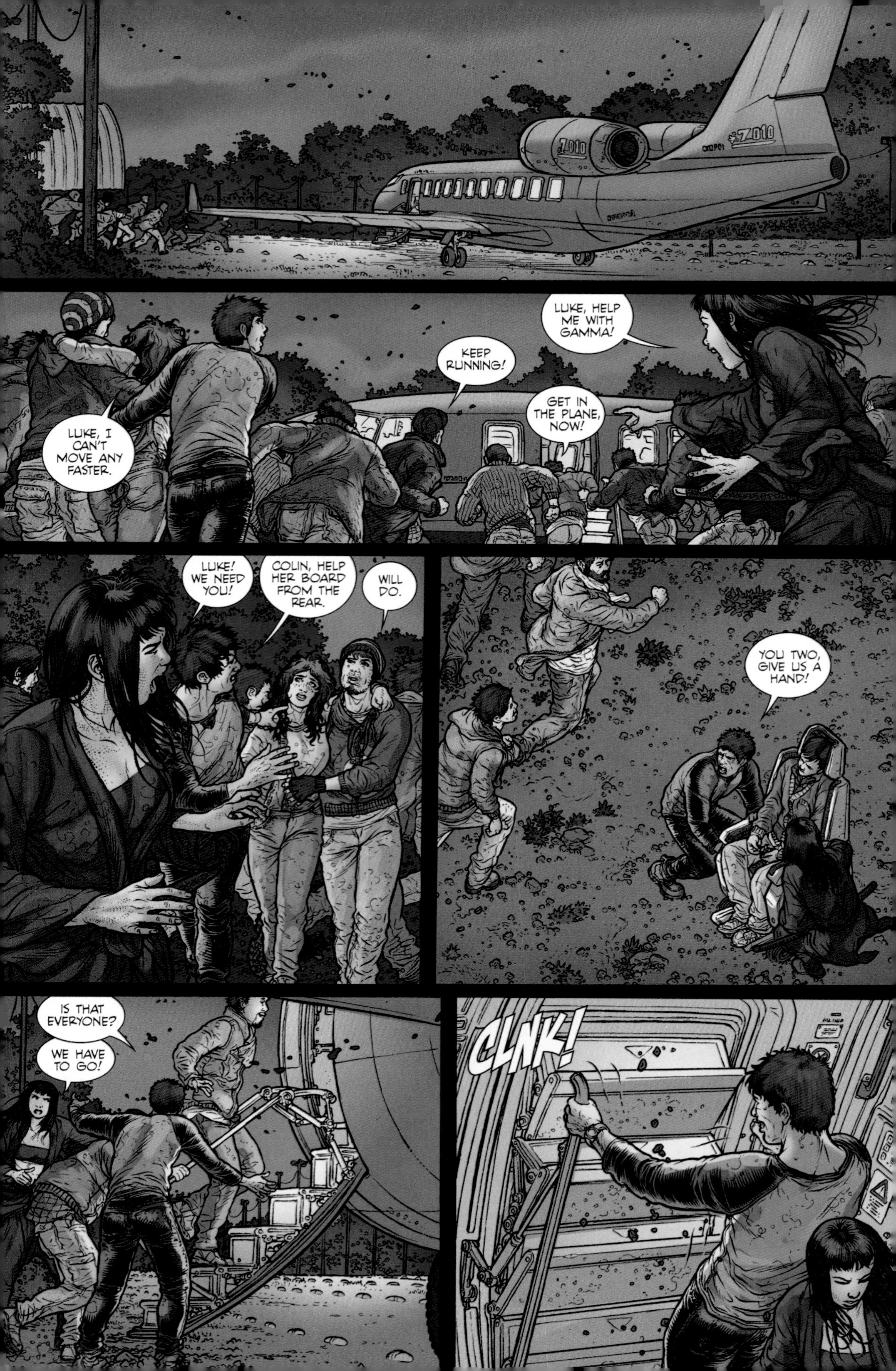
LUKE, HELP ME WITH GAMMA!
KEEP RUNNING!
GET IN THE PLANE, NOW!
LUKE, I CAN'T MOVE ANY FASTER.
LUKE! WE NEED YOU!
COLIN, HELP HER BOARD FROM THE REAR.
WILL DO.
YOU TWO, GIVE US A HAND!
IS THAT EVERYONE?
WE HAVE TO GO!
CLNK!

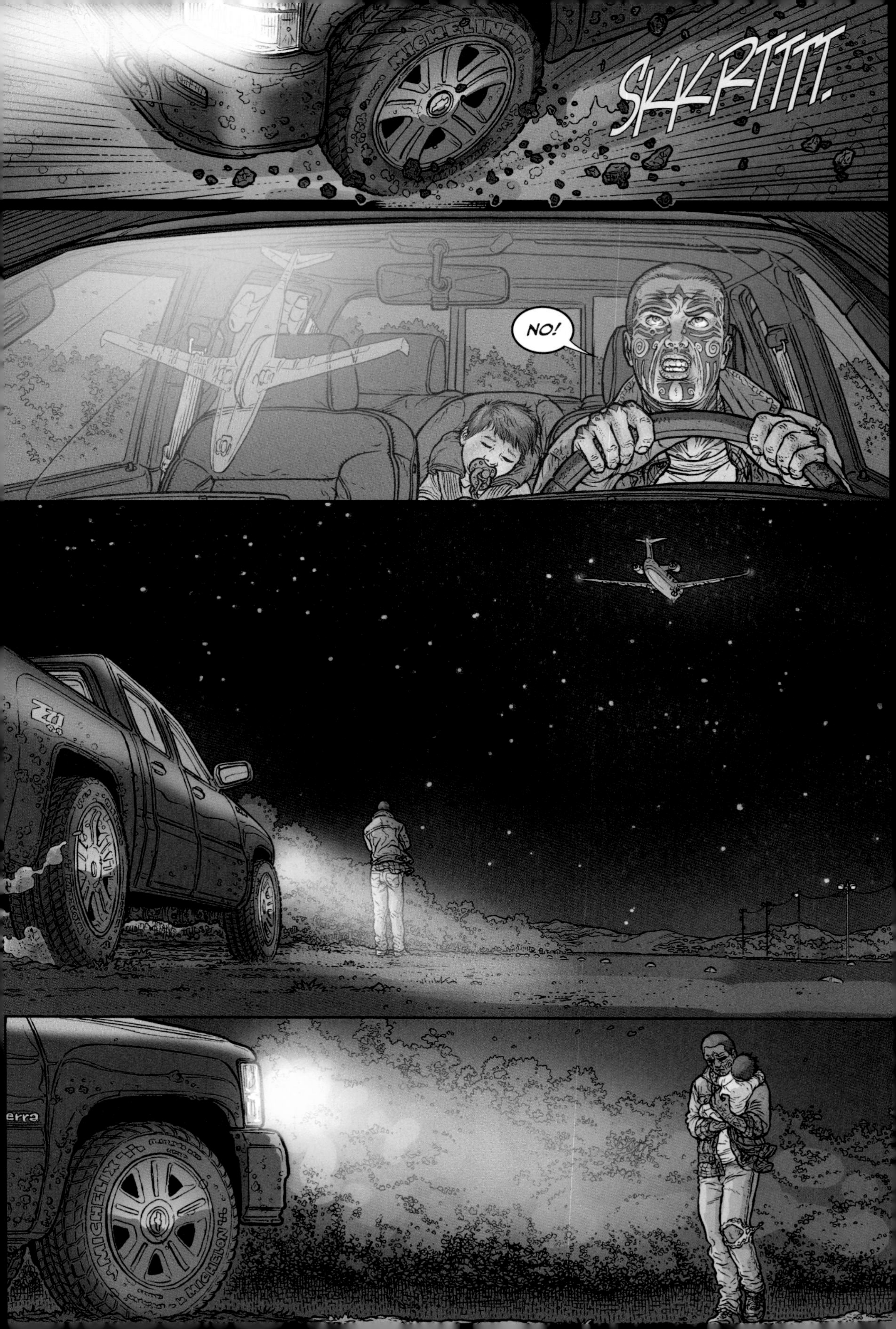
SKKRTTTT.
NO!

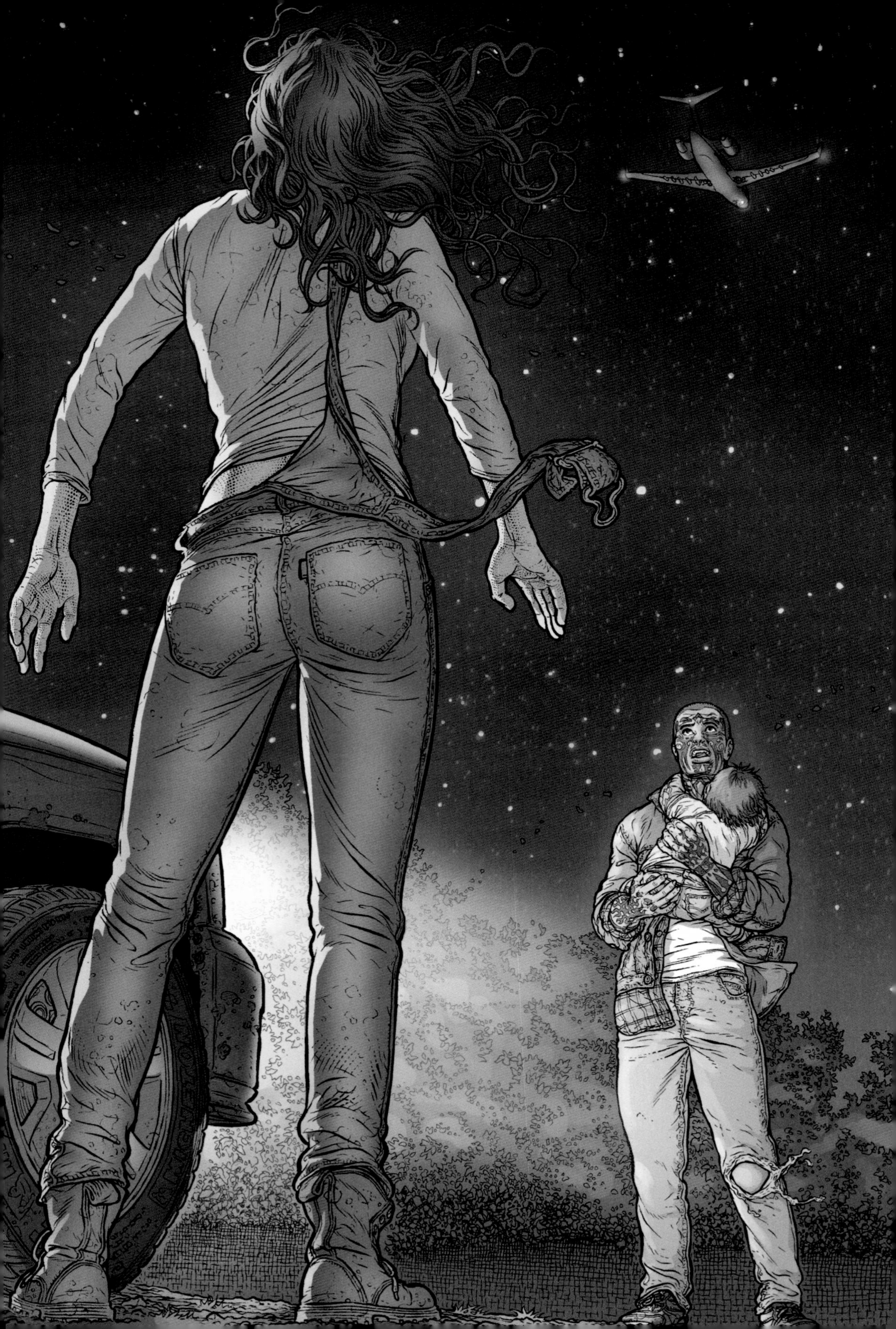

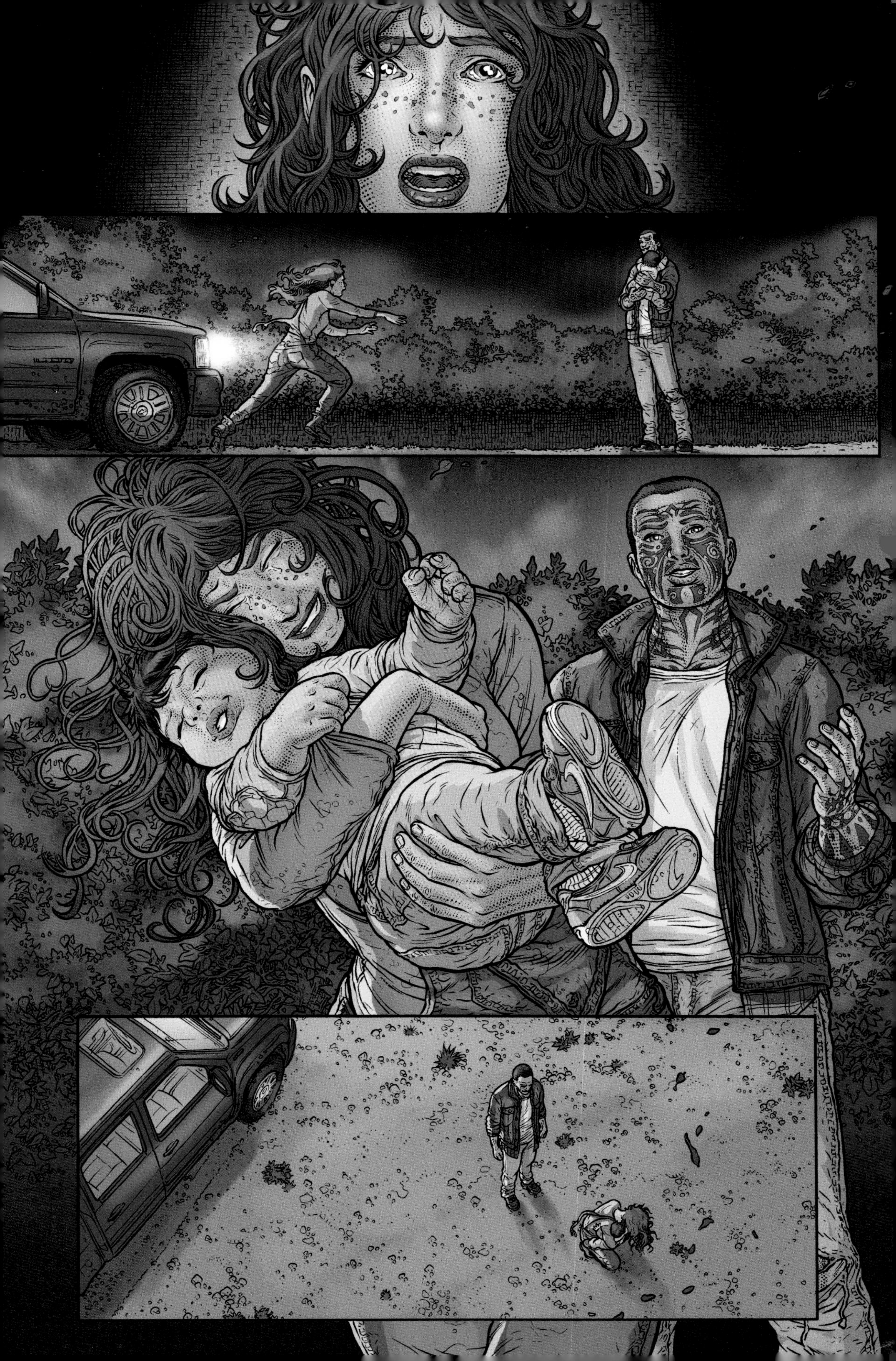

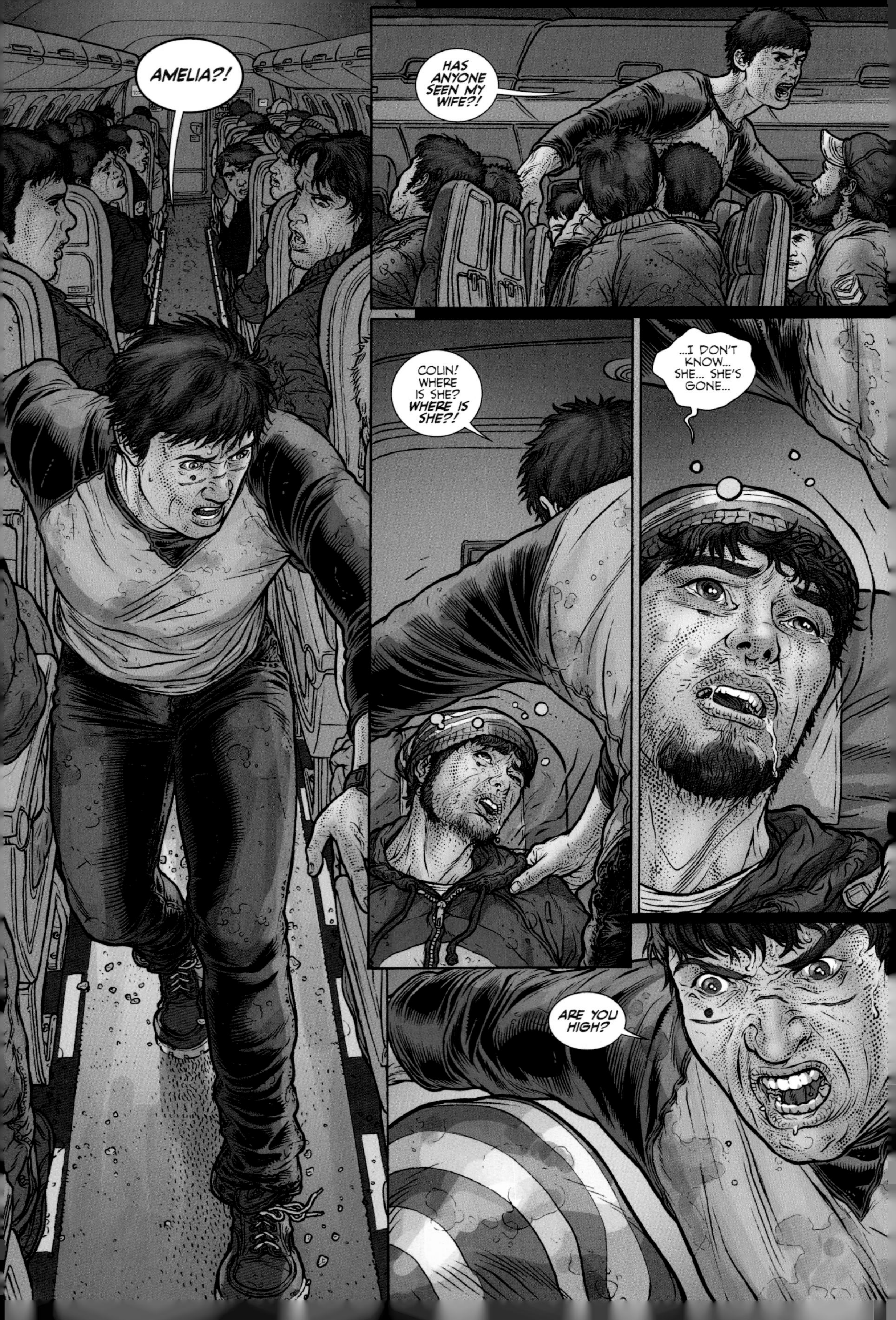
AMELIA?!
HAS ANYONE SEEN MY WIFE?!
COLIN! WHERE IS SHE? WHERE IS SHE?!
...I DON'T KNOW... SHE... SHE'S GONE...
ARE YOU HIGH?

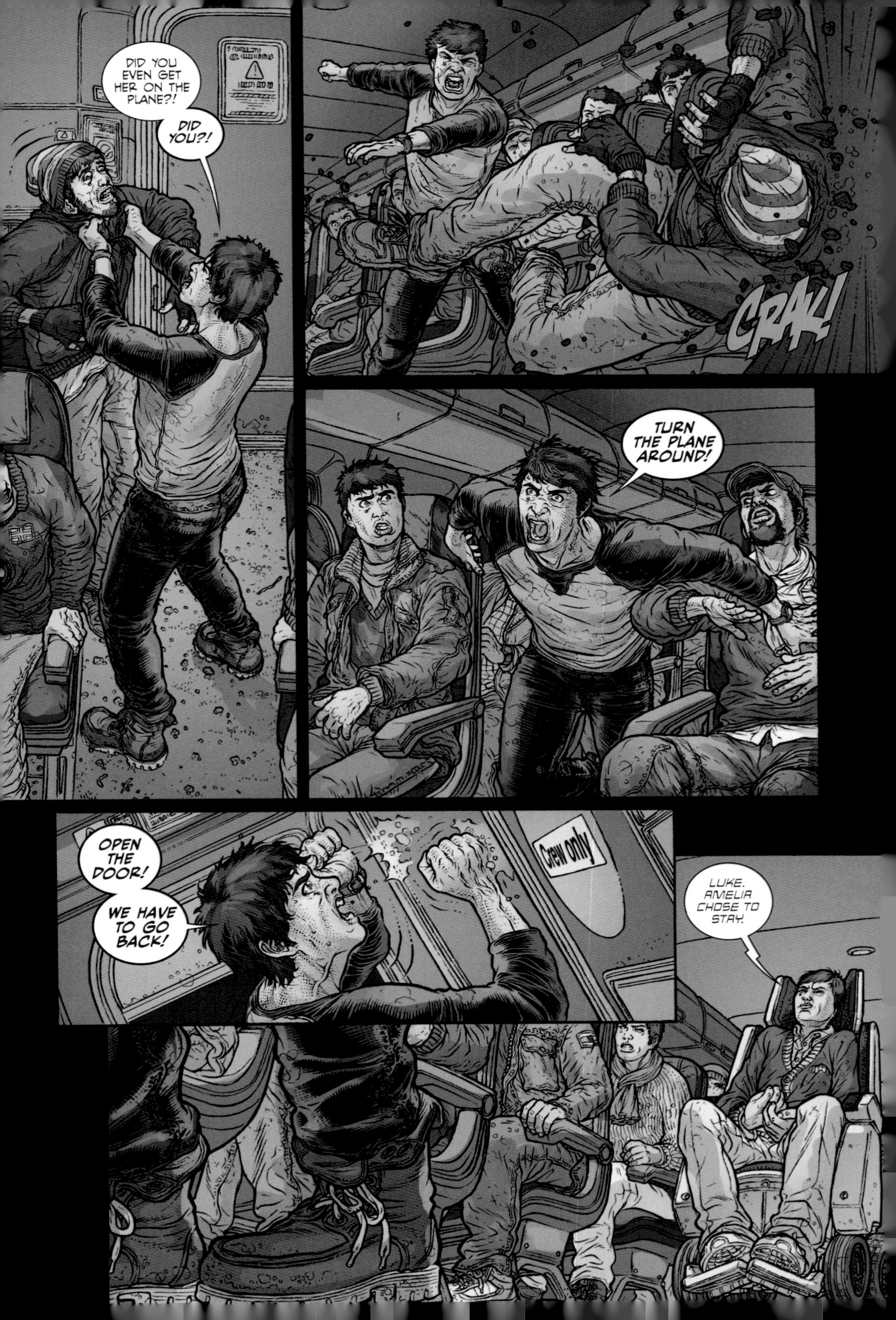
DID YOU EVEN GET HER ON THE PLANE?!
DID YOU?!
CRAK!
TURN THE PLANE AROUND!
OPEN THE DOOR!
WE HAVE TO GO BACK!
Crew only
LUKE. AMELIA CHOSE TO STAY.

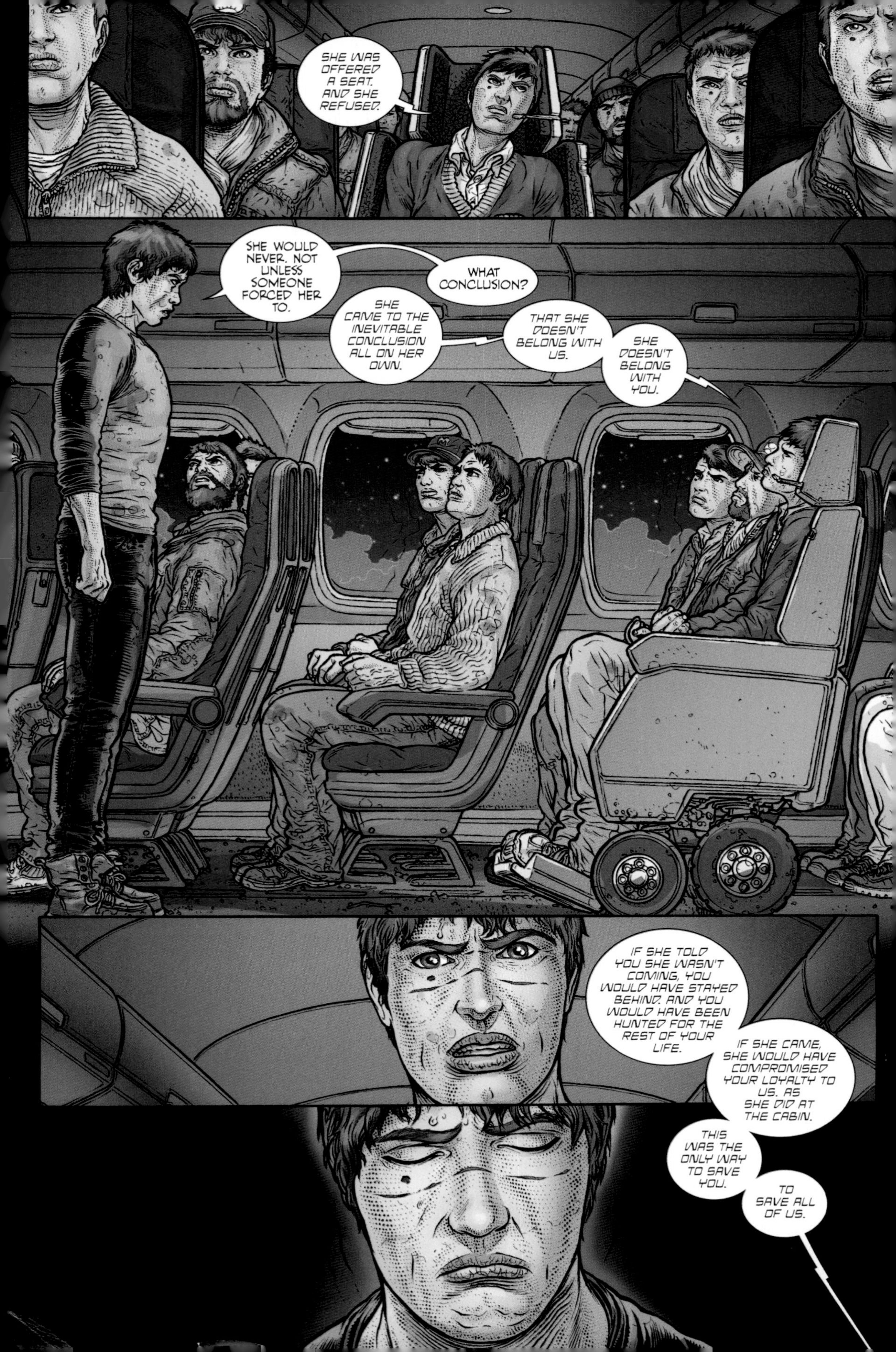
SHE WAS OFFERED A SEAT. AND SHE REFUSED.
SHE WOULD NEVER. NOT UNLESS SOMEONE FORCED HER TO.
SHE CAME TO THE INEVITABLE CONCLUSION ALL ON HER OWN.
WHAT CONCLUSION?
THAT SHE DOESN'T BELONG WITH US.
SHE DOESN'T BELONG WITH YOU.
IF SHE TOLD YOU SHE WASN'T COMING, YOU WOULD HAVE STAYED BEHIND. AND YOU WOULD HAVE BEEN HUNTED FOR THE REST OF YOUR LIFE.
IF SHE CAME, SHE WOULD HAVE COMPROMISED YOUR LOYALTY TO US. AS SHE DID AT THE CABIN.
THIS WAS THE ONLY WAY TO SAVE YOU.
TO SAVE ALL OF US.

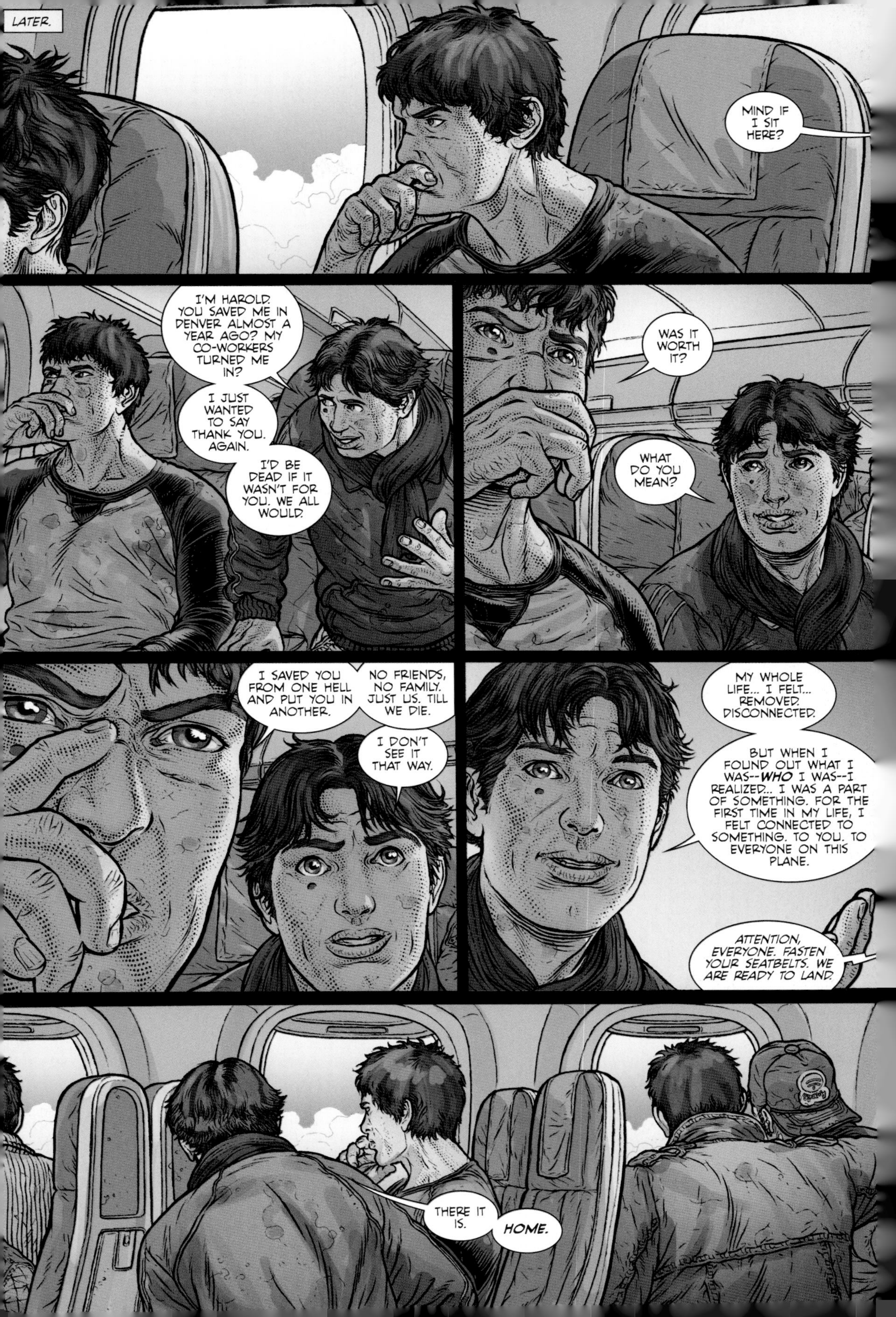
LATER.
MIND IF I SIT HERE?
I'M HAROLD. YOU SAVED ME IN DENVER ALMOST A YEAR AGO? MY CO-WORKERS TURNED ME IN?
I JUST WANTED TO SAY THANK YOU. AGAIN.
I'D BE DEAD IF IT WASN'T FOR YOU. WE ALL WOULD.
WAS IT WORTH IT?
WHAT DO YOU MEAN?
I SAVED YOU FROM ONE HELL AND PUT YOU IN ANOTHER.
NO FRIENDS, NO FAMILY. JUST US. TILL WE DIE.
I DON'T SEE IT THAT WAY.
MY WHOLE LIFE... I FELT... REMOVED. DISCONNECTED.
BUT WHEN I FOUND OUT WHAT I WAS--WHO I WAS--I REALIZED... I WAS A PART OF SOMETHING. FOR THE FIRST TIME IN MY LIFE, I FELT CONNECTED TO SOMETHING. TO YOU. TO EVERYONE ON THIS PLANE.
ATTENTION, EVERYONE. FASTEN YOUR SEATBELTS. WE ARE READY TO LAND.
THERE IT IS.
HOME.

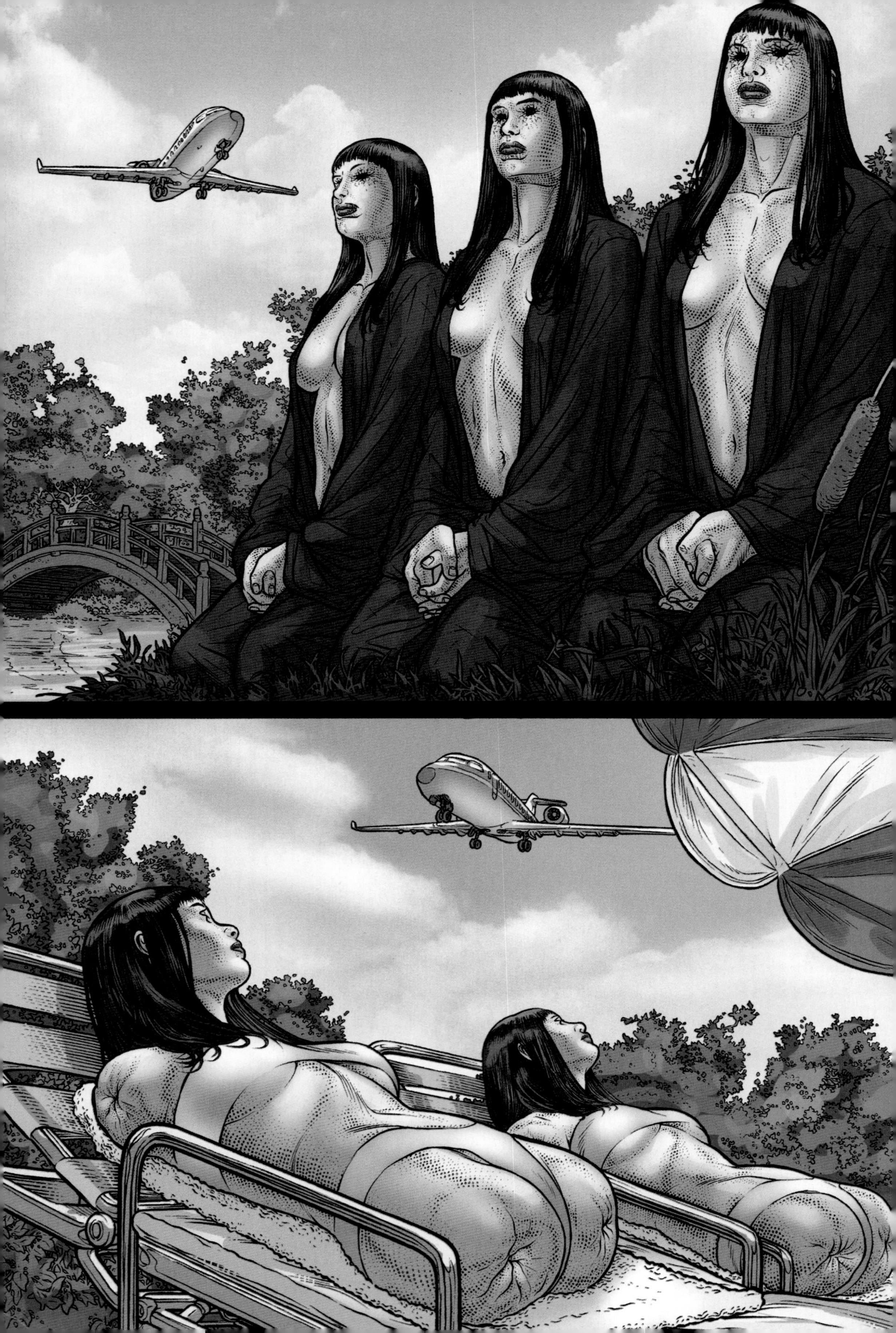

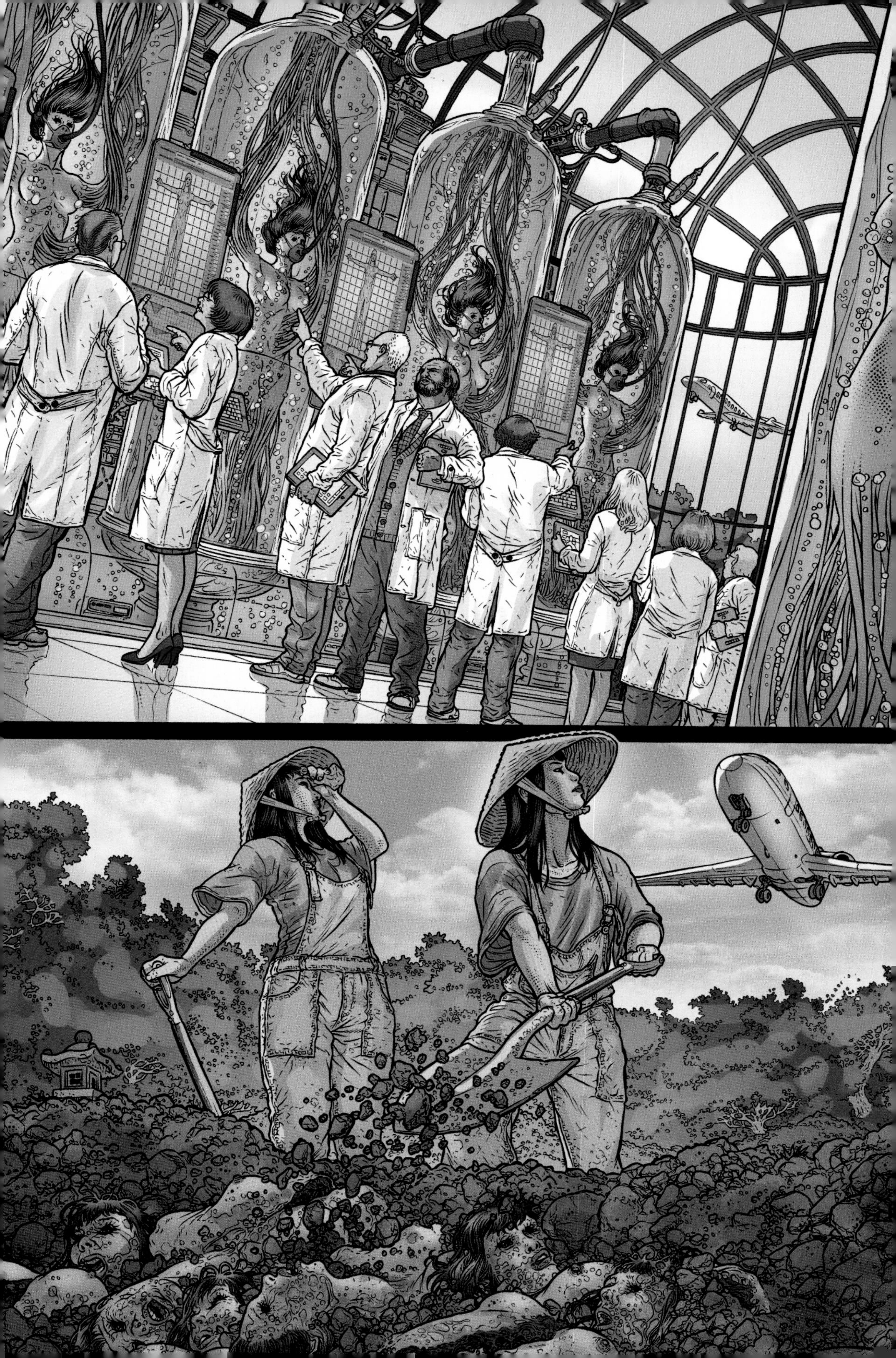

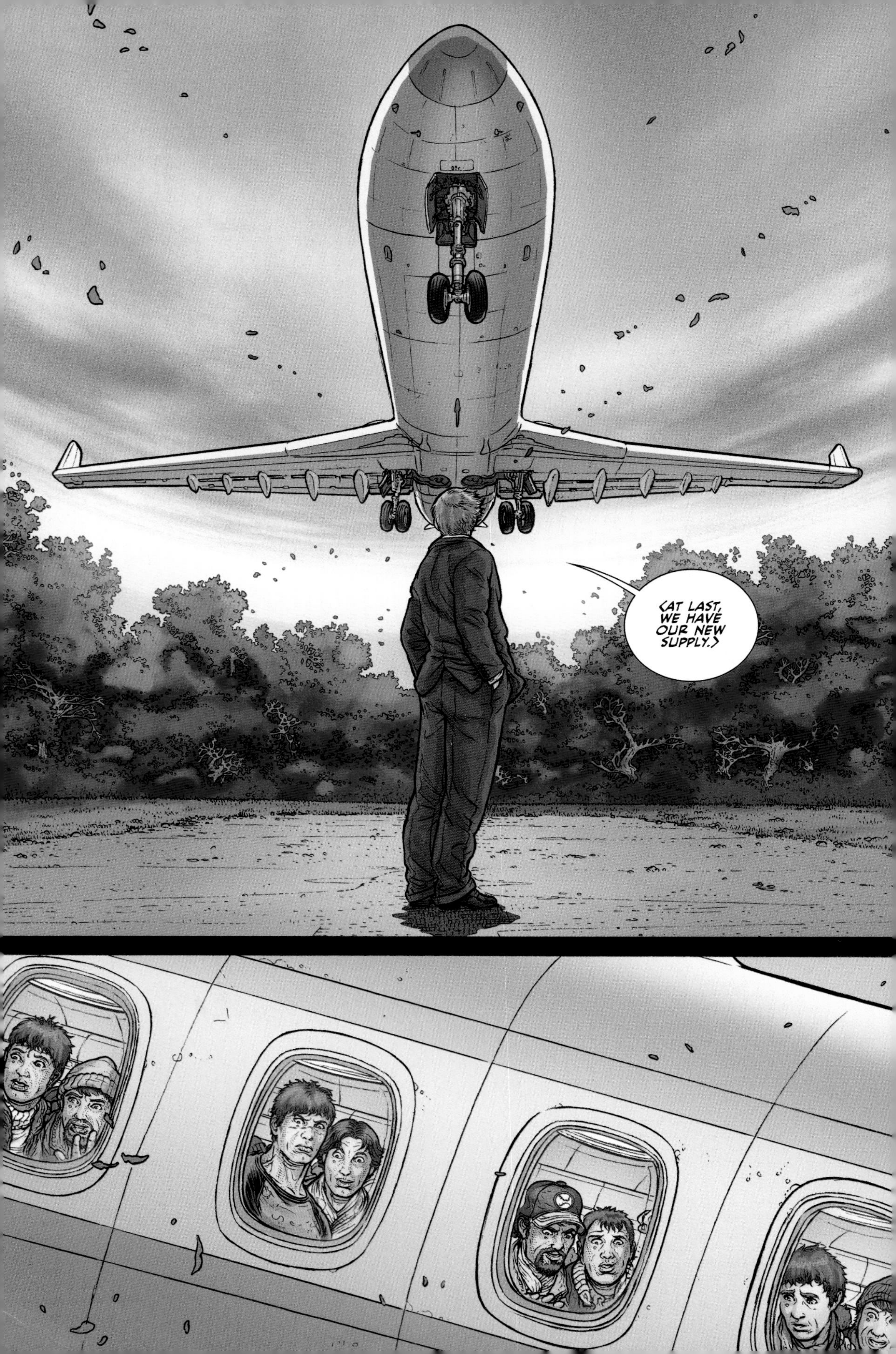
<AT LAST, WE HAVE OUR NEW SUPPLY.>

SKETCHBOOK

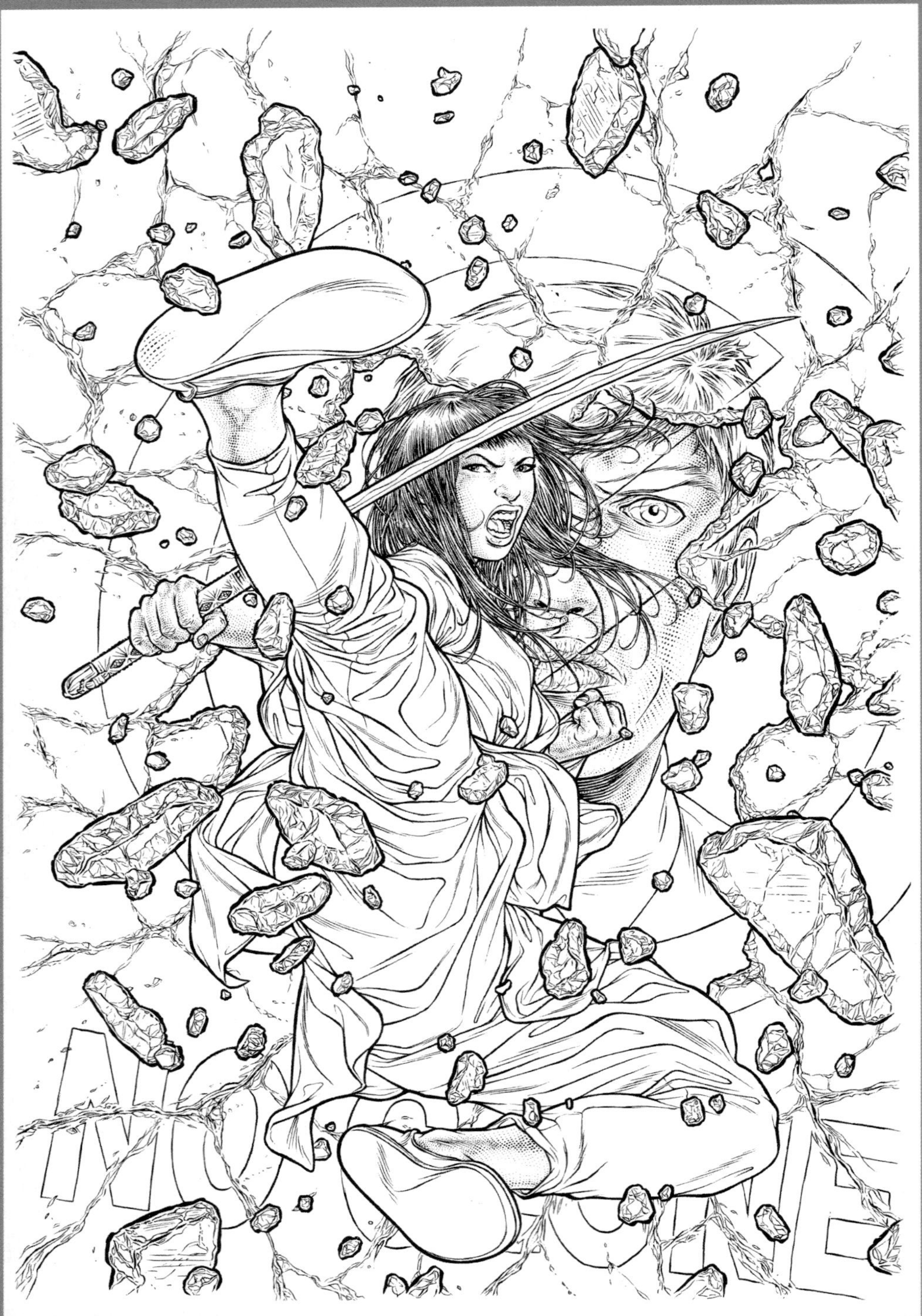

DAVID SCHULNER: These covers are always the hardest. You're trying to convey the arc of the series, make it attention grabbing, but without giving anything away. And make it recognizable as a *Clone* trade cover. *The Walking Dead* is really successful at this. I love those covers with the main characters staring back at you while underneath that image is their zombie selves. For *Clone*, our signature is one character leaping, running or jumping off the page — with glass breaking or blood spilling to convey the urgency and recklessness. It made sense for Meiko to grace the cover this time, since the overall arc of this trade is about her attempts to bring Luke and his clones to the island sanctuary. Juanjo draws this stuff brilliantly. And accurately. I love that Meiko's non-sword-wielding hand is in the perfect chamber position. And just look how every strand of hair is individually drawn. And has to be individually colored by Andy!

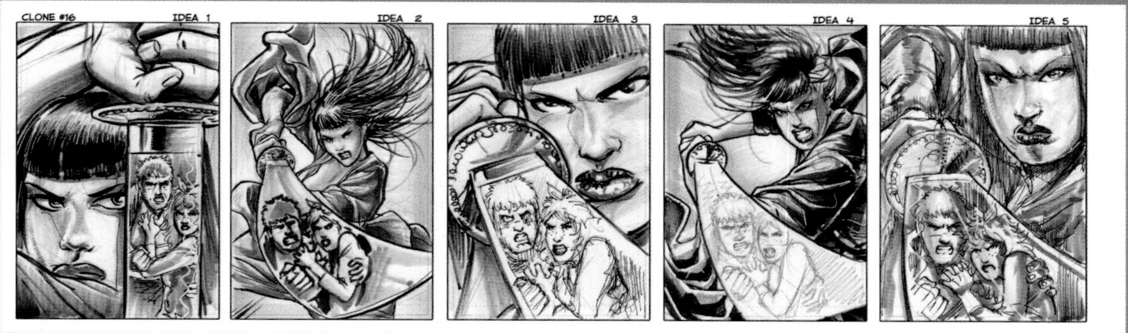
CLONE #16
IDEA 1
IDEA 2
IDEA 3
IDEA 4
IDEA 5

WADE MCINTYRE: We settled on the idea for this cover fairly quickly: we knew we wanted to kick off the fourth arc by emphasizing the threat to Luke and Amelia from Meiko and her clone sisters. Juan came back with this great series of sketches with the raised blade and the reflection of Luke and Amelia. Unfortunately, we'd already used a reflection in a blade on the cover of issue #13, and felt like we needed something new.

I believe it was our fearless editor Sean who came up with the brilliant (and slightly creepy?) suggestion to indicate Amelia's presence with only wisps of her distinctive red hair. After some initial concern that that we might need to see a bit more of her to tell the story (note her hand in this sketch which was removed for the final cover) it became clear that less is more. Just the hair is enough. Leave everything else to the imagination.

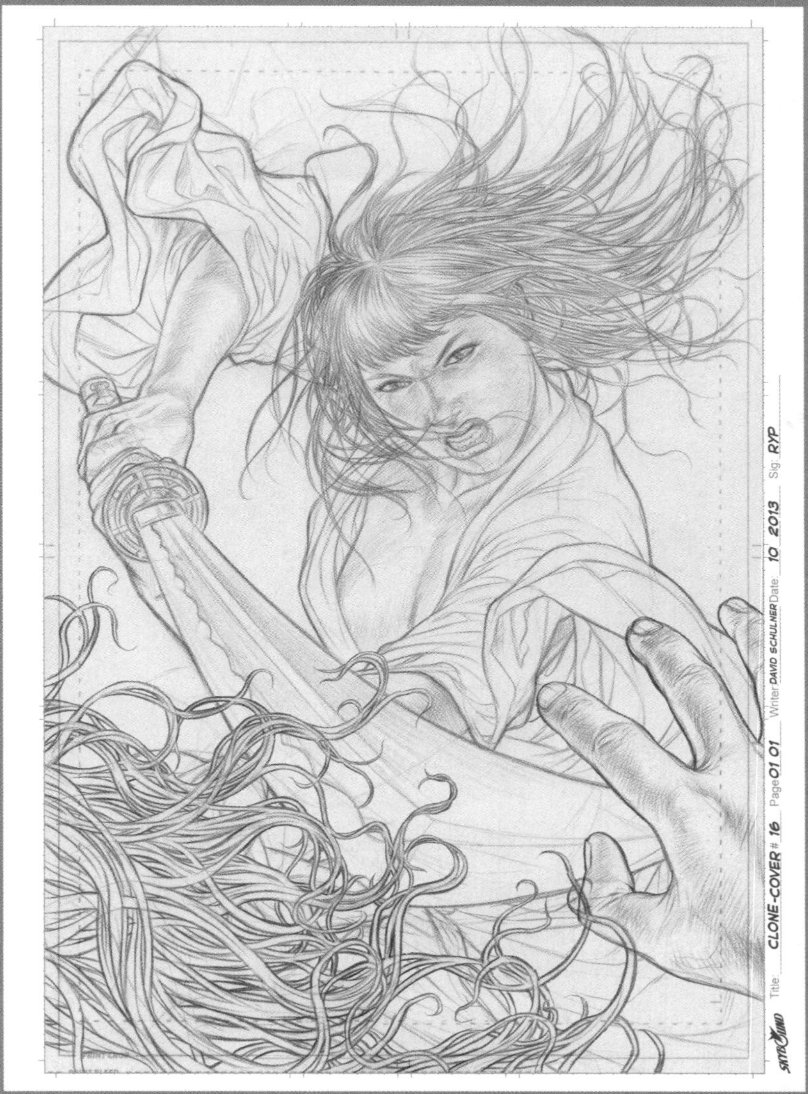
Title: CLONE-COVER # 16 Page 01 01 Writer DAVID SCHULNER Date: 10 2013 Sig: RYP

The final result is a great dynamic composition. Everything is whirling in motion: the hair is flinging, the sword is swinging, even her clothes are flying off a little bit... It was a true collaboration between artists, writing team, and editorial. Except for me. I didn't do anything other than chime in at the last minute, admiring them all. Great job, guys! Glad I could help.

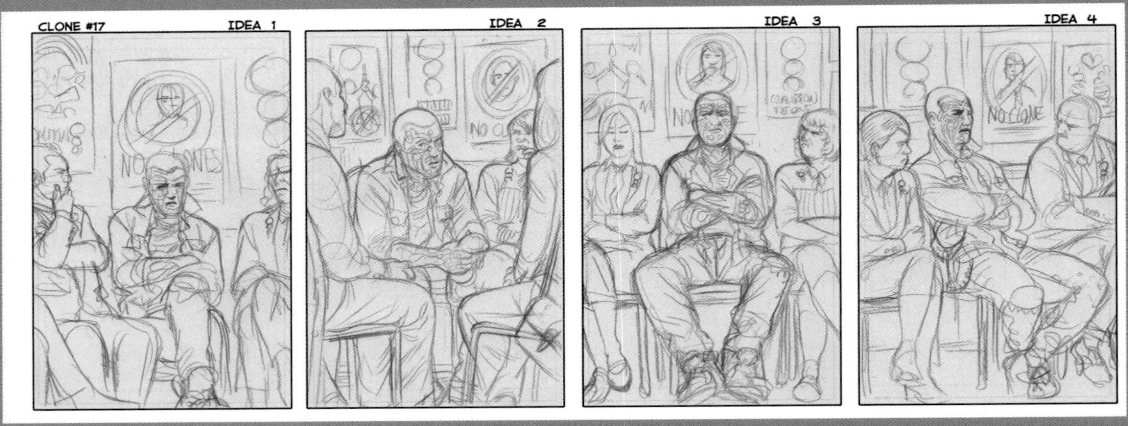
CLONE #17
IDEA 1
IDEA 2
IDEA 3
IDEA 4

AARON GINSBURG: Not gonna lie - there was much debate about the cover of Issue 17.

The issue is jam-packed with big character moments, shocking turns, and the core foundation is established for what would be the book's nightmarish conclusion... but we couldn't show any of that without completely spoiling a killer page turn. So, what to do? We discussed dozens of options, some esoteric, some downright confusing, but nothing felt right.

Then one of us pitched the idea of Eric (or "Tat" as he's affectionately known) sitting casually in a anti-clone Coalition meeting. It was quirky, it was weird, it was a real contrast to the action-packed covers we'd done in the past. Hell, it was even... funny.

Now, as you're aware, *Clone* is a series with little room for humor. The stakes are so high, the characters are always backed into corners, and every moment balances on the knife's edge between life and death... Yet, this idea of Eric just kicking back in some dingy church basement, relaxing beneath anti-clone posters that displayed HIS face, was hilarious.

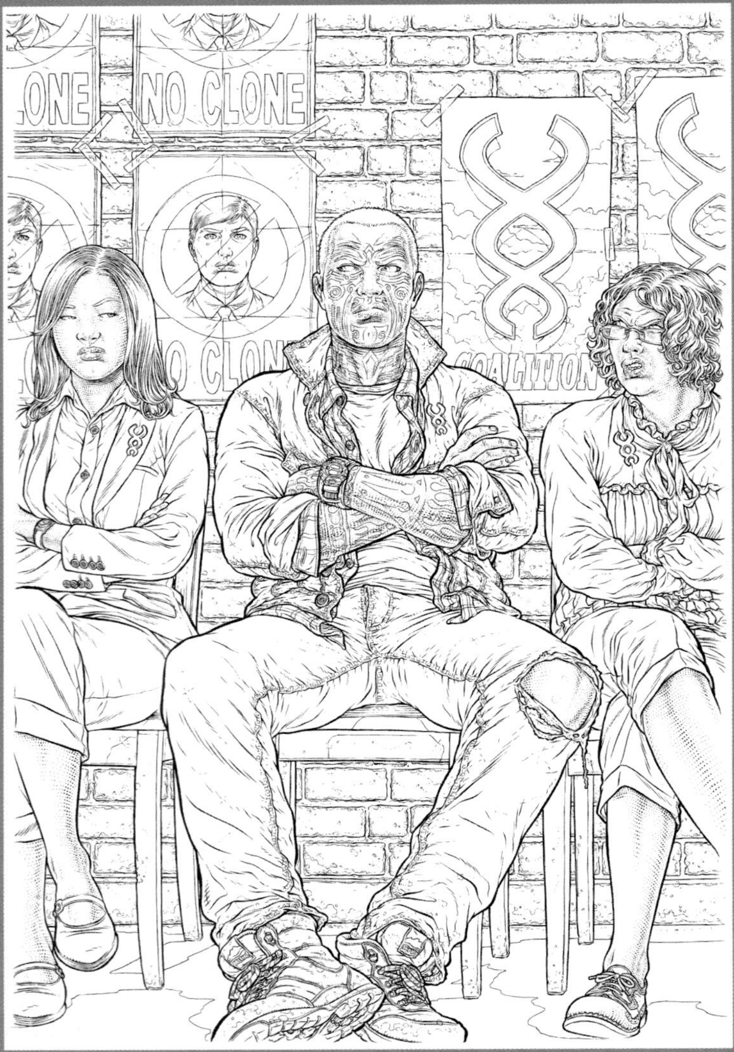
NO CLONE
COALITION

Juan didn't miss a step — and he shot back a bunch of options (seen above) for this fateful meeting. Once we were faced with the choices, idea #3 just popped off the page. As you can see, Juan managed to capture a Norman Rockwell still-life, an almost-quaint window into our twisted version of a post-clone America. Just a bunch of well-meaning citizens doing their part to stop the ethical scourge of genetic manipulation...

Oh, yeah, and Eric.

WADE: We admit it. This cover is a bit of a fake out. The previous issue ended with Amelia being shot and now we have Luke clearly digging a grave. Could she really be dead!?! Better buy the book to find out — no wait! Luke is actually just burying some incriminating evidence. Okay... Well, you already have the book in your hand anyway. Mwahahaha, etc.

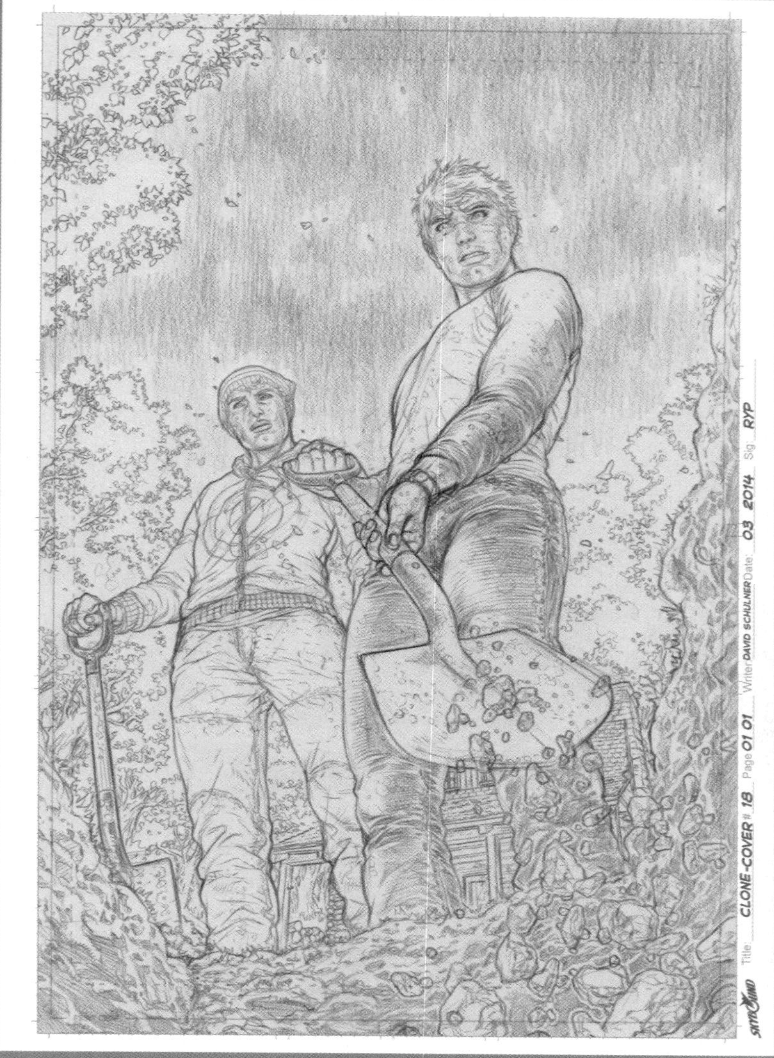
Title: CLONE-COVER # 18 Page 01 01 Writer DAVID SCHULNER Date: 03 2014 Sig: RYP

It wasn't quite that calculated, but we knew we had to get a little creative with this cover. Issue 18 is one of our more character and emotion-based issues, which can make for a great story, but it does make it slightly harder to come up with a compelling cover image. Even though we don't have a lot of guns and swords and mayhem in this one, I think Juanjo has created a foreboding and intriguing image.

As you can see from the initial sketches, the trick was finding the right angle to show the digging without revealing that it wasn't a grave. The solution turned out to be to look up from the point of view of what we don't want you to see. It's similar to a camera perspective they used a lot on one of our favorite TV shows, *Breaking Bad*. Putting a shovel full of dirt in Luke's hands was a last-minute addition, and it made a big difference.

Finally, we gave the artist a bit of challenge here with Luke's facial expression. He needs to look like he's burying the love of his life... or he could also just be burying a bunch of incriminating pamphlets. Somehow or another, as always, Juanjo managed to pull it off.

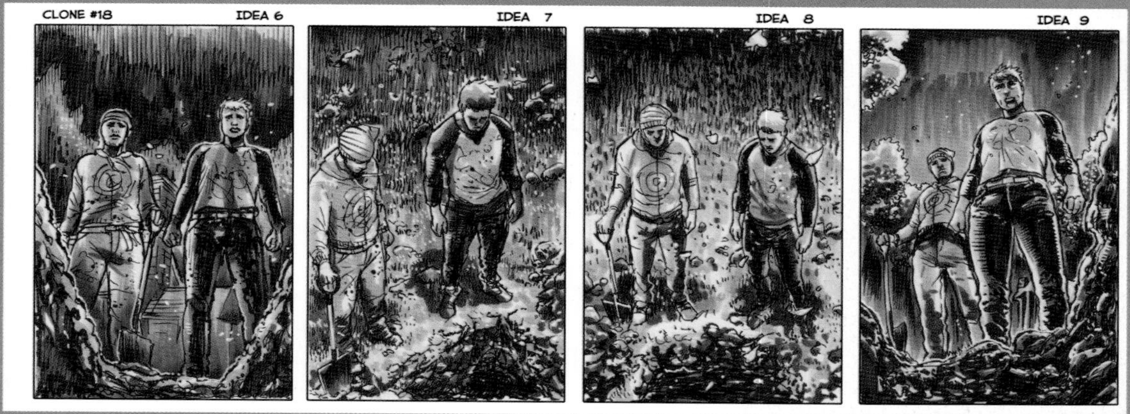
CLONE #18
IDEA 6
IDEA 7
IDEA 8
IDEA 9

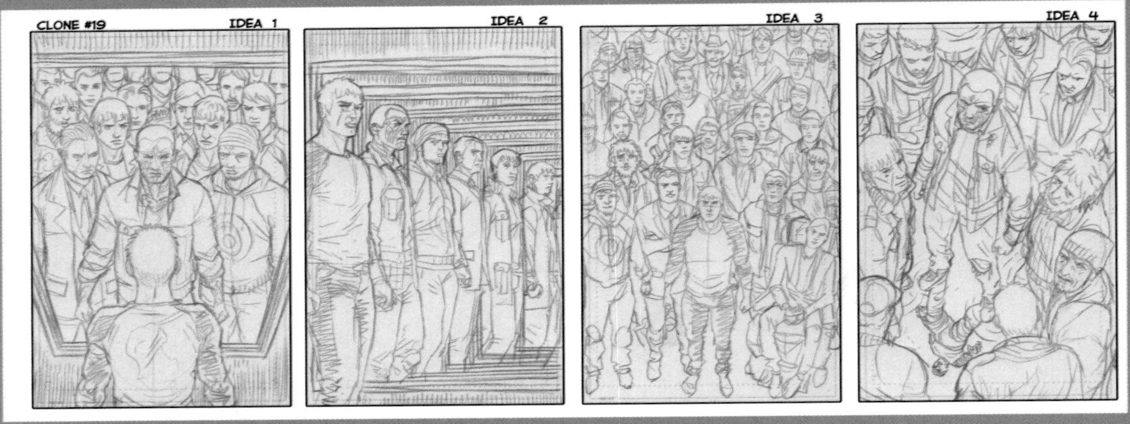
CLONE #19
IDEA 1
IDEA 2
IDEA 3
IDEA 4

AARON: This is going to sound crazy, but it's true.

For 19 action-packed issues, Juan had been churning out some of the most incredibly detailed art any of us had ever seen. Every single panel he draws overflows with incredible specificity — from individual shards of glass exploding from a broken window to ornate tattoos covering every square inch of a man's body... Juan always manages to immerse the reader in hyper-realistic images that, let's be honest, must be absolutely backbreaking to create.

So, when Issue 19 rolled around, we assumed that he might be happy for a break — you know, an easy cover concept that he could just whip up without taking years off of his life. But, instead, Juan came to us and asked — he seriously asked — for a cover that would showcase a veritable hand-drawn tidal wave of infinitesimal detail. He genuinely and specifically requested a concept that would include as many characters as we could reasonably fit on the page.

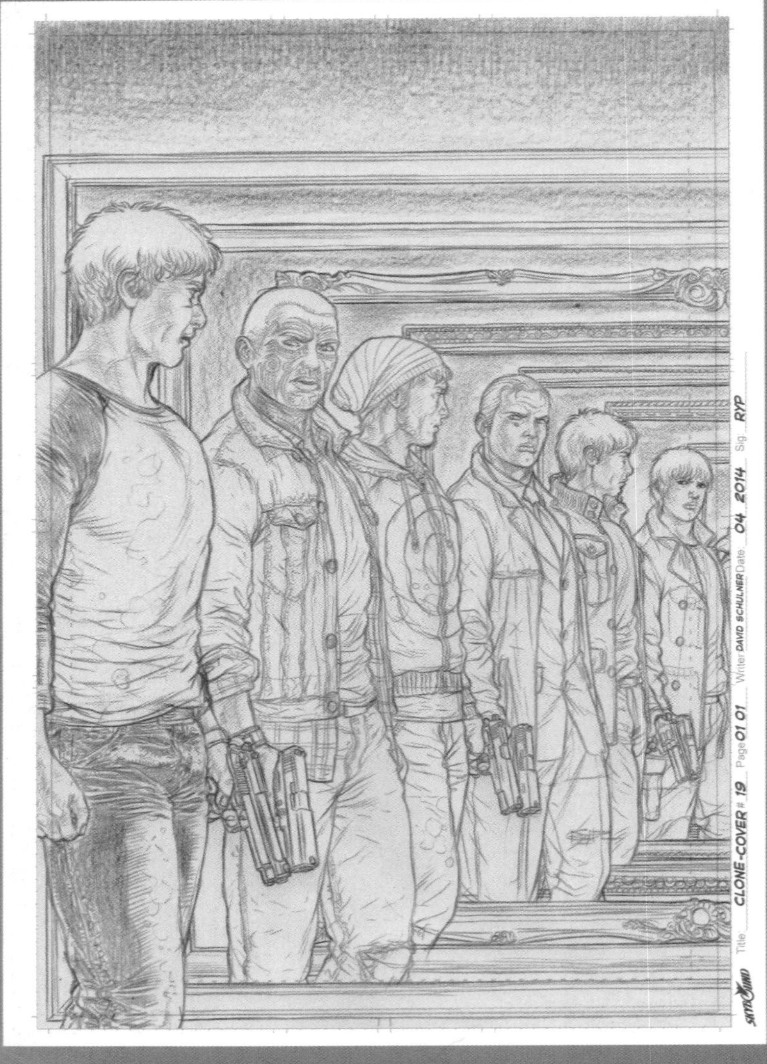
Title: CLONE-COVER # 19 Page 01 01 Writer DAVID SCHULNER Date: 04 2014 Sig. RYP

Hey, his funeral, right? As it turned out, we had just the idea in mind. At one time, we'd considered an image of Reverend Wayne Snyder (or maybe Vice President David, remember him?) getting his suit tailored — standing in front of a tryptic of mirrors — all reflecting his visage from various angles, going on and on for infinity... Never found a way to use that, but it got us thinking... What if Issue 19 depicted a cool twist on this mirror reflection concept, but with Luke — and instead of an actual reflection, ad nauseam, Luke would be confronting all of the literal versions of himself?

Sounded pretty hard to us, but hey, Juan did ask for it...